The Struggle for World Markets

NEW HORIZONS IN INTERNATIONAL BUSINESS

General Editor: Peter J. Buckley
Centre for International Business,
University of Leeds (CIBUL), UK

This series is aimed at the frontiers of international business research. The study of international business is important not least because it gives researchers the opportunity to innovate in theory, technique, empirical investigation and interpretation. The area is fruitful for interdisciplinary and comparative research. This series is established as a central forum for the presentation of new ideas in international business.

Titles in the series include:

Transnational Corporations in Southeast Asia
An Institutional Approach to Industrial Organization
Hans Jansson

European Integration and Competitiveness
Acquisitions and Alliances in Industry
Edited by Frédérique Sachwald

The State and Transnational Corporations
A Network Approach to Industrial Policy in India
Hans Jansson, M. Saqib and D. Deo Sharma

Competitive and Cooperative Macromanagement
The Challenges of Structural Interdependence
Edited by Gavin Boyd

Foreign Direct Investment in Japan
Edited by Masaru Yoshitomi and Edward M. Graham

Structural Competitiveness in the Pacific
Corporate and State Rivalries
Edited by Gavin Boyd

Euro-Pacific Investment and Trade
Strategies and Structural Interdependencies
Edited by Gavin Boyd and Alan M. Rugman

Multinational Firms and International Relocation
Edited by Peter J. Buckley and Jean-Louis Mucchielli

Current Issues in International Business
Edited by Iyanatul Islam and William Shepherd

The Struggle for World Markets
Edited by Gavin Boyd

Japanese Multinationals in the Global Economy
Paul W. Beamish, Andrew Delios and Donald J. Lecraw

Global Competitive Strategies in the New World Economy
Multilateralism, Regionalisation and the Transnational Firm
Edited by Hafiz Mirza

The Struggle for World Markets

Competition and Cooperation between NAFTA and the European Union

Edited by
Gavin Boyd

Honorary Professor Political Science Department, Rutgers University, US, and Research Associate, Centre for International Business Studies, University of Montreal, Canada

NEW HORIZONS IN INTERNATIONAL BUSINESS

Edward Elgar
Cheltenham, UK • Northampton, MA, USA

Published by
Edward Elgar Publishing Limited
8 Lansdown Place
Cheltenham
Glos GL50 2HU
UK

Edward Elgar Publishing, Inc.
6 Market Street
Northampton
Massachusetts 01060
USA

A catalogue record for this book is available from the British Library

Library of Congress Cataloguing in Publication Data
The struggle for world markets: competition and cooperation between
  NAFTA and the European Union/edited by Gavin Boyd.
  (New horizons in international business)
  Includes index.
  1. International trade. 2. North America—Foreign economic
  relations—European Union countries. 3. European Union countries—
  Foreign economic relations—North America. 4. Competition,
  International. 5. International cooperation. I. Boyd, Gavin.
  II. Series.
  HF1379.S79   1998
  337.407—dc21   97–18422
                                                                                     CIP

ISBN 1 85898 549 8

Printed and bound in Great Britain by
Biddles Limited, Guildford and King's Lynn

Contents

List of figures		vi
List of tables		vii
Notes on contributors		ix
Foreword		xi
Preface		xiii

1 Re-energizing the transatlantic connection
John H. Dunning — 1

2 Atlantic interdependencies and free trade — 12
Stephen Blank and Anne Taillandier

3 Structural interdependence between the European Union and the United States: technological positions — 32
Pierre Buigues and Alexis Jacquemin

4 North American sectoral profiles and corporate strategy in the automobile industry — 59
Alan M. Rugman and Gavin Boyd

5 Atlantic systems of corporate finance and governance — 80
Stephen Prowse

6 Atlantic sectoral linkage potentials — 110
Maria Papadakis

7 Atlantic high-technology complementarities — 141
Jorge Niosi and Benoit Godin

8 Atlantic foreign direct investment flows — 155
Peter J. Buckley and Jeremy Clegg

9 Atlantic strategic technology alliances — 177
John Hagedoorn

10 Systemic approaches to managing interdependencies — 192
Gavin Boyd

11 Planning Atlantic direct investment conferences — 222
Gavin Boyd

Index — 243

Figures

3.1 Employment and value added (1990 prices) in EU and USA,
1985–94   41
3.2 Alliances and R&D by sector: Europe   49
4.1 The five partners business network   68
5.1 Percentage of salary and wage earners in small enterprises 100
9.1 Growth of international strategic technology alliances,
EU-NAFTA and other international alliances, 1980–94   183

Tables

3.1	Western Europe and North America, 1992	33
3.2	The interpenetration of EU and US economies	34
3.3	Labour productivity and wages, 1994	38
3.4	Productivity and demand, wages and production prices (average percentage annual growth rate 1985–94)	39
3.5	Value added, employment and investment	42
3.6	Trade in high, medium and low tech	45
3.7	Transborder mergers and acquisitions: EU versus US in high-, medium- and low-tech sectors	48
3.8	International distribution of strategic technology alliances, overall figures, total information technologies, computers, microelectronics, telecommunications (as percentages) 1980–84 and 1985–89	50
3.9	Share of total manufacturing by size class	52
3.10	Small, medium and large enterprises in the high-tech sector	52
5.1	Stock market capitalization, 1994	84
5.2	Gross public issuance of equity	84
5.3	Corporate bond and commercial paper markets	85
5.4	Composition of companies' credit market debt, 1994	85
5.5	Ownership of common stock of listed companies	86
5.6	Summary statistics of ownership concentration of large non-financial corporations	87
5.7	Average annual volume of completed domestic mergers and corporate transactions with disclosed values, 1985–89	87
5.8	Hostile takeovers and leveraged buyouts as a percentage of all attempted transactions, 1985–89	88
5.9	Legal and regulatory constraints on corporate control	91
5.10	German legal and regulatory constraints on non-financial firms' access to non-bank finance	94
5.11	Selected results from a survey of the implementation of the OECD guidelines on the disclosure of information by multinational enterprises	95
5.12	Life insurance and pension fund assets	102
6.1	International business arrangements that constitute strategic alliances	113

6.2   Import penetration and export-to-production ratios for the
      manufacturing sector, EU and NAFTA   117
6.3   Sectors with limited transatlantic alliance potential   120
6.4   Profile of industries with good transatlantic alliance potential 122
6.A1 Alliance potential indicators for the EU and NAFTA   130
7.1   Revealed technological advantages of Canadian firms, 1988–91   145
7.2   US FDI in Europe, 1995   146
7.3   European FDI in the United States, 1995   146
7.4   Patents granted in the USA in 1993 in selected countries and
      industries (total numbers)   147
7.5   Patents granted in the USA in 1993 in selected countries and
      industries (averaged by population)   147
7.6   R&D expenditure and employment by affiliates of foreign
      companies in the US, 1993   151
7.7   US expenditure for R&D abroad, by country, 1993   151
8.1   Outward foreign direct investment stock of Canada and the
      USA into Europe, percentage distribution, 1985–95   159
8.2   Outward foreign direct investment stock of Canada into the UK,
      other EU, and the world, percentage distribution, 1985–95   161
8.3   Outward foreign direct investment stock of the USA into Europe
      and the world, percentage distribution, 1985–95   163
8.4   Outward foreign direct investment stock of the USA into the UK,
      France, Germany, the Netherlands and Switzerland, percentage
      distribution, 1985–95   164
8.5   Inward foreign direct investment stock of Canada and the USA
      from Europe, percentage distribution, 1985–95   166
8.6   Inward foreign direct investment stock of Canada from the UK,
      other EU, and the world, percentage distribution 1985–95   167
8.7   Inward foreign direct investment stock in the USA by Europe
      and the world, percentage distribution, 1985–95   168
8.8   Inward foreign direct investment stock in the USA by the UK,
      France, Germany, the Netherlands and Switzerland, percentage
      distribution, 1985–95   169
8.9   Inward foreign direct investment stock of Mexico for available
      European countries, value and percentage distribution, 1995   170
9.1   Distribution of R&D and market-focused international strategic
      technology alliances, EU-NAFTA and other international
      alliances, 1980–94   185
9.2   Distribution of joint ventures and contractual international
      strategic technology alliances, EU-NAFTA and other
      international alliances, 1980–94   185
9.3   Sectoral distribution of international strategic technology alliances,
      EU-NAFTA and other international alliances, 1980–94   187

Notes on contributors

Stephen Blank is Professor of Management and International Business at the Lubin School of Business, Pace University, New York, and teaches regularly at L'Ecole des Hautes Etudes Commerciales, University of Montreal. He has written extensively on corporate structure and strategy in North America.

Peter J. Buckley is Director of the Centre for International Business, University of Leeds, UK, and editor of the series *New Horizons in International Business* for Edward Elgar Publishing.

Pierre Buigues is Director of the Planning Unit, DGXII, European Commission, Brussels.

Jeremy Clegg is Jean Monnet Senior Lecturer in European Integration and International Business Management, Centre for International Business, University of Leeds, UK.

John H. Dunning is Professor of International Business, Rutgers University, New Jersey, USA, and Professor Economics Emeritus, University of Reading, UK. He has published very extensively on the structures and strategies of international firms.

Benoit Godin is Professor of the Sociology of Science, National Institute for Scientific Research, University of Quebec at Montreal.

John Hagedoorn is Professorial Research Fellow, Maastricht Economic Research Institute on Innovation and Technology, Faculty of Economics, University of Limburg.

Alexis Jacquemin is Chief Advisor, Planning Unit, DGXII, European Commission, Brussels.

Jorge Niosi is Professor of Technology Management, Department of Administrative Science, University of Quebec at Montreal, and Principal

Investigator, Centre for Interdisciplinary Research on Science and Technology, University of Quebec at Montreal and University of Montreal.

Maria Papadakis is Associate Professor of Integrated Science and Technology at James Madison University, Virginia.

Stephen Prowse is Senior Economist and Policy Advisor, Federal Reserve Bank of Dallas, Texas, USA.

Alan M. Rugman is Professor, Faculty of Management, University of Toronto. His collected works are being published by Edward Elgar.

Anne Taillandier is at Citibank, New York; she received her MBA from the Lubin School of Business at Pace University, New York.

Foreword

With the multiplication of structural linkages in the world economy, business schools have to offer specializations with wider interdisciplinary coverage, extending into areas of economic policy that regulate, influence and support corporate activities. Managers are being obliged to become closely acquainted with macro and microeconomic policy trends and issues in the home and host countries of their firms, while decision makers in economic ministries are being challenged to study intently the planning of investment, production and marketing strategies by firms. There is a degree of convergence between the knowledge-intensive learning requirements at the corporate and government levels

The Centre for International Business Studies of l'Ecole des Hautes Etudes Commerciales, affiliated with the University of Montreal, is expanding its operations in line with the dual trend of imperatives for corporate and government learning. Research is focusing on complementarities between the entrepreneurial, technological and financial skills of corporate managements and the matching skills at the policy levels which are being demanded by public sector management reforms in industrialized states.

The potential efficiencies of interactive learning, based on the complementarities between the two levels of capabilities and task orientations, have aroused interest in the planning of conferences for exchanges between international business scholars, economists with macro and micro specializations, and political scientists. Most of the chapters in this volume were presented as papers at a conference which the Centre sponsored in November 1996. It had an Atlantic focus and explored the evolution of the North American and European economies, and the structural links between them. There was much interest in potentials for the further development of strategic alliances between European and North American firms, and in ways of coordinating policies to facilitate the formation of such alliances.

The financing of the conference was aided by generous grants from the Quebec government, the European Union Delegation in Ottawa, and the Canadian Federal government. There was strong representation from the Federal and Provincial governments and business groups in Quebec and from universities in the USA and Europe. The operational significance of the conference assumed additional significance after a presentation on the TransAtlantic Business Dialogue sponsored by the European Commission and the US Department of

Commerce. This presentation was given by Ellen Frost, Senior Fellow, Institute for International Economics, Washington, DC. The European Commission was represented at the conference by Pierre Buigues, Head of the Planning Unit, DG XII, who presented a paper on 'Structural Interdependence between the European Union and the United States: Technological Positions'. The paper, co-authored with Alexis Jacquemin, Chief Advisor to the Planning Unit, has been included in this volume.

Some warm friendships began at the conference, and I am sure that these will lead to very productive encounters at future meetings. I was pleased to meet Peter J. Buckley, Director of the Centre for International Business at the University of Leeds, the General Editor of the series in which this book has been published, and I was very grateful to John H. Dunning, State of New Jersey Professor of Management at Rutgers University, Newark, who gave a luncheon address on Alliance Capitalism that has become the first chapter in this volume. The organizational work for the conference was performed very efficiently by the Centre's staff, for whose cooperation I am especially grateful.

Alain Lapointe
Director, Centre for International Business Studies, HEC, Montreal

Preface

This book has been planned for the study of Atlantic interdependencies, which are being given larger and more complex dimensions by the competitive and cooperative activities of firms and governments. There are imbalances in these interdependencies, which have cumulative effects on growth, employment, and stability on each side of the Atlantic, and accordingly the examination of trends at the corporate and government levels raises questions about what might be done to promote greater complementarities between the European Union and North America. Studies of sectoral linkage potentials and of strategic technology alliances are therefore central chapters in the volume.

European and American corporate activities, especially in high-technology sectors, evolve under the influence of national policies that are in varying degrees restrictive and supportive. As firms expand their international operations, through transnational production and trade, their ranges of strategic options in dealings with governments are widened, and their choices have extensive consequences in the development of national economic systems. Governments respond with differing structural policy measures, and these reflect contrasts in commitments and administrative capabilities. They also reflect policy orientations emphasizing reliance on market forces and the avoidance of interventionist methods, which are generally considered to be counterproductive. A trend in structural policies, accordingly, is innovation at the policy level to induce corporate cooperation through building consultative links, providing administrative favours, and offering attractive business environments. This trend is stronger in Europe than in the USA, and shows the influence of traditionally close government-corporate relations in Europe, as well as European concerns about lagging competitiveness in world markets.

Structural policy rivalry between governments tends to be exploited by firms in their efforts to maximize the use of location advantages, spread risks, and increase access to markets. Corporate rivalries are exploited by governments, but in general less effectively: elements of economic sovereignty are lost by governments, and firms have incentives to form alliances with each other that are not matched at the policy level by collaborative cross-border structural measures. These alliances, moreover, benefit from the flexibility associated with widely spread international corporate operations.

The interactions between corporate strategies and structural policies can become more productive in the common interest if governments cooperate with each other as they implement those policies. This possibility has much significance in Europe, especially because of the influence of the European Commission on the policies of member countries in the European Union. In the larger Atlantic context the possibility of structural policy cooperation has greater significance, although the orientation of American policy can be seen as a challenge for European decision makers. The greater American emphasis on corporate freedom is advantageous for US firms. In Europe, moreover, US firms operate increasingly on the basis of global strategies directed against Japan, while the strategies of European firms are less active outside their own region and North America.

All these factors in Atlantic economic relations occasioned exchanges between the contributing authors of this volume when speaking to their drafts in the very convivial atmosphere of a conference on Atlantic trade, economic integration, and strategic alliances. This was sponsored by the Centre for International Business Studies (CETAI) at the beautiful new campus of the Ecole des Hautes Etudes Commerciales (HEC), affiliated with the University of Montreal, and took place on 7–9 November 1996. All wish to express their thanks for the excellent hospitality of the Director, Dr Alain Lapointe, and his staff, and for the stimulation provided by intensive discussions during the conference.

Gavin Boyd

1. Re-energizing the transatlantic connection

John H. Dunning

How are the economic relationships between Europe and North America being affected by the globalization of firms and markets? In attempting to answer this question, I would like to set it within a historical perspective. I do so because I believe that the level and pattern of contemporary transatlantic trade, investment and technology flows are not only the outcome of recent economic forces, but are a reflection of the ideologies and values of the European and American people, their institutions and their forms of economic governance, which were initially crafted more than three centuries ago, and which only now are being challenged by the advent of the global village.

For the most part, the moral and social architecture of the nations bordering the North Atlantic are very similar, which is not surprising, as each stems from a common root. However, the spirit and course of democratic capitalism in North America – and particularly in the US – has followed a rather different trajectory to that of most Western European nations. I would argue this is due not so much to any disagreement about the virtues of a market economy *per se*, but rather about the means by which these virtues can best be promoted and preserved. More specifically, I would suggest that the somewhat ambivalent relationship between European and American civic society and interest groups lies in the different emphasis each places on the respective roles of individualism (in the form of persons and firms) and communitarianism (in the form of government and non-profit organizations) in the value-forming and systemic decision-taking processes underpinning economic activity. I would further assert that world events of the closing years of the twentieth century are not only leading to much deeper transatlantic connections, but to a re-evaluation of the tenets of individualism and communitarianism, so that each may blend into a new set of organizing principles, which elsewhere (Dunning 1997) I have referred to as alliance capitalism or, to coin a new word, 'alliancism'.

Alliancism, like individualism, focuses on the person, family or commercial institution as the main initiators and beneficiaries of economic activity, but also suggests that in the pursuit of self-interest, private economic agents need to cooperate with each other. Like communitarianism, alliancism recognizes the

1

worth of collective goals, systemic cohesion and social institutions. It further accepts the critical task of government in economic activities, but regards that task as less to regulate or participate in the creation and deployment of indigenous resources and capabilities, and more to set goals, help build institutions, and facilitate the workings of an efficient market system. It also acknowledges the increasing role of the not-for-profit sector in many capitalist countries as a provider of social capital and as a promoter of a civil society (Rifkin 1995).

With these thoughts in mind, let me offer you a thumbnail sketch of the history of transatlantic economic relationships, before turning to consider how these are being affected by contributory events; and also the response of the business community and of national and/or regional governments – and particularly of the European Union (EU) and the US – to these effects.

The hallmark of the transatlantic economic connection for the first two and a half centuries following the European settlement of North America was that of asymmetrical economic interdependence; although, after the American Revolution, the ideologies, political systems and institutions supporting this interdependence began to diverge. Most commercial intercourse took the form of arm's-length trade in goods and assets, and of the westward migration of people and enterprises. In the US, the organization of everyday life evolved in the mid nineteenth century from an elemental subsistence economy in the north, and a more internationally oriented plantation economy in the south, to a predominantly free market industrial economy built on the principles enunciated in the Declaration of Independence, and those espoused by Thomas Jefferson, John Locke and Adam Smith.

From the very beginning of the new American republic, there was a bottom-up attitude to the functions and power of government, which was quite different from the top-down philosophy of Colbert and much of European mercantilism (Lodge and Vogel 1987). Although for most of the nineteenth century both Federal and state governments played a major entrepreneurial, and sometimes protective, role in shaping American economic development (Kozul-Wright 1995), the importance placed on the liberty of the individual and of interest groups, rather than on collective responsibility and social equality, was considerably greater than that then evolving in Western Europe (Novak 1982). There, in most countries, after a brief embracement of *laissez faire* principles, the earlier spirit of communitarianism returned – this time in the guise of the socialism of Marx, Engels and F.D. Maurice. Due possibly to the greater social unrest and political upheaval following the industrial revolution in Europe, relative to that in North America, issues of equality and brotherhood were given at least as much attention as those of liberty; and, in the leading continental European countries, that of the state's role in curbing or redressing the less desirable consequences of free markets.

Yet such ideological issues probably had little effect on the economic links then being forged between the North Atlantic economies. This, I believe, was due to the fact that, for much of the nineteenth century, these links were less determined by the cultural mindsets and domestic economic strategies of the participating nations, and more by the discipline of the internationally accepted gold standard. In such conditions, assets, goods and people moved freely across the Atlantic Ocean; and, by the First World War, closer trade and investment ties had been established between the major European nations and the US than between those countries and the rest of the world.[1] At the same time, by the late nineteenth century, not only had the US economy overtaken the major European economies, but it was rapidly becoming less dependent on them for its prosperity. In spite of concerns expressed, in some US quarters, about the increasing domination by European investors of several US industries (Wilkins 1989), by 1914, the combined value of trade and the inward and outward foreign direct investment (FDI) stock of the US, expressed as a proportion of its GNP, was only 15 per cent, compared with around 50 per cent in the case of the leading European nations (Lewis 1938).

The late nineteenth century and the early twentieth century were also a time of quantum leaps in technological and organizational styles, which presented new challenges to European democratic capitalism. The emergence of managerial hierarchies coincided – indeed may have been fostered by – the enormous private wealth of such family dynasties as the Rockefellers, Astors, Vanderbilts and Pierpoint Morgans. The ideology of individualism not only reached its zenith in these years, it also helped fashion the mass production system – better known as Fordism – which the US later exported to the rest of the world. By contrast, in Europe, markets were more fragmented, family businesses were less scale intensive. and less professionally managed; and governments were increasingly taking communitarian postures towards markets, and becoming more predatory in their actions.

While the First World War helped promote closer social affinities between the transatlantic allies, the inter-war years saw a retrenchment of Euro-American trade and investment, as, on both sides of the Atlantic, the attention of governments and markets was given over to internal economic problems. It was in the 1930s that the individualistic philosophy of the American founding fathers was most put to the test; and particularly so through the 'new deal' of Franklin Roosevelt, which, along with the earlier abandonment of the gold standard, brought some aspects of European communitarianism to the US. At the same time, on both continents and in transatlantic commercial transactions, there was little sign of alliance capitalism; indeed, if anything, there was a strengthening of competitive and adversarial relationships between interest groups, such as management and labour, suppliers and customers, and firms and national governments. In such conditions, not only was there little transatlantic greenfield foreign investment, but there were very few Euro-American mergers and acquisitions or strategic alliances, designed either to exploit or to augment the competitive advantages of the acquiring or partner firms.

In the years following the Second World War, the US shared its growing hegemony with an economically ravaged Western Europe, mainly through government-sponsored schemes, such as the Marshall Plan, and through direct investment by US multinational enterprises (MNEs). Indeed, by the mid 1960s, so much of European industry had fallen into US hands that several writers, such as Jacques Servan-Schreiber (1968), were predicting that Europe would soon become a technological satellite of the US. These forebodings were premature. Less than twenty years later, European firms were investing as much in the US as the US was in Europe.[2] In the mid 1990s, west-east flows of goods, services and assets across the North Atlantic were almost perfectly balanced by east-west flows (UNCTAD 1996). Aggregate Euro-US trade and the sales of US affiliates in Europe and European affiliates in the US, in 1994, totalled over $1.5 trillion – 50 per cent higher than their transpacific equivalent. In that same year, not only was one-half of the total US FDI stock and three-fifths of Canadian FDI stock outside North America directed to the European Union, but over two-thirds of the inbound FDI into the US and Canada originated from the European Union (UNCTAD 1996).

In 1995, the US was the largest non-European foreign investor in all EU countries, while Europe was the largest foreign investor in forty-one US states and the second largest in the remaining nine states. Europe is also the leading, or second leading, export market for forty-two states and – outside the US – for Canada as well (European-American Chamber of Commerce 1996). Moreover, much of the transatlantic FDI is high quality investment. In 1992, for example, the US subsidiaries of European firms accounted for nearly two thirds of the research and development (R&D) expenditures of all foreign firms in the US, while three-fifths of the foreign R&D expenditures of US MNEs was undertaken in their European affiliates (Dunning and Narula 1995). In that same year, royalties and fees paid by US corporations to European firms and vice versa accounted for two-thirds of the global royalties and fees paid or received by US corporations.

While these data all point to a growing deepening of transatlantic economic relationships, they neither confirm nor deny the proposition that these links are becoming more cooperative and less adversarial, or that they are more in keeping with alliance capitalism than with hierarchical capitalism, or that they are symptomatic of a convergence or harmonization in the political and social architecture supporting democratic capitalism in Europe and North America. To give force to this proposition, I shall turn to consider some of the more significant events now occurring in the world economy.

Most of us live in a closely knit globalizing economy, the prosperity of which is being increasingly driven by advances in human creativity, and made possible by the liberalization of crossborder markets and fast falling transport and communication costs. Information, knowledge and skills embodied in human and physical capital in the late 1990s are what land was to the early European settlers in North America, and what the ownership of the means of production – and particularly that of machine power – was to our ancestors in the last century. Together with the emergence of new economies, today's globalizing environment is challenging some of our cherished notions about both the organization of economic activity and the moral and political foundations of democratic capitalism (Dunning 1994). Such an ideological reconfiguration is seen, first, in a new interpretation of the role of markets and non-market institutions (especially governments and voluntary associations) in the creation and deployment of human and physical capital; and second, as a response to the paradox that while some of these assets – especially all kinds of information – have become more mobile over geographical space, others, notably most kinds of knowledge-supportive infrastructure and social capital, have not only become less mobile, but have become more embedded in agglomerative clusters of economic and social activities.

Due primarily to the kinds of economic motors now driving globalization, this is demanding changes to the established international division of labour. Originally this division – including that between North America and Europe – was based on the spatial distribution of *natural* assets and on relatively free arm's-length trade. Over the last century, it has been increasingly determined by the distribution of *created* assets; while, in the high-technology and scale-related commercial sectors, trade is increasingly taking place *within* firms rather than *between* firms. Today, the specialization of economic and social tasks and the pattern of cross-border transactions are determined not just by the location-specific resource endowments and institutions of countries and the core competencies of firms, but by the way in which these are combined with each other, and with the assets, competencies and institutions of other countries and firms, through a network of formal and informal alliances. Let me explain what I mean.

Globalization is causing corporations to question a purely individualistic approach towards their production and marketing systems for two reasons. First, more intensive competition resulting from the liberalization of markets, reduced cross-border transport costs and the emergence of new producers from third world countries is compelling them to search for new ways to reduce their production and transaction costs, to upgrade the quality of their existing products and innovate new ones, and to seek out new markets. Frequently, to achieve these goals speedily and effectively, producers have had, not only to streamline the range of their own value-added activities, but to engage in on-going collaborative arrangements with other producers – including those supplying the products previously manufactured within their own organizations.

Such alliancism is being further stimulated by the nature of contemporary technological advances. First, many of the new technologies are generic in the sense that they can be put to multiple uses. Telecommunication and computer-aided design and manufacturing equipment are no less applicable to the food processing and business consultancy industries as they are to the biotechnology and semiconductor sectors. Second, many kinds of economic activity require a variety of technological inputs; genetic engineering and the exploration of space are two cases in point. Such activities prompt collaboration both between the various suppliers of the technologies and between them and user firms. Third, in today's innovatory global environment, not only is the upgrading of technological capacity a competitive necessity for most firms; it is becoming increasingly expensive and is becoming obsolete more quickly. To spread the costs, or speed up the rate, of innovation, to share its risks and to capture new markets, firms are engaging in asset-acquiring investments or alliances, both along and between value chains. Fourth, the success of the use of the core competencies of firms is increasingly resting on their being able to gain access to a wide range of enabling competencies, which are sometimes supplied by nonmarket institutions. This is leading both to a spatial clustering of complementary activities and to increased pressure on the public sector and various non-profit interest groups to provide the social capital necessary to support an efficient market economy.

The idea of 'cooperating to compete', and that alliancism should be regarded as complementary to individualism and to a strong civil sector (Rifkin 1995) applies no less to intra-firm than to inter-firm relationships. The individualistic or adversarial relationships between managers and workers, and the lack of cooperation between different departments within the same firm, is not just less tolerable in today's environment; it is totally counterproductive. Labour under Fordism was primarily treated as a passive factor input like a raw material or a machine. In today's age of flexible production, it is better regarded as an active partner in the productive process and a potential source of creative ideas and programmes. Outside the marketplace the role of the individual, and of small groups of individuals, is also under scrutiny, as the principle of subsidiarity in government and the contribution of non-profit organizations to social well-being are being increasingly recognized. Today, too, it is inconceivable to think of a billion-dollar R&D programme for a new aircraft, or drug, or generation of computers, being conducted without the close and active cooperation between the manufacturer of the product, its main suppliers and its leading industrial customers. Each association is a facet of alliancism.

Perhaps what I am saying is not particularly controversial; and certainly when one examines the evolving pattern of the Euro-American connection over the past decade or so, the evidence, scant as it is, points to a major thrust – which is perhaps more pronounced than in any other part of the world – towards asset-acquiring FDI and inter-firm alliance formation. Let me give just one example. Walter Kuemmerle of Harvard University, in a recent paper (Kuemmerle 1996), has examined both the geographical distribution of the R&D activities of thirty-two leading MNEs in the pharmaceutical and electronics industries over the period 1980–95, and the extent to which the R&D directors of the participating firms perceived that the main purpose of their foreign-based laboratories was to exploit or augment their home-based assets. Kuemmerle not only found that 80 per cent of the innovatory activity of these MNEs was located in the US, Canada and the EU, but a significant, and increasing, proportion of this activity was undertaken outside their home countries, and was designed to add to, rather than utilize, their existing technological capabilities.

If the interaction between alliancism and individualism is fairly evident at a corporate level – and to some extent too in the non-profit sectors[3] – it is much less so at either a corporate-government or an inter-government level. Yet it is here that, if the North American and European economies are to sustain, let alone improve, their competitive positions in today's globalizing economy, there needs to be some convergence in the ideologies and institutions underpinning their approach to economic management – and particularly microeconomic management. Or, putting it rather differently, more attention needs to be given to reducing transatlantic 'system friction' (Ostry 1990).

I am not unduly optimistic that this will be accomplished in the near future, at least not as far as EU-US relations are concerned. This is primarily because, in spite of the growing internationalization of several sectors of the US economy over the last two decades, and the blurring of the economic policies of the left and right of politics on both sides of the Atlantic, by far the greater amount of US economic activity remains firmly wedded to the satisfaction of domestic needs, and is supportive of the ideology of individualism. Only if and when the interests of US citizens and interest groups are better identified with those of the global economy is individualism likely to be modified by alliancism, and domestic policies towards foreign competition and dispute settlement with foreign interests likely to become less adversarial or contractual (Chang and Rowthorn 1995). In Europe there is much less evidence of such dualist philosophy, as most nations are highly dependent on foreign markets for their prosperity. But, even in Europe, it is becoming increasingly clear, despite statements by the European Parliament and the European Commission about issues such as the Social Charter, that the communitarianism of the past needs remodelling if the Union is to combat the competitive challenges from both East Asian and North American firms.

How might cross-border cooperation between the European and North American governments increase, and what form might it take? How far, indeed, is such cooperation necessary or desirable to extract the benefits of inter-firm alliancism?

To what extent might such alliancism be a trail-blazer for a transatlantic free trade area? How formal should it be? How might it differ from existing intra-European and intra-North-American regional integration schemes, or from the multilateral agreements now being drawn up by such organizations as the WTO and the OECD?

These are all questions yet to be resolved, but to conclude, I would like to very briefly describe one initiative in alliance capitalism which is designed, first, to promote a more coordinated approach by the EU and US governments to reducing or eliminating non-tariff barriers in transatlantic trade and investment, and, second, to energize the reform of the social and institutional frameworks underpinning these, and related domestic markets.

The experiment is the Transatlantic Business Dialogue (TABD), which is an unprecedented form of government-business partnership, specifically aimed at encouraging the US and EU governments to work together to enable their companies to better take advantage of the new realities of the global marketplace. TABD has been variously called an experiment in entrepreneurial diplomacy and 'a quadrilateral negotiating forum'.[4] It is a business-level dialogue, yet it is intended to influence the participating governments in their policy formation. It was first launched at a meeting sponsored by the EC Committee of the American Chamber of Commerce in December 1994 by the late US Secretary of Commerce, Ron Brown. A year later, at Seville in Spain, a group of CEOs from the leading US and European MNEs got together to discuss practical ways in which obstacles to transatlantic trade and investment might be removed or reduced. More precisely, the goal of the TABD

> is to encourage the political leaders to analyze the competitive situation on both sides of the Atlantic to ensure that laws and regulations converge wherever possible to allow market forces to accelerate economic growth and job creation and improve international competitiveness. (Jackson 1996, p. 22)

Shortly after the conference in Spain, there was a summit meeting between US President Bill Clinton and EU Commission President Jacques Santer at which many of the seventy specific recommendations which emerged from Seville were incorporated into a new transatlantic agenda, and into a strategic US-EU action plan agreed upon by both parties. These recommendations included the increased transparency of, and cooperation on, environmental standards and regulatory policies; the adoption of a common approach to strengthening the multilateral trading and investment regimes, and to the future work of the WTO; the mutual recognition of conformity assessment procedures; the extension of US-EU customs cooperation and procurement procedures; the establishment of common eligibility standards to govern access to European and US R&D programmes; the development of a global information infrastructure and the removal of all market access barriers for information technology; the initiation of a transatlantic labour dialogue, and the setting up of a task force on EU-US employment-related issues; and a commitment to better harmonize the tax treatment of foreign earned income to encourage more transatlantic investment. By November 1996 – a year after the Seville conference – some progress had been made on several of these issues, in particular the successful conclusion of an EU/US Customs Cooperation and Mutual Assistance Agreement, and the launching of a Transatlantic Small Business Initiative. Sector-specific initiatives include the conclusion, or near conclusion, of Euro-US Mutual Recognition Agreements in the information technology, medical devices and pharmaceutical industries. Less satisfactory progress has been made on harmonization of standards and technical regulations.[5]

As yet, TABD cannot be regarded as more than a small – albeit important – step towards reconciling the different cultural mindsets of the US and European governments towards global democratic capitalism: nor, indeed, is it its main purpose to do so. But, most certainly, in so far as the consequences of this unique and pragmatic model of inter-governmental transatlantic negotiations – which, incidentally, go well beyond trade and investment issues – spill over into other – including domestic – domains of economic activity, they will help transform at least some of the individualistic values of the US and the communitarian tendencies of the EU into the kind of alliancism I am arguing for, without destroying the virtues of either.

Already, international corporations are well aware of the benefits of cross-border alliance formation in their efforts to improve their global competitive positions. So, indeed, are several non-profit clubs or organizations invested in promoting a variety of social objectives,[6] while, for obvious reasons, governments have been reluctant to do so. However, I believe the content and consequences of globalization will eventually force them to cooperate. Indeed, I would argue, it is not so much a question of whether governments will work together with each other, but how – how much and what form such cooperation will take. While I am not arguing that alliance capitalism will, or indeed should, lead to a complete homogenization of the ideological philosophies and institutional superstructures underpinning different national economies, I am suggesting that the successful embrace of globalization will demand some movement in this direction. In this respect, because of their innate political and cultural empathies, North Atlantic rim countries – Canada and the UK in particular[7] – offer an excellent experimental ground both for tackling the challenges and opportunities of alliance capitalism, and for fashioning a new social architecture in a focused and coordinated way.

NOTES

1. With the possible exception of those between the metropolitan powers and their colonial territories (Svedberg 1981).

2. Further details on the post-war history of transatlantic FDI and trade flows are set out in Chapter 7 of Dunning (1993) and in Wallace and Kline (1991). See also the chapter by Peter Buckley and Jeremy Clegg in this volume.
3. The 'not-for-profit' sector is one of the fastest growing sectors of both the US and European economics and well illustrates how the spirit of individualism can be used to promote the interests of groups of individuals. For the most part, however, this non-government-sponsored communitarism is strongly oriented to domestic, rather than cross-border, issues. Notable exceptions include the International Red Cross, the World Council of Churches and several associations fighting crime, terrorism and drug trafficking.
4. There are few published details on the TABD, but what there are are available on the internet at http://iepnt1.itaiep.doc.gov/tabd/tabdrpt.htm. See also an unpublished paper by Cowles (1996).
5. These and other issues were discussed by Euro-US business leaders and government representatives at a conference held in Chicago on 8–9 November 1996.
6. For an account of the role of internationally oriented clubs in a globalizing economy, see especially Eden and Hampson (1990) and Lawrence, Bressand and Ito (1996).
7. Canada because its cultural and political philosophy is more communitarian than that of the US, and the UK because its philosophy is more individualistic than the rest of Europe.

REFERENCES

Chang, H.-J. and R. Rowthorn (eds) (1995), *The Role of the State in Economic Change*, Oxford: Clarendon Press.

Cowles, M.G. (1996), *The Collective Action of Transatlantic Business: The Transatlantic Business Dialogue*, Charlotte, North Carolina: University of North Carolina mimeo.

Dunning, J.H. (ed.) (1993), *The Globalization of Business*, London and New York: Routledge.

Dunning, J.H. (1994), *Globalization. Economic Restructuring and Development*, Geneva: UNCTAD (the 6th Prebisch Lecture).

Dunning, J.H. (1997), *Alliance Capitalism and Global Business*, London and New York: Routledge.

Dunning, J.H. and R. Narula (1995), 'The R&D activities of foreign firms in the US', *International Studies of Management and Organization*, 25 (1–2), Spring–Summer, 39–75.

Eden, L. and F.O. Hampson (1990) *Clubs are Trumps: Towards a Taxonomy of International Regimes*, Ottawa: Carleton University Center for International Trade and Investment Policy Studies, Working Paper 90–102.

European-American Chamber of Commerce (1996), *The United States and Europe: Jobs. Trade and Investment*, Washington: European-American Chamber of Commerce.

Jackson, S. (1996), 'The TABD: an Entrepreneurial force behind the new transatlantic agenda', *ECSA Review*, IX (3), Fall, 21–3.

Kozul-Wright, R. (1995), 'The myth of Anglo-Saxon capitalism: reconstructing the history of the American state', in H.-J. Chang and R. Rowthorn (eds), *The Role of the State in Economic Change*, Oxford: Clarendon Press.

Kuemmerle, W. (1996), *The Drivers of Foreign Direct Investment into Research and Development: An Empirical Investigation*, Boston: Harvard Business School Working Paper No. 96:062.

Lawrence, R.Z., A. Bressand and T. Ito (1996), *A Vision for the World Economy*, Washington, DC: Brookings Institution.

Lewis, C. (1938), *America's Stake in International Investment*, Washington, DC: Brookings Institution.

Lodge, G.C. and E. Vogel (1987), *Ideology and National Competitiveness*, Boston, MA: Harvard Business School Press.

Novak, M. (1982), *The Spirit of Democratic Capitalism*, New York: Simon and Schuster.

Ostry, S. (1990), *Governments and Corporations in a Shrinking World: Trade and Innovation Policies in the United States, Europe and Japan*, New York and London: Council on Foreign Relations.

Rifkin, J. (1995), *The End of Work*, New York: G.P. Putnam's Sons.

Servan-Schreiber, J.J. (1968), *The American Challenge*, London: Hamish Hamilton.

Svedberg, P. (1981) 'Colonial enforcement of foreign direct investment', *Manchester School of Economic & Social Studies*, 49, 21–38.

UNCTAD (1996), *World Investment Report 1996: Investment. Trade and International Policy Arrangements*, New York and Geneva: UN.

Wallace, C.D. and J.M. Kline (1991), *EC 1992 and Changing Global Investment Patterns: Implications for the US-EC Relationship*, Washington Center for Strategic and International Studies, Significant Issues Series, Vol XIV, No. 2.

Wilkins, M. (1989), *The History of Foreign Investment in the United States before 1914*, Cambridge, MA: Harvard University Press.

2. Atlantic interdependencies and free trade

Stephen Blank and Anne Taillandier

In exploring Atlantic interdependencies, participants in this volume confronted a series of profound contradictions. Some of these have been commented upon widely – the complex relationship between states and markets in an environment of market liberalization and state strategies to enhance competitiveness, and the conflicting requirements of differing forms of corporate governance, affected by pressures for convergence but also for continued differentiation. This chapter examines one of the most important contradictions – that between the high levels of Atlantic structural interdependence and the political distances affecting policy interdependencies between Europe and North America. Recommendations for Atlantic free trade are then assessed.

Patterns of transatlantic trade and investment are characterized by 'deep' integration.[1] Two-way trade between the United States and the European Union rose from $190 billion in 1990 to $351 billion in 1994, when the EU received 23 per cent of US exports and the US received 18 per cent of EU exports. Intra-firm commerce, which is a high proportion of this trade, is related to a high level of interdependence in foreign direct investment. In 1996 about 50 per cent of the US foreign direct investment position was in the EU, and almost 60 per cent of EU foreign direct investment was in the USA.[2]

These economic linkages overlay a much more complex historical relationship of isolation and integration. In the seventeenth century, the New World was viewed as an adjunct of Europe. But Americans were soon deeply instilled with a sense of the uniqueness of their own society and in the early 1800s, the American people, in George Dangerfield's words, 'endeavoured to turn their backs upon Europe, insofar as Europe represented the kind of world history they most detested'.[3] Few immigrants to America retained effective loyalties to their lands of birth, and ties across the Atlantic have more often been symbolic and mythical than intimate and informed.[4]

The rejection of Atlantic interdependence was most vivid in the isolationism of the 1920s and 1930s. The lesson of the First World War, widely assimilated by Americans in the decades following the war, was to avoid involvement in European conflicts ever again. The American presidency became an object of

Congressional mistrust in this period largely because excessive presidential discretion in foreign affairs was viewed as the cause of our involvement in the First World War. By 1937, according to a Gallup poll, three-quarters of the country favoured a so-called Peace Amendment which provided that except in the event of an actual invasion 'the authority of Congress to declare war shall not become effective until confirmed by a majority of all votes cast in a Nationwide referendum'. The Peace Amendment was defeated in the House of Representatives in 1937 by a vote of only 209 to 188. In 1937 more than 70 per cent of those questioned in a poll thought that the USA should not have entered the First World War.[5]

This brief history suggests how remarkable was the shift in policy after World War II which brought the US into an intimate fifty-year strategic and economic relationship with Western Europe. Driven by the Soviet menace, the US crossed 'the massive barrier between traditional isolation and global leadership'.[6] Americans were deeply reluctant to address this challenge. It was not at all clear in February 1947, when the British government delivered a note to the State Department which, in effect, declared Britain's inability to continue to stabilize the eastern Mediterranean – which would open the entire area to Communist control – that the US would step into this breach. America's rise to global leadership and the creation of the Atlantic Alliance, which seemed inevitable in retrospect, did not appear to be so at the time.

The West European states were dependent partners, and Atlantic economic ties developed because of US support for regional integration in Europe that was expected to provide a structural foundation for a substantial military capability. On the European side policies toward America's leadership role were for the most part deferential. Germany, emerging as the core industrialized state of the European Community, avoided assertiveness in foreign relations, and combined association with France in the leadership of the Community with support for the USA's containment policy, despite difficulties caused by strong expressions of French nationalism under de Gaulle. Gaullist policy sought to emphasize France's independence within the European Community and the Community's need to avoid American domination. Britain, unwilling at first to join the European Community, found its efforts to maintain a special relationship across the Atlantic neutralized as US policy focused increasingly on Germany as the leading European economic power and as a partner in attempts at global monetary cooperation.

RECENT HISTORY

Several interacting sequences of change affected the Atlantic Alliance and Atlantic economic ties after the mid 1960s. Structural interdependencies between

Europe and North America continued to rise, especially because the European Community remained the main destination of US foreign direct investment, while trade and transnational production links across the Atlantic grew substantially, partly because the persistence of non-tariff barriers in intra-Community trade made commerce with the US more significant for Community members. The Community entered a period of stagnant growth, losing competitiveness in world markets, and imbalances developed in the structural interdependence with North America. Meanwhile détente in Europe began to weaken political foundations of the Atlantic alliance, opening up opportunities for relatively independent European and American endeavours to reach understandings with the USSR.

America

American policy shifts were caused principally by the Vietnam war and by the changing economic environment in America. The Vietnam conflict struck deeply into many fundamentals of American life – relationships between government and governed, between generations, races, and genders. Patterns of social disintegration were accentuated, and the social consensus of the post-war era broke down. Political divisions were deepened and insecurities rose. In foreign and security policy Americans became less decisive, cautious lest another foreign entanglement produce a similar wrenching experience. Between 1964 and 1970, confidence in government and in America's capacity for global leadership declined precipitately.[7]

Economic change during the 1980s and continuing into the present decade also affected the dynamics of policy making, weakening confidence and consensus. Large fiscal and trade deficits, increasing unemployment, and rising economic inequalities raised difficult questions about policy mixes which seemed unable to cope with a series of domestic economic and social problems. It is difficult not to believe that the transition from George Bush, whose generation came of age in the ultimate triumphs of the Second World War, to Bill Clinton, whose generation came of age during the defeat in Vietnam, is of defining importance in understanding how the United States views itself today. American leaders are far less optimistic about the efficacy of projecting US force abroad and have less confidence in dealing with overseas partners. Mistrust of government is heightened by a sense of gridlock and frustration that froze the legislative process in the last years of the Bush administration and all but overwhelmed Clinton's first administration.

Problems of economic management in a more competitive world assumed large dimensions as the European Community opted for complete internal market integration during the late 1980s, absorbed new members, and made progress towards monetary union. Asymmetries in bargaining strengths across the

Atlantic were altered, and meanwhile the Japanese challenge in world markets became a more formidable problem.

America's modern political system emerged from a long crisis, beginning with the depression in the 1930s and continuing through World War II and the Cold War. Power was centralized in Washington, and there, in the executive, although executive dominance in policy making was never deeply institutionalized. For almost half a century, foreign and security policy objectives set parameters for domestic policy, and overriding security requirements of the Cold War provided discipline in organizing the vast array of interests that competed for access to the policy-making process. The collapse of the Soviet bloc had a tremendous impact not only on US policy but on the nature of the policy-making process as well.

Power is now flowing from the executive to Congress, and from Washington back to states, while at all levels policy processes have become more fragmented. Presidential leadership has declined sharply.[8] Congress has become an independent power, attempting to 'micromanage' foreign policy issues.[9] Developments since the Nixon presidency and the end of the Cold War have opened the policy process widely to interest penetration, and the social and economic changes of recent decades have greatly enlarged the number of groups seeking to influence policy.

Trade policy especially has been affected by interest group pressures, as different sections of American society have experienced vulnerabilities associated with foreign trade and foreign direct investment. Aggressive demands are made for 'fair' trade – demands which previously would have been restrained by political and strategic concerns. Securing passage of the North America Free Trade Area agreement revealed the new dynamics of trade policy making. NAFTA, it appears, was not so much sold to Congress as a policy ideal as bought from individual Congressmen in return for favours on an unprecedented scale.

This trade policy activism has involved state and local governments, asserting interests in promoting exports, attracting foreign direct investment, and restricting disruptive imports. This activism has been in effect encouraged by shifts of federal power to the states, in accordance with a rationale for increased responsiveness by state governments to local needs, but difficulties in engagement with those requirements have contributed to the state-level efforts to influence the federal government's management of foreign economic relations.[10]

Europe

European policy shifts have responded principally to the logic of deepening and widening regional integration. The objectives have been to increase growth and attain greater international competitiveness by forming a large single market in which the national firms of member countries will achieve efficiencies comparable with those of their American and Japanese rivals. The development of consensus for complete market integration was slow, but was pushed forward by Jacque Delors' energetic leadership of the European Commission. Major advances towards complete regional market integration posed questions about competition policy, foreign direct investment policy, industrial policy, and the structuring of common institutions, but on these matters agreement was difficult. Progress in policy learning resulted in commitments to monetary union, which would facilitate operations in the single market, but engagement with problems of structural competitiveness for the Union as a whole was hampered by uncertainties and conflicting preferences regarding the potential benefits of wider collaboration in economic management.

Consensus for deeper integration was hindered during the first half of the 1990s by a recession which limited the gains from the operation of the single market. The recession was attributable mainly to German monetary tightening, necessitated by the heavy costs of rehabilitating the former East German economy. In the context of the recession the attitudes of policy makers in member countries tended to become more ambivalent towards options for increased economic cooperation within the Union, but also more absorbed in those options. Interest in questions of economic cooperation with the USA thus appeared to be less active than it might have been in conditions of less strain and uncertainty. Meanwhile the evolution of the Union was changing as it was enlarged by the accession of new northern members and as the reunified Germany consolidated its position as the dominant economic power of the region.

Deepening integration and enlargement meant that the European Union had to devote more attention to its external environment, and especially to Atlantic relations, but awareness of this imperative remained limited, and the difficulties of decision making at the Union level tended to prevent the taking of major external initiatives. Issues in the external environment were, however, becoming more significant and had major implications for the Union's relations with the US. During the mid 1990s, the United States became committed to a drive for Asia Pacific trade liberalization, as part of a regional strategy that had been evident in the formation of the North America Free Trade Area. This dramatized the wide scope for American economic diplomacy: the European Union had few opportunities for intrusive economic diplomacy in the Asia Pacific area, in which most of its members had long been losing market shares. The Union was expanding economic links with Mediterranean and East European countries, but these promised only moderate benefits over the long term.

CURRENT ATLANTIC TIES

The weakening of Atlantic security bonds since the end of the Cold War has adversely affected political ties that could help sustain cooperative management of the deep structural links between the European Union and the US. Differences over economic issues now threaten the Atlantic political ties under strain, and a new transregional security consensus is not in prospect. Major security problems for each side call for intensive collaborative short-term and long-term planning, but do not command high priorities in US and European policy making. Domestic economic problems, in conditions of intensified pluralism, tend to give an inward-looking orientation to US policy processes. Intra-regional problems of growth and employment have a similar effect in the European Union.

The North Atlantic Treaty Organization is evolving reactively, in response to localized crises, without consensus on how it should grow and how it should relate to potential new members in Eastern Europe and to the transitional Russian political economy. There is a degree of consensus that the development of a market economy in Russia must be further encouraged through multilateral aid and the expansion of trade links, but little apparent optimism that this will help to form a viable democracy. Opportunities for dialogue on fundamentals with Russian political elites are not being seized, although NATO enlargements under consideration clearly risk stirring Russian nationalism – a potent unifying force that could activate an authoritarian solution for the country's acute problems of transitional adjustment and growth.

Organizational adaptation and development require leadership, but, while there are questions about continuity in the inward preoccupations noted in Europe and the US, there are also questions about shifts of American attention to the Pacific and to Latin America. Europe is increasingly preoccupied by awkward triangular policy interactions between Germany, France, and Britain which are linked with diverging views and preferences regarding the further enlargement of the European Union and its association with the evolution of NATO. Internal concerns in the USA allow more freedom in the choice of foreign policy options, as the American administration acts alone on the basis of a strong global presence, with opportunities in the high growth area of East Asia where attention focuses on rivalry with Japan. The competitive challenges in this rivalry are more potent than those that can be envisaged if European firms substantially increase their efficiencies through operations in their single market.

In the European context, German policy is committed to the deepening and enlargement of the Union, with emphasis on the acceptance of East European countries, the preservation of strong political and security ties with the USA, and continued partnership with France in the leadership of the Union. That partnership, however, requires consideration of French preferences for the development of a Union that will be very independent, maintaining relatively weak ties with the US. British policy, active mainly outside the Franco-German connection, and with less influence on Union decision making, supports the enlargement of the Union but is reluctant to contribute to its deepening, and emphasizes the preservation of links with the US. The interests motivating retention of those links partially coincide with Germany's, but diverge because of use of the connection to strengthen Britain's status in the Union as a member with confederal preferences.

For the US, dialogue with Germany appears to have the most productive potential, while the differing policy orientations of the three major European Union members prevent the evolution of a common Union foreign and security policy. Substantively, Germany policy is more closely aligned with US political, security, and economic interests, is sustained by relatively stable policy processes, and is implemented with a very strong presence in the dynamics of Union decision making. For cultural reasons, however, the scope for comprehensive understandings is greater in US relations with Britain, in which policy communities on each side are influenced by large two-way flows of research literature. The utility of rapport that may be attained with British decision makers is significant in the security area mainly as it complements US understandings with Germany, but is of less value in the economic area because of the priority that US policy has to give to interaction with Germany and to consideration of Franco-German preferences.

The complexities and uncertainties that must be reckoned with in US Atlantic relations raise questions about possible reorientations of American policy. America has extensive interests in the dynamic Asia Pacific area. American firms export twice as much to Asian markets as to European.[11] Between 1992 and 2000, 40 per cent of the world's new purchasing power will be in East Asia, and that area will absorb between 35 and 40 per cent of the global increase in imports. Latin America's prospects are less promising, but US interest is being attracted by recovery from the disruptive effects of the Mexican currency crisis, by the efforts of the Mercosur countries to integrate their markets and by vigorous growth in many Latin securities markets.

There is much evidence of rising inwardness of US policy interests. With the end of the Cold War, the perception has grown among publics and elites alike that the US has few fundamental security interests at stake in the world, and that much more attention should be focused on domestic problems. A recent *Wall Street Journal*/NBC News poll found that some 78 per cent of Americans do not believe that they or their spouses work for a company that exports, and that 73 per cent reject the view that they or their spouses work for a company that faces foreign competition. National security focuses increasingly on domestic economic and social issues rather than foreign policy. The debate over the impact of globalization has increased significantly in recent years. It cuts across party lines and further reduces party coherence and makes American politics even less manageable.

Nationalism has become more acceptable. A new 'American Liberal Nationalism' is posed as '*the* alternative to the fissioning that the multiculturalists celebrate as pluralism and the democratic universalists condemn as Balkanization', and would involve 'a new union of cultural and economic nationalism in the interest of the transracial middle class'. Key economic policies would include strict restriction of immigration to raise wages at the bottom of the income ladder, checks on the expatriation of American industry and the institution of a 'social tariff' to deter American employers from responding in a tight labour market to rising wages at home by transferring production abroad, and to preserve middle-class living standards. The leading exponent of this view writes that a 'high-skill, high-wage strategy of selective multilateralism that realistically addresses the need for government regulation of cross-border flows of goods, labour, and capital, while preserving the ideal of free trade among the industrial democracies, will probably become increasingly attractive to policymakers responding to pressure from the wage-earning majority'.[12]

LOOKING FORWARD: POSSIBLE SCENARIOS

American leaders continue to promote ties across the Atlantic despite the uncertainty of transatlantic relations in the aftermath of the Cold War. But those who have spoken in favour of strengthening the relationship on both sides of the Atlantic are aware that it can no longer rely solely on the old framework. Atlantic trade and investment relationships are deep, mature and balanced. But they are also ambiguous. Transatlantic trade and investment operate on 'two planes, corporate and political'. 'On the corporate plane, trade and above all investment continue to grow, with the result that economic interdependence increases ... The political plane, by contrast, is characterized by some shrill language and mutual recrimination.' At times it seems that the two heavyweights of international trade are 'more than ready to stand and trade blows'.[13] Defining a new common objective is at the core of the debate on transatlantic relations. Many believe that the EU and the US should set a new, pragmatic, geoeconomic objective and build on their existing trade and investment interdependencies.

As the world economy seemed to be dividing into economic blocs in the second half of the 1980s, and as American firms were battered by global competitors, economic cooperation across the Atlantic became increasingly uncertain. Uncertainty was heightened by the European unity project. Later, with the launching of the European agenda of 1992, political tensions began to centre on the perception in certain sections of the US policy community that the EC's internal market programme was contributing to the construction of a 'Fortress Europe'. The US responded to what it perceived as unfair trading practices of its partners and sought to construct a safety belt of non-tariff barriers and retaliatory measures – in particular the 'Super 301'. Relations, already frayed, were much aggravated by difficulties in concluding the Uruguay round.

Americans blamed the Europeans for foot-dragging, and several crises almost put an end to the Uruguay round enterprise. The US-Canada free trade agreement was no sooner concluded than Washington and Mexico City launched NAFTA negotiations, and some American leaders pressed immediately to extend NAFTA throughout the hemisphere.

Fred Bergsten observed that ultimate failure in the Uruguay round 'would have discredited the entire global system and raised the spectre of competing blocs'. He felt that APEC – by joining East Asia and North America – could eliminate the possibility of a three-bloc world so widely feared in the early 1990s. But the potential for trade bloc competition was by no means ended. A two-bloc world that would convey substantial dangers could still arise if APEC and Europe failed to work out satisfactory accommodation. 'The EU frequently seems to focus so heavily on its regional agenda that it forgets its global responsibilities', wrote Bergsten. 'The United States is often viewed as preoccupied with NAFTA or APEC – or as turning protectionist more generally, a fear heightened by the early successes of Pat Buchanan in this year's Republican primaries.'[14]

From the perspective of US-Europe relations, several scenarios seem possible in the near future. They include incompatible trade blocs and future trade wars, compatible trade regions and perhaps, a transatlantic FTA.

Incompatible Trade Blocs

One scenario, popular with journalists at the end of the 1980s, envisaged a world organized by hostile trade blocs – 'Fortress Europe', 'Fortress North America' and a new 'Greater East Asia Co-Prosperity Sphere'. A rash of books anticipated a new 'struggle for supremacy' among Japan, Germany and the US, together with their client countries.[15]

Several strands were bundled together in this scenario. One was the fear that balance of power politics would revive among the three major players in the global system with the collapse of Cold War bipolarism. A second was a growing concern about inwardness in all three major centres. A key goal in the European agenda was to achieve greater independence from the United States. Rising concerns in Europe about high levels of government expenditure, a worsening crisis of welfare spending and mounting unemployment suggested that the core countries of the EU might seek refuge in isolationism. At the same time, large numbers of Americans were turning their attention inward, and Japanese were faltering in their efforts to 'internationalize' business practices. Fred Bergsten summarized these fears well:

> A central question of the 1990s is whether the new structure of international relations will produce conflict over economic issues or healthy competition and cooperation. History suggests that there is considerable risk of conflict, even spilling over from the

economic sphere into new political rivalries ... The ultimate paradox of the 20th century would be a realization of the Marxist prophecy of inevitable conflict among the capitalist nations just as the political conflict spurred by Marxist ideology was waning.[16]

Compatible Regional Trade Organizations: TAFTA

The fear that old allies might drift apart with the end of the Cold War led to efforts to redefine the transatlantic bridge. Some thought about constructing an economic NATO, while others questioned whether strengthening economic relations would be a sufficient step to redefine the alliance. Soon after the formation of NAFTA, a number of Europeans and Americans began to explore the feasibility of constructing some sort of transatlantic free trade agreement or 'TAFTA' that would represent a combined output of $13 trillion and 700 million people on both sides of the ocean.

The idea seems to have been most fully developed by Canada's International Trade Minister Roy MacLaren at a meeting in London in May 1995 when he spoke of a transatlantic free trade area that would revitalize the global trading system and begin the crucial task of bridging potentially exclusionary blocs. MacLaren proposed the creation of a Transatlantic Eminent Persons group to examine priorities for future trade negotiations and identify gaps in existing structures and to report to a meeting of the Heads of Government in June 1996.

To some observers, the need for a transatlantic agreement was obvious. Clyde Prestowitz, for example, stated that the absence of a transatlantic free trade area and of any high-level push by the United States and the European Union to create it 'is a great mystery of modern international economic affairs'.[17] Ernest Preeg similarly observed that

> the bottom line for the trading system ... is that the regional free trade genie is irreversibly out of the bottle. The EU and NAFTA alone already account for 43 percent of world trade, and other ongoing free trade initiatives should push this figure well above 50 percent. It is only in this context that the full meaning – and potential – of a TAFTA can be understood.[18]

Official support for the idea remained cool, however. The Clinton Administration, having been handled so roughly by Congress on the ratification of NAFTA and the Uruguay Round, gave no signs that it was strongly committed to a TAFTA and produced no concrete proposals. Secretary of State Christopher suggested that the Atlantic partners start with less sensitive areas such as standards and then deal with issues left out of the Uruguay Round agreement, such as telecommunications and financial services. France remained aloof as well, fearing for the fate of the Common Agricultural Policy and for its role in the EU. Prime Minister Juppe and others felt that the Uruguay Round package had to be digested first, and that efforts should be made to strengthen the WTO before embarking on a TAFTA project. Europeans in general wanted discussions to include international monetary issues and the low value of the dollar. Business leaders showed greater interest: a hundred CEOs from both sides of the Atlantic met in Seville on 10–11 November 1995 for a Transatlantic Business Dialogue. And a number of think tanks – the Council on Foreign Relations and the British-North American Committee, for example – were asked by different political authorities to develop ideas and comments on a TAFTA plan.

A New Transatlantic Agenda was signed at the Madrid summit in December 1995. One key objective was to reinforce the relationship across the Atlantic in four critical political areas – to promote peace, political stability and development worldwide, fight against crime, drugs and pollution, advance science, education and cultural and professional transatlantic linkages and create a new transatlantic free marketplace. To achieve these goals, the new Agenda was accompanied by a Joint EU-US Action Plan committing the two parties to work together on 150 policy areas to each of which a separate declaration was dedicated.

Still, with all of the talk about a TAFTA, it was not clear what form it might take. The Economic Strategy Institute projects the trade gains from a TAFTA at $70 billion over seven years with a total boost to US GDP of $42 billion. A TAFTA mandate would phase out tariffs on all goods and services, liberalize agricultural trade and other sensitive sectors such as textiles, work toward suppression of non-tariff barriers and insure the protection of intellectual property rights investment. In the ESI's view, the most useful outcome of signing a TAFTA would be a joint transatlantic effort to work towards the elimination of NTBs, such as environmental or health regulations with trade-impeding effects. Eliminating all barriers to trade across the Atlantic could boost economic output in the United States by $142–$239 billion (between 1.6 and 2.8 per cent of GDP) and in the European Union by $94–$184 billion (between 1.0 and 1.9 per cent of total EU output).[19]

Others are more cautious and less optimistic. Tariff reductions, they say, would not generate large gains because Atlantic tariffs after the Uruguay Round will be generally very low. EU tariffs on US imports will average only 6.36 per cent and US tariffs on EU imports only 3.19 per cent. The removal of tariff barriers would be important only for the sensitive sectors left out of the last round of GATT negotiations. Even if a TAFTA were successful in phasing out all remaining tariff barriers, its success in removing existing non-tariff barriers or preventing new ones from being erected is more doubtful. The fears provoked by such an agreement may lead special interests to press for the creation of new inhibitions to trade and investment flows. This would be all the more tempting because important structural differences between the US and the EU which could be used as justifications for new barriers.

Although the debate on a TAFTA focuses largely on tariff barriers in sensitive sectors, the critical obstacle may well be barriers created by different social, economic and political structures and practices. The two sides have different visions of an economic community – differences between the EU, an economic union born out of a vision of peace in the midst of the Cold War, and NAFTA, a more pragmatic free trade agreement which recognized the deepening *de facto* economic integration of Canada, the US and Mexico. The European Union has a common commercial policy, with supranational institutions and a community law binding on the member nations, while the United States constitution recognizes the preeminence of state legislation. A TAFTA would have to accommodate the different regulatory policies and structural impediments already in existence. Subsidies are more likely to be viewed as legitimate policy instruments in Europe than in the US. Similarly, the US recognizes host country control over investment, while the EU applies home country control. Battles may well erupt over different policies on rules of origin. Sharp differences in the social dimensions of the European Union, which has a social charter, and NAFTA promise public discontent and controversy over labour and social issues. A TAFTA could be overwhelmed by the complexity of dissimilar labour laws and their implementation, by different levels of productivity and wages and, above all, by high unemployment levels in Europe and an already trying debate over immigration from Mexico to the United States.

Brian Hindley lays four main alternatives for a transatlantic alliance. A transatlantic free trade area with conditional most favoured nation clause would phase out tariffs on all trade sectors, even the most sensitive. Liberalizing these sectors would generate most of the gains of a TAFTA because they remain the only sectors with high tariffs, but political opposition on both sides of the Atlantic would abort this project. A second scenario would be to use the combined weight of the US and the EU to push a GATT-inconsistent TAFTA through the WTO. Such an agreement would violate Article XXIV by including only certain sectors of trade and by preventing the liberalization of other sensitive sectors such as agriculture. This enterprise, too, would probably fail and doom a TAFTA. Hindley fears that if it succeeded, it could open the way to numerous other partial agreements worldwide and eventually destroy the WTO. A third alternative would permit concessions made within TAFTA to be multilateralized. This is an option the transatlantic partners should consider, but Hindley feels it would also be rejected. A fourth alternative would be to restrict the project to areas in which there is no WTO involvement, and hence no MFN obligation to extend concessions to other WTO members.[20]

Patrick Messerlin says that a transatlantic agreement should focus on the removal of non-tariff barriers left out of the Uruguay Round negotiations. He differentiates three types of these NTBs: 'the Untouchables' (intellectual property rights, investment rules, steel, agriculture and public procurement –

especially public utilities in Europe and mass transportation in the US), 'the Reachables' (rules of origin, governmental norms and firm standards and services left of the General Agreement on Trade in Services such as air transport, audiovisual services and shipping) and 'the Questionables' (commitments on the removal of NTBs that do not seem likely to be honoured in the foreseeable future).[21]

A smooth transition to a TAFTA with no obvious threat to industrial jobs in Europe or the United States is a misleadingly rosy scenario. Still, enthusiasts like MacLaren tend to downplay the importance of these structural differences and suggest ways around them. When confronting the problem that NAFTA is not a customs union like the EU, MacLaren suggests that a precedent was established several years ago during EU negotiations with the member states of the European Free Trade Association. This, he said, could involve separate bilateral negotiations on levels of discipline in such areas as services, intellectual property, and investment.

TAFTA Implications

Would a TAFTA be an exclusive club denying access to Asian countries? Some at least are motivated to build a transatlantic entity able to speak on trade matters with a single voice and powerful enough to protect itself from the Asian commercial threat and perhaps even to dictate its rules to the rest of the world. To others, the aim of a TAFTA would not be to exclude Asians, but to bring together Europeans and Americans with historic and intimate cultural as well as economic linkages. For Prestowitz, for example, the rationale for a TAFTA is that Europeans are the 'most like us' and play the free trade game by the same rules. Asian countries have accounted for a large part of the US trade deficit while the EU and the US have conducted a balanced two-way trade, and have large, roughly balanced investment portfolios in each other's countries. TAFTA, therefore, is a 'trade policy natural'.

> A TAFTA would link countries that are already at comparable levels of socioeconomic development and already share a strong commitment to free-market practices. Thanks largely to this common ground, as well as to deep cultural affinities, economic relations between the two regions represent the world's greatest combined two-way flow of goods, services, capital, and technology. Indeed, due to the balanced nature of these economic flows, the US- EU economic relationship stands as a model of mutually beneficial international commerce.[22]

Another issue is consistency with the WTO and the promotion of global free trade. Would a TAFTA be a building block for global trade or a transatlantic economic fortress? To some, regional trade agreements serve as an impetus for promoting world trade by keeping the bicycle moving forward – by maintaining momentum in trade liberalization. Others disagree strongly. Jagdish Bhagwati argues that 'this obsession with free-trade areas strikes a blow at the multilateral system in ways that are either ill-understood or deliberately discounted, disregarded and distorted by politicians and lobbyists'. The wisest course of action would be to concentrate on the WTO. TAFTA, along with other preferential-trading areas, should be a 'trial balloon' and 'reshaped into a worldwide, multilateral trade negotiation'.[23] Jeffrey Schott is concerned that a TAFTA might not be consistent with the WTO, might erect new obstacles to multilateral trade and might adversely affect trade with developing nations. As an alternative, he proposes the launching of a new round of WTO trade negotiations. To him, the 'WTO-2000' initiative, a new round of multilateral trade negotiations by the year 2000, 'would avoid a process implicit in a WTO-consistent TAFTA that puts a spotlight on politically sensitive issues that could well exacerbate bilateral trade frictions'.[24]

Others oppose making TAFTA a priority in the renewal of NAFTA-EU relations. After assessing the feasibility of a TAFTA, Hindley concludes that 'the idea of closer transatlantic links is attractive, but TAFTA is a distraction. Neither the EU nor NAFTA has any good alternative to the multilateral trading system, nor any actual interest with respect to it other than to strengthen it.'[25] Others, Gary Hufbauer and Barbara Kotschwar, advocate a 'TAP' – a Transatlantic Partnership. Like TAFTA, a TAP would aim at reducing tariffs and liberalize trade but would do so with the broader objective of promoting the WTO. In addition, it could foster the establishment of 'systems to ensure non-discriminatory product standards and to create mutually recognized conformity assessment procedures (usually laboratory tests), [which] could set the stage for a future WTO accord'.[26]

Patrick Messerlin envisages a transatlantic free trade agenda that would focus on the non-tariff barriers left by the Uruguay Round. His agenda would launch a kind of 'free trade by instalments' earlier advocated by Hugh Corbet for the APEC. It would include a package of MRAs – mutual recognition agreements – that entail a minimal level of harmonization and a set of common rules on competition, investment, norms and audiovisual issues. The advantage of the MRAs is that they are consistent with the WTO and do not impinge on national sovereignty.[27]

What would the impact of a TAFTA be on global trade patterns? Some fear that the proliferation of regional arrangements would make it more difficult to maintain consistency with the global system. Bergsten fears that a TAFTA could have a very negative effect on the global trading system by encompassing new discrimination by rich against poor and reversing all the progress toward North-South trade cooperation. Excluding emerging economic giants such as India or China would be a grave mistake because it risks reversing the process of heightening the integration of the South in the global trading system.[28] TAFTA proponents, however, believe that its advantages would outweigh these problems. A critical role for TAFTA would be to defend the position of market-oriented economies and the values that support them in the changing world economy.

> Without greatly intensified cooperative transatlantic economic efforts to influence the integration process, the market oriented economies of the West could be fatally divided during the various negotiations that will write the rules for the new global economy. Moreover, if market oriented values do not predominate in this new economy, political support in Western Europe and North America for continued trade liberalization will be endangered.[29]

TAFTA or TAP would establish patterns of behaviour for other countries – a 'trade yardstick'. The Atlantic partners, like two older sisters, would set examples for their novice siblings and provide them with a 'handout' of proper trade conduct. The overwhelming size of a common transatlantic economic area would pressure others into conforming to North American and European trade standards. The WTO presently is incapable of dealing with problems that result from accelerating 'deep integration'. TAFTA, negotiated between two regions already sharing many economic values and practices, would show the rest of the word how to address these problems constructively and efficiently.[30] 'Once the US and EU agree on new trade rules', write Clayton Yeutter and Warren Maruyama, 'uncooperative developing countries would face a rapidly diminishing set of choices – basically either to sign up or go it alone without attractive access to US and EU markets.'[31]

A debate which poses TAFTA simply as either endangering the WTO or strengthening it as a building block toward multilateral free trade may well fail to illuminate the wider stakes involved. Preeg, for example, argues that a TAFTA could lead to a fundamental transformation of the trading system. A relatively quickly negotiated TAFTA which included an OECD investment agreement would facilitate the broadening of regional free trade in Europe and the Western Hemisphere and would also provide the impetus for an 'OECD-wide free trade agreement' by leaving Japan little choice but to join in.[32]

Could TAFTA become a new framework for transatlantic relations? Experts are divided. James Dobbins observes that 'the forging of a trade alliance between the United States and Europe may represent a natural means of adapting the Atlantic community to a new world order, one in which geoeconomics is replacing, or at least competing on equal terms with, geopolitics as a central determinant of international relations'.[33] By contrast, Hufbauer and Kotschwar believe that a TAFTA would lack sufficient substance to serve as a new framework for Atlantic relations. A TAFTA limited to trade and investment would be too narrow to replace NATO in transatlantic relations.

A stronger economic alliance, some argue, would allay security disagreements. We are skeptical. Economics is economics and geopolitics remain geopolitics. Although the twain can sometimes meet, and while bad relations in one area can spill over to the other, it seems improbable that transatlantic disputes over regional security will be resolved by stronger economic glue.[34]

TAFTA may lack inspirational power – especially enough to keep the US a vital participant in the Atlantic and global communities.

At least some proposals for both sides of the Atlantic may be motivated by a sense of a need to find a means of holding US interests, and reinvigorating US involvement, in the rest of the world ... TAFTA, though, almost certainly, is not a cure. If lack of US interest in the rest of the world is the problem, TAFTA is too small to solve it. Solutions to a problem of that magnitude call for projects that offer more to the imagination of Americans, and engage the interests of enough of them to change the balance.[35]

The Normalization of Interdependence: the 'End of Geography'

A third scenario is also a possibility. In this scenario, technological innovation makes high levels of integration possible without the need for physical presence. Key elements that differentiate national from international business activities would diminish. The result might be termed the 'normalization of globalization'.

Richard O'Brien has written about the 'end of geography' in financial markets. 'The end of geography, as a concept applied to international financial relationships', he observes, 'refers to a state of economic development where geographical location no longer matters in finance, or matters much less than hitherto.' [36] New technology in communications and computing 'makes it less necessary for firms to be everywhere – what is necessary is to be plugged into the interconnected networks'. Greater access to markets, O'Brien observes, has not automatically meant greater market share. Rather, greater access has heightened competition, making market share even more difficult to gain and squeezing profits margins everywhere. With intensifying competition and declining margins, firms are struggling to identify ways of widening their business without bearing the cost of establishing many new operations.

The same evolution seems to hold true in manufacturing. Hypercompetition is a response to dramatic environmental changes such as customization, globalization, rapid technological change, deregulation and shifting workforce demographics. These changes in the environment drive the transformation of organizational forms from command and control to information-based organization.[37] The result is that here, too, strategic outsourcing and a wide array of other alliance structures may preclude the necessity for physical presence in overseas markets, and also contribute to the capture of much greater efficiencies. Or, as Charles Handy observes, the 'intellectual organization' of the future might become 'a collection of project teams, harnessing the intellectual assets around a task or an assignment, rather as a consultancy company or an advertising agency now does'.[38]

The Ford 2000 project seeks to normalize global activities as well, although using a much different platform. Once again, technology is the key which, in this case, makes possible high levels of real-time integration across the Atlantic in all critical aspects of auto design and development.

> Thanks to video conferencing and linked computer networks, Ford no longer needs to bring together every member of each team at a single site. Engineers and designers, working with the same Silicon Graphics Inc. terminal that generated the dinosaurs for the firm *Jurassic Park*, can in effect be wired into a single studio.[39]

The bottom line in this scenario is that technological innovation could transform the entire process of international commerce, eliminating many of those elements that specifically characterize international business. New forms of business organizations would be able to carry on a wide array of activities around the world either with little physical presence at all in overseas locations or as if everyone, no matter where they are located, were sitting together at the same time. In any case, the need for complex trade relationships such as a TAFTA would be greatly reduced.

CONCLUSIONS: TAFTA AS A SUPPORT TO CORPORATE EXPANSION AND INTEGRATION

The third scenario is fascinating but probably premature, and it is unlikely that the 'end of geography' would mean the end of government involvement in economic affairs. The likelihood of the first scenario, hostile trade blocs, materializing is fairly low, most specialists would agree. So we conclude with comments on the second. It would be difficult and probably impossible for a TAFTA – or any kind of transatlantic trade agreement for that matter – to take on the role and prominence of an 'economic NATO'. But we can still examine what role a new US-EU trade agreement could play in sustaining corporate expansion and globalization.

An initiative along these lines was launched in June 1995 by Commerce Department Undersecretary Jeffrey Garten who, in preparation for the Transatlantic Business Dialog, convened meetings with European and American business executives and the Transatlantic Policy Network. The Network is composed of major American and European multinational firms and their representatives in Washington and Brussels. The American members of the Network are Apple Computer, AT&T, Digital Equipment, Johnson & Johnson,

Mobil, Morgan Stanley, Motorola, Pfizer, 3M and Time Warner; the European members are British Rank Xerox, ICI, British Petroleum, Daimler-Benz, VEBA AG, IRI, Pechiney, Rhone-Poulenc and Unilever. The members of the Network have exerted a good deal of influence on the transatlantic business agenda.

The meetings followed a survey undertaken in February 1995 by Commerce Secretary Ronald H. Brown and EC Commissioners Leon Brittan and Martin Bangemann which sought to survey the concerns of American and European corporations in their efforts to develop business across the Atlantic. In response to their inquiries, 40 per cent of the companies said that standardizing and clarifying regulations ranging from computer privacy to ketchup labelling should be at the top of a transatlantic agenda.

In general, companies on both sides of the Atlantic felt that regulatory reform to enhance trade and investment flows remained a top priority. In particular, while European firms underlined the need for the reform of American taxation policy and regulations that raised hurdles to investments in banking and other sensitive areas where foreign ownership is limited by Congress, American companies sought the elimination of similar public procurement policies in European telecommunications and public utilities. Commenting on the US and EU companies who answered the letter, Frank Vargo, Garten's deputy for Europe, observed that 'they didn't much care whether the box had TAFTA written on it, so much as they wanted to be pragmatic about what was inside'.[40]

Most of all, European and American firms want their governments to focus on the removal of non-tariff barriers to trade and restraints on investment. To achieve these objectives by negotiating several MRAs (mutual recognition agreements) may be less glamorous than creating a full-blown transatlantic free trade agreement, but is probably more acceptable to domestic constituencies. The European Commission and Washington are already negotiating several MRAs, including an agreement that would cover telephone terminal and information technology equipment. They are also discussing electromagnetic compatibility issues. If an MRA is agreed to, laboratories in the United States could test and approve equipment destined for Europe. In return European manufacturers and tests labs would be able to approve equipment destined for the United States.[41]

Some experts believe that governments should focus their attention on promoting competition and interconnections, and that they usually fail if they go beyond these tasks to micromanage their economies. By agreeing on the recognition of standards, governments would successfully develop both competition and cooperation across the Atlantic.

As competition develops and thrives, markets increasingly can replace regulation as the key force guiding growth and development. Only by encouraging the growth of competition so that in time multiple vendors compete freely across sectors and borders to meet the demands of end-users will a true North American free trade market grow and flourish.[42]

By setting mutually recognized standards, the EU and the US would promote bilateral trade and would also leave little choice to other countries but to conform if they want their products to be sold in the transatlantic market.

NOTES

1. On the concept of 'deep' integration, see Robert Z. Lawrence, *Regionalism, Multilateralism, and Deeper Integration* (Washington, DC: Brookings Institution, 1996).
2. Data from Clyde Prestowitz, Lawrence Chimerine and Andrew Azamosszegi, 'The case for a transatlantic free trade area', in Bruce Stokes (ed.), *Open for Business: Creating a Transatlantic Marketplace* (New York: Council on Foreign Relations, 1996)
3. George Dangerfield, *The Awakening of American Nationalism, 1815–1828* (New York: Harper Torchbooks. 1965), p. 1.
4. English Canadians who continued to feel strong colonial ties to Britain are, of course, one exception to this rule. Through the 1930s, only francophone Quebecers called themselves 'Canadiens', while anglophones generally considered themselves British. Until 1947, Canadian passports carried the description 'British subject' rather than 'Canadian citizen'.
5. Arthur Schlesinger Jr, *The Imperial Presidency* (New York: Popular Library Edition, 1974), pp. 101, 103–4.
6. Theodore H. Von Laue, *The World Revolution of Westernization* (Oxford: Oxford University Press, 1987), p. l67.
7. Seymour Martin Lipset and William Schneider, *The Confidence Gap* (Baltimore: The Johns Hopkins Press, revised edition 1987), p. 16.
8. Joseph S. Nye, *Bound to Lead: The Changing Nature of American Power* (New York: Basic Books, 1990), p. 2.
9. Allan Gottlieb, *I'll Be with You in a Minute. Mr. Ambassador: The Education of a Canadian Diplomat in Washington* (Toronto: University of Toronto Press, 1991), pp. 27–9.
10. Earl Fry, 'States in the international economy: An American overview', in Douglas Brown and Earl Fry (eds), *States and Provinces in the International Economy* (Berkeley: Institute of Governmental Studies Press, 1993), p. 28.
11. See Klaus Schwab and Clade Smadja, 'Power and policy: the new economic world order', *Harvard Business Review* (Nov.–Dec. 1994), and Thomas Duesterberg, 'Prospects for an EU-NAFTA free trade agreement', *The Washington Quarterly*, 18:2, 1995.
12. Michael Lind, *The Next American Nation; The New Nationalism and the Fourth American Revolution* (New York: Free Press, 1995), pp. 1–15, and Michael Lind, 'Sphere of Affluence', *The American Prospect*, Winter 1994, p. 97.
13. Stephen Woolcock, 'Interdependence and political rhetoric', in *Market Access Issues in EC-US Relations: Trading Partners or Trading Blows?* (London: Royal Institute of International Affairs, 1991), pp. 25–6.
14. C. Fred Bergsten, 'Globalizing Free Trade', *Foreign Affairs*, May–June, 1996, p. 108.
15. See, for example, Jeffrey Garten, *A Cold Peace: America, Japan and Germany and the Struggle for Supremacy* (New York: Twentieth Century Fund, 1992); Lester Thurow, *Head to Head: The Coming Economic Battle among Japan. Europe and America* (New York: William Morrow & Co., 1992); Michel Albert, *Capitalism vs. Capitalism* (American edition, New York: Four Wall Eight Window, 1992).
16. C. Fred Bergsten, 'From Cold War to Trade War?', *Economic Insights*, July–August 1990.
17. Clyde Prestowitz Jr, 'Prepared testimony before the House Committee on International Relations', *Federal News Service*, 14 December 1995.

18. Ernest, H. Preeg, 'Policy forum: transatlantic free trade', *The Washington Quarterly*, Spring 1996, p. 108.
19. Data from Prestowitz, Chimerine and Azamosszegi, 'The case for a transatlantic free trade area'.
20. Brian Hindley, *Transatlantic Free Trade and Multilateralism*, Issue Paper No. 5, British-North American Committee, April 1996.
21. Patrick Messerlin, 'A transatlantic free trade agenda on non-tariff barriers', in Bruce Stokes (ed.), *Open for Business: Creating a Transatlantic Marketplace* (New York: Council on Foreign Relations Press, 1996).
22. Prestowitz, Chimerine and Azamosszegi, 'The case for a transatlantic free trade area', p. 20.
23. Jagdish Bhagwati, 'The high cost of free trade areas', *Financial Times*, 31 May 1995.
24. Jeffrey J. Schott, 'Reflections on TAFTA', in Bruce Stokes (ed.), *Open for Business: Creating a Transatlantic Marketplace* (New York: Council on Foreign Relations Press, 1996), p. 41.
25. Hindley, *Transatlantic Free Trade and Multilateralism*.
26. Gary Hufbauer and Barbara Kotschwar, 'Policy forum: transatlantic free trade', *The Washington Quarterly*, Spring 1996, p. 116.
27. Messerlin, 'A transatlantic free trade agenda'.
28. C. Fred Bergsten, 'Prepared statement before the House Ways and Means Committee Subcommittee on Trade', *Federal News Service*, 11 September 1996.
29. Prestowitz, 'Prepared testimony before the house committee on international relations'.
30. *Ibid.*
31. Clayton K. Yeutter and Warren H. Maruyama, 'A NAFTA for Europe', *The Wall Street Journal*, 19 May 1995.
32. Preeg, 'Policy forum'.
33. James F. Dobbins, 'TAFTA: An idea whose time has come?', in Bruce Stokes (ed.), *Open for Business: Creating a Transatlantic Marketplace* (New York: Council on Foreign Relations Press, 1996), p. 10.
34. Hufbauer and Kotschwar, 'Policy forum: transatlantic free trade', p. 115.
35. Hindley, *Transatlantic Free Trade and Multilateralism*, p. 8.
36. Richard O'Brien, *Global Financial Integration: The End Of Geography* (London: Royal Institute of International Affairs, 1992), p. 1.
37. James Brian Quinn, Philip Anderson and Sydney Finkelstein, 'New forms of organization', in Henry Minzberg and James Brian Quinn, *The Strategy Process*, 3rd edition (Upper Saddle Ridge, New Jersey: Prentice Hall, 1996).
38. Charles Handy, 'The intellectual organization', *Financial Times*, 2 December 1996.
39. 'Ford's new product teams span globe', *The Globe and Mail*, 10 January 1995.
40. Lawrence Malkin, 'Europe's search for security; will Atlantic proposal prove it matters?', *International Herald Tribune*, 8 June 1995.
41. Jonathan D. Aronson, 'A transatlantic information society', in Bruce Stokes (ed.), *Open for Business: Creating a Transatlantic Marketplace* (New York: Council on Foreign Relations Press, 1996), p. 78.
42. *Ibid.*, p. 87.

3. Structural interdependence between the European Union and the United States: technological positions

Pierre Buigues and Alexis Jacquemin

From a historical viewpoint transatlantic relations are unique and have demonstrated their capacity to withstand political and economic turbulence. In recent years, however, the United States has formed the North America Free Trade Area with Canada and Mexico and has led a drive for regional trade liberalization in the Asia Pacific Economic Cooperation forum (APEC). In the European Union regional integration is deepening and widening, while major economic and political challenges are being posed in the Union's external relations, especially with East European and Mediterranean countries. Links between the European Union and the United States are thus exposed to strains because of diverging regional interests but they are based on fundamental common values and should not be jeopardized by those diverging interests (Bail *et al.* 1996).

The sources of strain that must be reckoned with are asymmetries in structural interdependence which for Europe are evident especially in high unemployment, and a weaker capacity to adapt to competitive pressures in the international economy. The asymmetries may well become greater, as those competitive pressures increase, while regional interests on each side of the Atlantic occasion new rivalries.

In this context, this chapter examines the dimensions of economic interdependence between the United States and the European Union, and assesses their capacities to adapt to technological change while seizing opportunities presented by advances on research frontiers. We shall give much attention to European industrial structures and the strategies of European firms, in terms of high-, medium- and low-tech activities.

The first section describes the interdependence between the United States and the European Union in terms of trade and direct investment flows in manufacturing industry and the services sector. The second section provides a comparison of the economic importance and performance of the high-, medium- and low-tech sectors in the United States and the European Union. The third section uses this classification based on technological intensity and provides data for assessing the differences between the United States and the European Union in terms of corporate strategies and market structures. The final section sets out the main conclusions and economic-policy implications.

THE INTERDEPENDENCE OF THE EUROPEAN UNION AND THE UNITED STATES

We are currently witnessing a growing globalization of markets and production. At world level, foreign direct investment (FDI) increased from US$ 68 billion in 1960 to US$ 1650 billion in 1993. During that period, FDI grew four times more quickly than GDP and three times more quickly than international trade in goods and services. International trade in goods and services is increasingly based on the intra-firm trade of multinationals: this trade amounts to 40 per cent of the total (EC, 1996). In this context, the question which arises is to establish the respective economic weight of the European Union and the United States and to identify where the interdependence between the two blocs lies.

In both blocs, services account for more than half of the economic wealth created, although transatlantic trade consists principally of trade in industrial products of a similar nature: 40 per cent of such trade consists of machinery, cars and transport equipment. Finally, the population of Western Europe (EU-15 and EFTA) is some 25 per cent higher than that of North America (United States and Canada), although the two areas have a comparable GDP (approximately US$ 7 trillion), with Europe having a lower per capita GDP than the United States (see Table 3.1).

Table 3.1   Western Europe and North America, 1992

	Western Europe	**North America**
Population (millions)	350	283
PIB (billion dollars)	7 105	6 503
Total exports (billion dollars)	1 686	583
World share of		
GDP (%)	28	26
population (%)	6	5
exports (%)	46	16
Per capita GDP (dollars)	20 291	22 995
Exports/GDP (%)	24	9
Extra-regional exports/GDP (%)	7	6

Note: Western Europe = EU + EFTA; North America = US + Canada.
Source: Baldwin and François 1996.

Western Europe alone accounts for almost half of world trade in goods and services (46 per cent compared with 16 per cent for North America), although most European trade is regional (trade between European countries). If only extra-regional trade is taken into account, the two blocs have a similar degree of openness: extra-regional exports are equivalent to 6% of GDP in the case of North America and 7% in the case of Western Europe.

In 1994 trade in goods between Western Europe and North America amounted to US$ 276 billion, the bulk of this trade being carried out between the European Union and the United States (more than 80 per cent). The other countries (Canada, EFTA) therefore account for less than 20 per cent of total transatlantic trade. The focus here will be mainly on trade between the European Union and the United States (see Table 3.2).

Table 3.2   The interpenetration of EU and US economies

	US as a share of EU total exports and FDI[a]		EU as a share of US total exports and FDI[a]	
	1985	1994	1985	1994
Manufacturing exports				
value (billion US$)	49.5	96.6	33.2	75.7
% vis-à-vis world[b]	21.7	18.1	23.1	20.2
FDI flows (Manufacturing)				
value (billion US$)	n/a	3.9[c]	7.3	8.9
% vis-à-vis world[b]	n/a	58.8[c]	80.5	35.8
Services exports				
value (billion US$)	32.3	64.0[c]	17.0	52.9[c]
% vis-à-vis world[b]	34.7	32.7[c]	28.2	31.6[c]
FDI flows (services)				
value (billion US$)	n/a	7.1[c]	3.4	1.6
% vis-à-vis world[b]	n/a	45.8[c]	33.6	10.9
Total goods and services exports				
value (billion US$)	91.0	162.2[c]	63.5	140.7[c]
% vis-à-vis world[b]	24.9	21.5[c]	23.9	23.9[c]
FDI flows				
value (billion US$)	7.7	11.9[c]	12.0	12.4
% vis-à-vis world[b]	66.6	46.5[c]	69.4	26.1

Notes:
a   FDI flows are more volatile than FDI stocks.
b   Vis-à-vis extra-EU for US position in EU.
c   1993.

Sources: VOLIMEX (Trade in Manufacturing); ITS (Trade in Services); BOP (EU FDI); Survey.

Manufacturing Sector

The European Union is the United States' main trading partner for manufactured goods (US$ 76 billion or 20.2 per cent of American exports in 1994). Over the period from 1985 to 1994, that proportion remained relatively stable: after increasing from 23.1 per cent in 1985 to 26.5 per cent in 1989, it fell again to 20.2 per cent in 1994. The European Union accounts for an even greater share of American investment outside the United States in the manufacturing sector (36.4 per cent of American FDI in 1994 or US$ 8.9 billion). In 1985, however, this percentage was appreciably higher (81 per cent).

The United States' share of the European Union's exports of manufactured products is of a similar order (18.1 per cent in 1994 or US$ 97 billion) despite a fall from the figure of 21.7 per cent recorded in 1985. In FDI terms, the United States is even better placed since, out of the total direct flows from the Union to other countries, it accounts for the equivalent of US$ 4 billion (i.e. 58.8 per cent of the Union's FDI in third countries).

The Services Sector

The economic interpenetration in terms of trade between the United States and the Union is as strong in the services sector as in manufacturing industry. In 1994, the Union's share of American companies' exports of services amounted to US$53 billion (32 per cent of exports of services from the United States). In FDI terms, however, the 1994 figures are more modest, showing US$ 1.6 billion invested directly in Europe by American companies, which accounts for only 11 per cent of American FDI in the services sector, as against some 34 per cent in 1985.

Conversely, the United States represents a US$ 64 billion market for the Union's services companies, accounting for 33 per cent of Community exports of services, which is comparable with the above percentage. However, the American market accounts for by far the largest share of the Union's direct investment in services, with US$ 7 billion. This represents 46 per cent of Community FDI in this sector, which differs from American FDI in Europe (11 per cent instead of 46 per cent).

In conclusion, the interpenetration of the Union and the United States in trade is clearly such that their interdependence is vitally important on both sides of the Atlantic. Each bloc constitutes the other's principal partner. Furthermore, there has been relative stability over the last decade in each bloc's relative importance to the other.

The situation is different for American FDI in Europe: the European Union's share has fallen appreciably over the last decade both for manufactured products and for services. Furthermore, the pattern in the FDI field is asymmetrical:

European investment in the United States, whether in the manufacturing industry or in the services sector, is proportionally higher than American investment in Europe. This difference could be due to the longer American presence in Europe and to the growth in American investment in south east Asia. This may partly explain why the proportion of American FDI in Europe fell appreciably between 1985 and 1994.

THE HIGH-TECH SECTORS COMPARED WITH THE MEDIUM- AND LOW-TECH SECTORS: A COMPARISON BETWEEN THE EUROPEAN UNION AND THE UNITED STATES

The constant development of new technologies leading to new products and processes is seen as a key factor in the improvement of competitiveness and living standards. This is the main reason why the Competitive Policy Council in the United States (Council on Competitiveness, 1995) and the Competitiveness Advisory Group (1996) in the European Union have consistently favoured a technological research policy based on the complementary roles of the public authorities and industry.

At the sectoral level, the links between productivity, new skills and new jobs appear. 'Overall the evidence suggests that high-performance firms and high-technology industries, characterized by more innovative behaviour or use of more advanced technologies, have above-average productivity and employment growth, and employ more highly skilled workers' (OECD, 1996). Furthermore, high-tech activities have a positive impact on the economy as a whole. These external effects create new opportunities in such varied fields as steel, cars and agriculture: productivity depends not only on spending by the industries themselves on technology but also on whether user industries have access to the technologies developed by others. It is from that point of view that we shall examine the relative positions of the EU and the US, at different levels of technology.

The definition of high, medium and low technology has been the subject of a number of studies and articles (OECD 1995, 1996). The criteria for the technological classification of sectors are generally based on R&D expenditure. However, various criticisms are made of this classification method. For example, is the same classification meant to be used, without modification, for the entire period studied and for all countries, even if it does not necessarily reflect the actual situation in each country? Furthermore, an activity branch classified among the low-tech sectors may in fact show high-tech characteristics. Finally, the role of technology is extremely complex, and advanced techniques could prove crucial for traditional sectors by giving them access to new processes and thus enabling them to make spectacular progress in productivity terms. The method of classifying high-, medium- or low-tech sectors used here is that traditionally applied by the OECD and is based on R&D expenditure by sector. In analysing the results, however, it will be necessary to bear in mind the limits of such a classification based on R&D expenditure.

Manufacturing sectors have therefore been grouped together on the basis of their R&D intensity defined as the ratio of R&D expenditure to production:

- *High-tech sectors*: aerospace equipment manufacturing and repairing (NACE[1] 364), manufacture of pharmaceutical products (NACE 257), manufacture of office machinery and dataprocessing machinery (NACE 33), electrical engineering (NACE 34), instrument engineering (NACE 37);
- *Medium-tech sectors*: chemical industry (NACE 25, 26, except for 257), mechanical engineering (NACE 32), manufacture of motor vehicles and motor vehicle parts and accessories (NACE 35), processing of rubber and plastics (NACE 48), production and preliminary processing of nonferrous metals (NACE 224), manufacture of other means of transport (NACE 36, except for 361 and 364);
- *Low-tech sectors*: mineral oil refining (NACE 14), manufacture of metal articles (except for mechanical engineering and vehicles) (NACE 31), production and preliminary processing of metals (NACE 22, except for 224), building, repair and maintenance of sea-going vessels (NACE 361), food, drink and tobacco industry (NACE 41), textile industry, leather and leather goods industry, footwear and clothing industry (NACE 43, 44, 45), timber and wooden furniture industries (NACE 46), manufacture of paper and paper products, printing and publishing (NACE 47), other manufacturing industries (NACE 49).

Productivity, Prices, Wages and Sectoral Technological Intensity

An overall comparison (Table 3.3) between high-tech and low- or medium-tech sectors shows that, in employment terms, the first group is characterized by high wages and by their high labour productivity. The contrast is particularly marked for the low-tech industries, which are characterized by high labour intensity, an unskilled workforce and low wages. This is also one of the reasons why the high-tech sectors are regarded as being so important for the growth of the industrialized economy. The jobs created in them are highly skilled and well paid jobs. Finally, these sectors are generally protected from growing competition from low-wage-cost countries by their capital and skilled labour requirements

Table 3.3   Labour productivity and wages, 1994

	EU			
	Productivity (current prices)		Average wage (current prices)	
	1000 US$	Total = 100	1000 US$	Total = 100
High tech	60.57	114	33.42	117
Medium tech	58.81	110	32.68	115
Low tech	47.45	89	24.32	85
Total manufacturing	53.23	100	28.47	100

	USA			
	Productivity (current prices)		Average wage (current prices)	
	1000 US$	Total = 100	1000 US$	Total = 100
High tech	110.40	118	36.46	118
Medium tech	106.25	113	34.17	110
Low tech	80.55	86	26.97	87
Total manufacturing	93.93	100	30.94	100

Source: DEBA – authors' calculations.

(Buigues and Jacquemin 1995). Competition is therefore particularly fierce between industrialized countries in the high-tech field.

From a dynamic viewpoint, Table 3.4 provides a comparison, over the period from 1985 to 1994, of the trends of productivity, demand wages, production prices, and employment for the high-, medium- and low-tech sectors.

This shows, firstly, a sharp increase in *demand* (as measured by apparent consumption at constant prices, i.e. production less exports plus imports) for the products of the high-tech sectors both in the European Community and in the United States. In the high-tech sectors, demand even increased more sharply in Europe than in the United States (4.9 per cent a year compared with 3.9 per cent in the United States), although this was true also of manufactured products generally (2.5 per cent a year in Europe as compared with 1.8 per cent a year in the United States).

Secondly, there was a very sharp increase in *productivity* in the high-tech sectors. This increase was due in particular to the importance of technological progress and economies of scale in these sectors. It is interesting to note that

Table 3.4 *Productivity and demand, wages and production prices (average percentage annual growth rate 1985–94)*

EU

	Productivity (1990 prices)	Demand = apparent consumption (1990 prices)	Productivity (current prices)	Average wage (current prices)	Nominal unit labour costs	Production (1990 prices)	Employment
High tech	4.49	4.90	5.34	5.55	0.21	4.33	-1.09
Medium tech	3.19	2.50	5.36	5.37	0.01	1.95	-1.38
Low tech	3.73	1.78	5.35	4.77	-0.58	1.90	-1.40
Total manufacturing	3.70	2.50	5.35	5.14	-0.21	2.29	-1.34

US

	Productivity (1990 prices)	Demand = apparent consumption (1990 prices)	Productivity (current prices)	Average wage (current prices)	Nominal unit labour costs	Production (1990 prices)	Employment
High tech	5.27	3.87	7.34	4.94	-2.40	3.78	-1.51
Medium tech	3.77	1.51	5.86	3.77	-2.09	3.15	-0.10
Low tech	2.71	1.14	5.2	4.16	-1.04	1.92	-0.00
Total manufacturing	3.60	1.76	5.87	4.17	-1.70	2.68	-0.36

Note: Based on data in ECU for the EU and US$ for the USA.

productivity growth in the high-tech sectors was appreciably higher in the United States than in Europe (5.3 per cent a year in the United States compared with 4.5 per cent in Europe). The converse is true of the low-tech sectors (3.7 per cent in Europe compared with 2.7 per cent in the United States). This means that the productivity performances for manufactured products as a whole were apparently comparable in Europe and the United States but with quite different positions in high-tech versus low-tech sectors.

Thirdly, there was a sharper increase in *wages* in Europe than in the United States in the case of manufactured products (5.1 per cent a year on average compared with 4.2 per cent over the 1985–94 period). Wages of course increased more rapidly in the high-tech sectors than in the medium- or low-tech sectors. This is consistent with the relative labour productivity trends. In the high-tech sectors, however, labour productivity increased appreciably more quickly than wages in the United States, whereas in Europe wages increased more rapidly than productivity. In national currency terms, therefore, there was a deterioration in Europe's cost competitiveness in the high-tech sectors. Unit labour costs have increased by 0.2 per cent yearly on average in Europe but they have decreased in the United States (minus 2.4 per cent yearly).

Fourthly, *production prices* for manufactured goods increased more rapidly in the United States than in Europe (2.7 per cent a year on average compared with 2.3 per cent over the 1985–94 period). Furthermore, those prices increased more sharply in the high-tech sectors than in the medium- or low-tech sectors. This may be due in part to sustained demand for high-tech goods. In the high-tech sectors, however, it was Europe which recorded the higher increase in prices, contrary to the situation for manufactured products as a whole (4.3 per cent a year on average in Europe compared with 3.8 per cent in the United States over the 1985–94 period). As pointed out, however, the high-tech sectors were also those in which demand grew most sharply in Europe, particularly compared with the United States.

Finally, *industrial employment* fell more in Europe than in the United States (minus 1.3 per cent a year on average compared with minus 0.4 per cent in the United States over the 1985–94 period). In Europe, however, it was the low-tech sectors which recorded the largest employment reductions, contrary to the situation in the United States (minus 1.4 per cent a year on average in Europe compared with zero change in the United States over the 1985–94 period). This is also explained by the relative trends in labour productivity in these sectors. Faced with virtual stagnation of demand for low-tech products, with the constraints on the unskilled labour market in Europe and with fierce competition from low-wage countries in the low-tech sectors, European companies cut jobs in order to improve their productivity performances in those sectors (OECD 1996).

The Economic Weight of Sectors According to their Technological Intensity

Taking industry as a whole, in terms of employment and value added, the European Union and the United States showed similar situations in 1992. However, from 1991 American industry recorded spectacular growth, which contrasts sharply with the stagnation of European industrial output (see Figure 3.1).

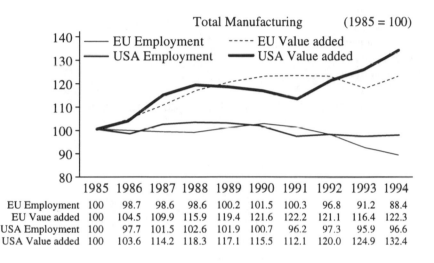

	1985	1986	1987	1988	1989	1990	1991	1992	1993	1994
EU Employment	100	98.7	98.6	98.6	100.2	101.5	100.3	96.8	91.2	88.4
EU Vaue added	100	104.5	109.9	115.9	119.4	121.6	122.2	121.1	116.4	122.3
USA Employment	100	97.7	101.5	102.6	101.9	100.7	96.2	97.3	95.9	96.6
USA Value added	100	103.6	114.2	118.3	117.1	115.5	112.1	120.0	124.9	132.4

Source: VISA/DEBA.

Figure 3.1   Employment and value added (1990 prices) in EU and USA, 1985–94

An analysis is made below of the importance in value added and employment terms of the various activity sectors according to their technological intensity. It should of course be borne in mind that the comparisons between 1994 and 1985 in fact cover two distinct periods (1985–91 and 1991–94).

High-tech sectors

Table 3.5 shows some differences between the Union and the United States as regards the position of the high-tech sectors in manufacturing industry. Viewed in relation to manufacturing industry in general, these activities, in 1994, accounted for 24.7 per cent of value added and 20.4 per cent of jobs in the United States, as against only 20.4 per cent and 18 per cent in the Union. Compared

Table 3.5　　Value added, employment and investment

	EU			USA			USA–EU[a]	
	1985	*1994*	*94–85[b]*	*1985*	*1994*	*94–85[b]*	*1985*	*1994*
High tech								
Value added								
(current price)	20.0	20.4	0.4	24.2	24.7	0.5	4.3	4.3
Employment	17.6	18.0	0.4	22.6	20.4	−2.2	5.0	2.3
Investment	18.1	16.1	−2.0	25.5	20.6	−4.9	7.3	4.4
(current price)								
Medium tech								
Value added								
(current price)	33.6	33.3	−0.2	31.0	31.7	0.6	−2.6	−1.7
Employment	30.3	30.1	−0.1	27.6	28.2	0.6	−2.6	−1.9
Investment								
(current price)	34.1	37.3	3.2	32.2	36.2	4.0	−1.9	−1.1
Low tech								
Value added								
(current price)	46.4	46.3	−0.2	44.8	43.6	−1.1	−1.7	−2.6
Employment	52.1	51.9	−0.3	49.8	51.4	1.6	−2.3	−0.5
Investment								
(current price)	47.7	46.5	−1.2	42.3	43.1	0.9	−5.4	−3.4
Total								
Manufacturing	100	100		100	100			

Notes:
[a]　Difference between USA and EU.
[b]　Difference between 1994 and 1985.

Source:　VISA/DEBA.

with the Union, the aerospace, data processing and electronics industries in particular occupy very important positions in the American economy.

In terms of trends, one would expect a shift in employment and value added from the low-tech and highly labour-intensive sectors to high-tech activities based on scientific research. In actual fact, the movement was not as marked as expected between the mid 1980s and the mid 1990s.

Furthermore, the trend was not identical in the United States and in Europe. Overall, the increase in value added was roughly the same in the United States and Europe (+ 0.5 per cent). However, the importance of the high-tech sectors for jobs declined in the United States (–2.2%), whereas it increased in the Union (+ 0.4%).[2]

In both Europe and the United States, the weight of the high-tech sectors in industrial value added is greater than that in total investment. Viewed overall, the high-tech sectors are less tangibly investment-intensive than the medium-tech sectors and even the low-tech sectors. By contrast, the high-tech sectors show particularly high levels of intangible investment intensity (research and development, marketing, distribution, after-sales services). From that viewpoint, the trend should reflect the importance of intangible investment compared with traditional tangible investment.

Medium-tech sectors

The medium-tech sectors (mainly the chemical, car and non-electronic equipment industries) have greater weight than the high-tech sectors in terms of value added and employment and occupy a more important position in the Union than in the United States, accounting for 33.3 per cent of the value added of the manufacturing sector, compared with 31.7 per cent in the United States. In employment terms, these sectors account for 30.1 per cent of total employment in manufacturing industries in the Union, 1.9 percentage points more than in the United States. They are more capital-intensive than the high-tech sectors. Finally, it is interesting to note that the weight of the medium-tech sectors has increased in the United States (+ 0.7 of a percentage point of total industrial value added), whereas it has fallen in Europe (–0.2 of a percentage point).

Low-tech sectors

Most of the fears relating to employment concern the low-tech traditional industries (steel, shipbuilding, textiles, agri-foodstuffs) in which technical developments and globalization are perceived as the main causes of the decline in employment. These industries retain a predominant position in the manufacturing sector (46.3 per cent in the European Union and 43.6 per cent in the United States in value added terms) and have lost little ground over the last ten years (–1.1 percentage points in the United States and –0.2 of a percentage point in the European Union). However, the proportion of value added accounted for by the low-tech sectors has fallen more sharply in the United States than in Europe, while their share of total industrial employment has increased in the United States and fallen in Europe (+ 1.6 percentage points in the United States as against –0.3 of a percentage point in Europe). This is of course explained by the widely differing trends in labour productivity in the low-tech sectors in Europe and the United States.

TRADE AND COMPETITIVENESS – THE HIGH-TECH SECTORS COMPARED WITH THE MEDIUM- AND LOW-TECH SECTORS

This section examines the changes in the situations of the Union and the United States from an international trade viewpoint over the period from 1985 to 1994. The analysis is based – for each of the three major sector groups (high-, medium- and low-tech sectors) – on four indicators (see Table 3.6): the share in exports, the share in imports, the export intensity (exports/production ratio) and the import penetration ratio (imports/apparent consumption ratio). The combined analysis of these indicators shows the degree of exposure of the Union and the United States to international competition, both from the viewpoint of imports and from that of exports. Finally, a relative specialization indicator has been calculated by relating the coverage ratio (export/import ratio) of each of the three above-mentioned sector groups to the coverage ratio of the manufacturing sector as a whole. In fact, these relative specialization indicators correspond quite simply to the relationship between the contribution of these sector groups to their share of exports and imports, which gives an idea of their relative performances. The differences in terms of trade are striking compared to what is observed in terms of value added.

High-tech Sectors

The high-tech sectors are export-oriented: their share of exports of manufactured goods is much greater than their contribution to the value added of those goods. This is especially true in the United States where, in 1994, high-tech industry accounted for 37.3 per cent of manufactured exports, as opposed to 24.7 per cent of their value added. In the case of the Union, the respective figures are 22.8 per cent and 20.4 per cent. The high-tech sectors are also much more open than the others to external competition on their national markets. The import penetration ratio[3] can be used to measure each sector's import intensity and degree of openness to the outside world. The results obtained (approximately 25 per cent in the United States and the European Union in 1994) are markedly higher than in the other sectors. A quarter of total demand for high-tech products is therefore covered by imports. The import penetration ratio increased at roughly the same rate in the United States and the European Union (i.e. by about 3.5 percentage points) over the four years.

The high level of specialization of the American manufacturing sector in high-tech industries is well known and is explained in particular by the preponderance of US companies in the aerospace and data-processing sectors. In 1993 the relative specialization or coverage ratio of the United States in the high-tech sectors stood at 122.7%, compared with 79.3% for the European Union. The difference is

Table 3.6   Trade in high, medium and low tech (%)

	EU			USA			USA–EU[a]	
	1989	*1993*	*93 – 89*	*1989*	*1993*	*93 – 89*	*1989*	*1993*
High tech								
Export share	20.0	22.8	2.8	37.9	37.3	–0.6	17.9	14.6
Import share	27.1	28.8	1.6	26.6	30.4	3.9	–0.6	1.8
Specialization[b]	73.6	79.3	5.7	142.7	122.7	–20.0		
Export intensity	18.8	24.0	5.3	21.1	23.0	1.9	2.3	–1.1
Import penetration ratio	22.2	25.5	3.3	20.2	24.2	3.9	–2.0	–1.3
Medium tech								
Export share	41.5	39.2	–2.2	40.9	41.9	1.0	–0.6	2.7
Import share	32.0	29.4	–2.6	41.5	38.1	–3.4	9.5	8.7
Specialization[b]	129.7	133.6	3.9	98.6	110.0	11.4		
Export intensity	18.4	21.8	3.4	12.9	15.6	2.7	–5.5	–6.2
Import penetration ratio	13.7	15.2	1.5	17.0	18.1	1.1	3.2	3.0
Low tech								
Export share	38.5	38.0	–0.5	21.2	20.8	–0.4	17.3	–17.2
Import share	40.9	41.9	1.0	32.0	31.5	–0.5	–8.9	–10.4
Specialization[b]	94.3	90.7	–3.6	66.4	66.0	–0.4		
Export intensity	11.2	12.9	1.7	4.7	5.5	0.8	–6.5	–7.3
Import penetration ratio	10.9	12.2	1.4	9.1	10.4	1.3	1.8	–1.8
Total manufacturing								
Export share	100	100		100	100			
Import share	100	100		100	100			
Export intensity	14.8	17.6	2.8	10.5	12.4	1.9	–4.2	–5.2
Import penetration ratio	13.7	15.4	1.8	13.8	15.7	1.9	0.1	0.3

Notes:
a   Difference US – EU.
b   Specialization: $X_i/M_i/X/M = X_i/X:M_i/M$.

Source: VISA/DEBA.

further accentuated by the fact that these sectors have the highest relative coverage ratio in the United States and the lowest in the European Union when compared with the average- or low-tech sectors.

The degree of specialization of the American manufacturing industries corresponds exactly to their technological content since it is high in the high-tech sectors, medium in the medium-tech sectors and low in the low-tech sectors. In the case of the European Union, specialization is relatively high in the medium-tech sectors, medium in the low-tech sectors and low in the high-tech sectors.

Between 1989 and 1994, however, the high-tech sectors' share of exports showed a more favourable trend in the European Union than in the United States (+ 2.8 percentage points, as against –0.6 of a percentage point). Furthermore, the relative coverage ratio improved by 5.7 percentage points in four years, whereas it fell markedly in the United States. These figures confirm the results obtained for export intensity. That indicator, which corresponds to the proportion of output exported, increased sharply in the European Union between 1989 and 1994 (+ 5.3 percentage points as against 1.9 percentage points in the United States). Clearly, this improvement in the European Union's exports in the hightech field is relative given the gap between the United States and the European Union as regards those sectors' share of exports.[4]

Medium-tech Sectors

The medium-tech sectors are more export-oriented than manufacturing industry in general. The proportion of output exported is markedly greater in the European Union than in the United States (21.8 per cent and 15.6 per cent respectively) but the import penetration ratio is lower (15.2 per cent and 18.1 per cent respectively). These figures are consistent with the relatively satisfactory results of Community manufacturing industry in the medium-tech sectors, whose coverage ratio (export/import ratio) is very much higher in the European Union than in the other sectors, which is not the case in the United States (this ratio was 133.6 per cent in the European Union in 1993, as against 110 per cent in the United States).

In terms of specialization, therefore, the European Union is more oriented towards medium-tech production (chemicals, cars, machine tools), whereas the United States specializes in high-tech products (aerospace, pharmaceuticals, data processing).

Low-tech Sectors

The low-tech sectors group is the only one whose share of exports is lower than its contribution to value added. Furthermore, the proportion of output exported is much more modest than in other sectors (12.9 per cent in the European Union, 5.5 per cent in the United States) and the proportion of demand covered by imports is low (12.6 per cent and 5.5 per cent respectively). These sectors (agri-foodstuffs, textiles, timber, paper, shipbuilding) are faced with increasing competition from low-wage-cost countries. It is interesting to note, however, that they are much more oriented towards the domestic market than the other activity sectors.

The fears concerning employment are quite understandable given the weight of these sectors in manufacturing production (more than 50 per cent). From that viewpoint, the European Union is much more exposed than the United States. The low-tech sectors account for 38 per cent of exports of manufactured goods in the European Union, as against 20.8 per cent in the United States. Both the Union and the United States have a coverage ratio of less than 100 per cent in these sectors, with the United States suffering, like the European Union, from a relative disadvantage in terms of international trade. This is particularly true of the United States where the relative coverage ratio was 66 per cent in 1993, as compared with 90.7 per cent in the European Union, even though this specialization coefficient is falling in both cases. These highly labour intensive and low-skilled sectors are the only ones in which the developing countries can compete on world markets. In the medium or long term, therefore, a reduction in these sectors' share of exports can be expected, as is currently the case (–0.5 of a percentage point in four years on both sides of the Atlantic).

CORPORATE STRATEGIES AND MARKET STRUCTURES

Mergers and Acquisitions

Earlier in this chapter (pp. 33–40), we saw the importance of FDI in the interrelationship between the United States and the European Union. Light is shed on the movements observed by the breakdown of merger and acquisition operations between the three groups of high-, medium- and low-tech sectors (see Table 3.7). First of all, *high-tech companies*, which are responsible for only 20 per cent of the value added of the manufacturing sector in the European Union, accounted for 28 per cent in 1986–91 and 30 per cent in 1992–95 of the merger/acquisition operations carried out by Community companies on the American market in the two periods covered. These companies are therefore particularly active in the merger and acquisition sphere, which is consistent with the fact that they are also export-oriented. The figures obtained for operations carried out by American companies in the European Union are similar (31 per cent for the 1986–91 period and 29 per cent for the 1992–95 period) but, as the weight of the high-tech sector in manufacturing industry is greater in the United States than in the European Union (approximately 24.5 per cent of manufactured goods), American high-tech companies in fact focus less on other countries than their European Union counterparts. This may be explained by the fact that one

Table 3.7   Transborder mergers and acquisitions: EU versus US in high-, medium- and low-tech sectors

| | 1986–91 | | | | 1992–95 | | | |
| | US targeting EU | | EU targeting US | | US targeting EU | | EU targeting US | |
	Number	%	Number	%	Number	%	Number	%
High tech	142	31	334	28	194	29	156	30
Medium tech	154	33	409	34	276	41	172	33
Low tech	167	36	457	38	210	31	193	37
Total	463	100	1200	100	680	100	521	100

Source: AMDATA, authors' calculation.

of the aims underlying European companies' mergers and acquisitions is to benefit from American technological advances.

By contrast, *the low-tech sectors*, which contribute 46.5 per cent of the value added in the manufacturing sector in the European Union, account for only some 36 per cent of the Community companies investing in the United States. These sectors are more oriented towards the domestic market. American companies in the European Union, both before and after 1991, showed a growing interest in the medium-tech sectors, where the European Union is best placed (increase from 33 per cent to 41 per cent of operations). This phenomenon can again be explained by the desire of American companies to focus their acquisitions on sectors in which European Union companies have a comparative advantage.

Secondly, it is interesting to note that the sectoral breakdown of cross-frontier mergers and acquisitions of Community origin remained the same between 1986 and 1991 and between 1992 and 1996, which indicates that, from a structural viewpoint, the roles of the different types of European company have remained unchanged.

Cooperation between Companies

A large proportion of the cooperation agreements between firms that have been identified in recent years contain provisions relating to R&D. This is a field in which world competition and costs have led companies – even the largest and most technologically advanced companies – not to depend purely on their own resources but to create strategic alliances that can improve their competitive positions.

Figure 3.2 suggests, in fact, that, by sector, there is a positive correlation between R&D intensity and alliance intensity. The high-tech sectors are characterized by a multiplicity of cooperation agreements (pharmaceuticals,

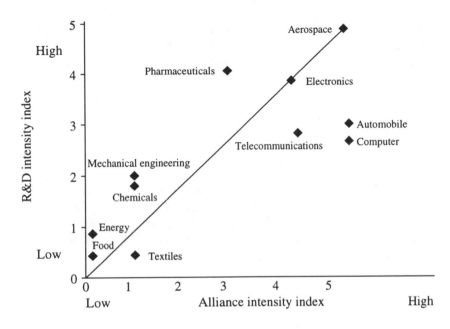

Note: R&D intensity is based on the relationship between the amount of R&D in each sector and the weight of that sector in the economy. Hence the aerospace sector has the highest R&D intensity, although the total spent is less than in electronics, for example. Alliance intensity is calculated in a similar way.

Source: OECD 'ANBERD' 1992, Braxton/Horack Adler analysis and European Commission, *Panorama of EU Industry*, Brussels, 1995/96, p. 33.

Figure 3.2   Alliances and R&D by sector: Europe

telecommunications, electronics, aerospace). By contrast, there are only a limited number of cooperation agreements in the low-tech sectors (textiles and agri-foodstuffs).

Two aspects are important for an understanding of the increase in transnational cooperation. The first relates to the fact that a company's R&D is characterized by the importance of its effects, both for other companies belonging to the same sector and for other sectors. According to certain estimates of these external effects, the social rate of return from R&D is between 20 per cent and 25 per cent, whereas the private return is between 10 per cent and 12 per cent (Torre 1990). But the external effects of R&D are also important on a geographical level. On the basis of a comprehensive econometric study, Coe and Helpman (1995) concluded that a quarter of the profits created by the R&D investment carried out in the seven largest economies (the G7) was appropriated by their business partners: the effects of R&D therefore have a major transnational dimension.

The second aspect relates to the consequence of a very partial appropriation of the profits by the companies carrying out the investment. This prompts a level of R&D expenditure that is insufficient from the viewpoint of the general interest. By internalizing these effects between the partners, cooperation agreements are able to improve the situation. This has been demonstrated by a number of theoretical studies (see in particular d'Aspremont and Jacquemin 1988).

It is in this context that the question of a growing internationalization of the alliances themselves arises. Since the 1980s, this type of R&D alliance has actually grown rapidly.

A prime characteristic of such cooperation concerns the main fields in which it has increased. According to Hagedoorn and Sadowiski (1996), the new core technologies – information technology, biotechnology, new materials – account for the bulk of this cooperation. More than 65 per cent of all the international alliances made since 1980 relate to these core technologies.

A further characteristic concerns the countries most involved. Taking the information technology sphere alone, which breaks down into computers, microelectronics and telecommunications, the geographical distribution of the alliances can be identified by major economic region and between those regions. Table 3.8, which provides this international breakdown of alliances, is based on 4192 cases (Duysters and Hagedoorn 1996).

Table 3.8 International distribution of strategic technology alliances, overall figures, total information technologies, computers, microelectronics, telecommunications (as percentages), 1980–84 and 1985–89 (total operation n = 4192)

		1980–84	1985–89
Intra	Europe	17.7	20.1
	US	22.9	25.3
	Japan	4.2	6.2
Inter	Europe-US	22.1	22.5
	Europe-Japan	6.5	5.7
	US-Japan	17.6	11.7
Other		9.1	8.4
Total		100.0	100.0

According to this table, the United States made the most technology alliances at national level (or at regional intra-group level). This situation existed both during the 1980–84 period (22.9 per cent of total alliances) and during the 1985–89 period (25.3 per cent). Europe (EU + EFTA) came second with 17.7 per cent and 20.1 per cent respectively.

In the case of regional inter-group alliances, the Europe/United States partnership came top of the three combinations used, with 22.1 per cent of the total in the 1980–84 period and 22.5 per cent between 1985 and 1989. Confirming the information relating to FDI (see pp. noted above), the number of Europe/United States alliances exceeded that of intra-European alliances during the 1985–89 period. By contrast, the EU/Japan alliances accounted for only 6.5 per cent and 5.7 per cent respectively during the two periods. US/Japan alliances accounted for 17.6 per cent and 11.7 per cent respectively of the totals for the two periods.

On the basis of this information, it can be concluded that Europe maintains a respectable position regarding technology alliances and that its cooperation with the United States still dominates. The ratio of the intra-regional partnership to the inter-regional partnership would also suggest that the internationalization of cooperation is gaining ground globally and is concentrated within the Triad.

The Role of Small Enterprises

The respective importance of small and large enterprises in the different levels of technology is a subject of debate. Table 3.9 shows the wide differences between the United States and the European Union regarding small, medium and large enterprises, in manufacturing. It indicates, firstly, that small enterprises (fewer than 100 employees) account for 97.9 per cent of the number of enterprises and for 31.6 per cent of turnover in Europe, whereas the corresponding figures in the United States are 91.9 per cent and 15.3 per cent. Compared with the United States, therefore, small enterprises seem to play a particularly important role in Europe. Conversely, in the US large enterprises are dominant (2.7 per cent for the number of enterprises but 71.7 per cent of turnover). This result is confirmed by a recent study which shows that US concentration is in general much higher than in the EU (Davies and Lyons 1996).

However, there is a considerable difference between the United States and Europe in the high-tech sectors: 22.7 per cent of American small enterprises belong to high-tech sectors, whereas the corresponding figure in Europe is only 13.3 per cent (see Table 3.10).

In the European Union, therefore, the proportion of small enterprises active in the high-tech sector is small, while the percentage of high-tech enterprises among the large enterprises is similar in the EU and in the US, contrary to the situation in manufacturing as a whole. The high-tech sector is the only one where the concentration at the EU level is close to US concentration levels.

Table 3.9 Share of total manufacturing by size class

	EU 1990			USA 1991		
	Number of enterprises	Employment	Turnover	Number of enterprises	Employment	Turnover
Small	97.9	41.1	31.6	91.9	21.8	15.3
Medium	1.8	20.6	21.1	5.4	16.0	13.0
Large	0.4	38.3	47.3	2.7	62.2	71.7
Total	100.0	100.0	100.0	100.0	100.0	100.0

Small: < 100 employees
Medium: 100–499 employees
Large: 500 or more employees

Source: Eurostat, authors' calculations.

Table 3.10   Small, medium and large enterprises in the high-tech sector (percentage of high-tech enterprises in the different categories)

	Small enterprises	Medium enterprises	Large enterprises
European Union	13.3%	22.8%	27.8%
United States	22.7%	24.0%	26.4%

Source: Eurostat, authors' calculations.

As an illustration, in the data-processing and electronics industries, the dynamism of American industry over the last few decades can be observed through the success of SMEs, which have seen spectacular growth in their activity. The European Union seems to encounter more difficulties in this field: in the data-processing and electronics industries, large enterprises have dominated and new operators have failed to change the established order. This situation can perhaps be explained by a competitive climate that is dominated by the major groups (frequently with the support of the public authorities), high barriers to market entry, difficulties encountered by SMEs in securing access to funding, and an inadequate spirit of enterprise.

CONCLUSIONS AND POLICY OUTLOOK

On the basis of a broad quantitative assessment, the first section of this chapter has shown that the economic sizes of the European Union and the United States are relatively similar, as is their degree of openness.

In terms of interdependence, each region maintains a strong presence on the other's market. The European Union is the United States' main partner for trade and FDI and vice versa. This shows just how crucial the relationship between the two economies is and will continue to be in the medium term.

However, the similarities start to break down when one looks more at the disaggregated aspects rather than the whole. This becomes particularly apparent when industries are classified by their level of technology. Although one can argue that the S&T knowledge base in the US and the EU – in fact in the Triad – is not radically different in each of the regions, such an obvious generalization may conceal significant differences in terms of specialization. A key area is high-tech industry, which is characterized by rapidly increasing demand, high productivity, a high-skill workforce and high wages. Against the background of analyses showing that the continued creation of new technologies, products and processes plays a key role in productivity and growth, our study has identified significant differences between the European Union and the United States in this respect.

Using the classification proposed by the OECD, we have mainly shown that, in manufacturing, high sectors account for 24.7 per cent of total US value added, compared to 20.4 per cent for the EU, in 1994, and they account for 20.4 per cent of US employment, compared to 18 per cent in the EU. Between 1985 and 1994, labour productivity growth in high-tech was 5.3 per cent per year in the US, compared to 4.5 per cent in the EU, with the difference becoming more marked since 1991. Moreover, in this domain, European wages are increasing more rapidly than productivity, contrary to the US case. Such a deterioration of unit labour cost could be an important handicap. In contrast, in medium-tech industries Europe is more strongly placed than the US in terms of both value added and employment, although the productivity growth rate between 1985 and 1994 was 3.2 per cent in the EU as opposed to 3.8 per cent in the US.

Low-tech industries account for a similar share of total manufacturing industry in both regions, although the productivity growth rate over the period 1985 to 1994 was much higher in the EU (3.7 per cent) than in the US (2.7 per cent). This contrast partially reflects the reactions of firms to competition from low-wage countries: a fall in employment in Europe and a low-wage policy for the unskilled in the United States.

These trends are reflected in trade. A breakdown of exports by technological level reveals that in 1993 high-tech goods accounted for 37.3 per cent of US exports, but 22.8 per cent of EU exports. This difference is mirrored in the high-tech specialization ratio (relative coverage ratio), which was 122.7 per cent in the US, but 79.3 per cent in the EU. Generally speaking, American specialization is at its highest in high-tech industry, medium in medium-tech and low in low-tech. Conversely, EU specialization is high in medium-tech, medium in low-tech and low in high-tech. However, between 1989 and 1994, the high-tech export share improved more in the EU (+2.8 points) than in the US (–0.6 points).

In terms of corporate strategies, American companies carry out fewer operations with European companies in high-tech industry than in medium-tech, whereas European companies concentrate their acquisitions on high-tech industries. In high-tech, it is the United States which has made the most corporate alliances on its national territory.

Finally, if one looks at the size of firms in relation to the line of business they are in, significant differences can be seen. In the US 22.7 per cent of small enterprises are in high-tech, whereas the proportion in Europe is only 13.3 per cent. It would appear that in Europe high-tech activities are more concentrated in large companies.[5]

These analytical data highlight several political challenges. A key element in this is the issue of competitive advantages. The preceding discussion would seem to suggest that the US has several advantages in the high-tech industry, whereas the EU is more geared up to specialization in medium- and low-tech industry. This state of affairs is not problematic *per se*, if viewed as an international division of labour based on initial endowments. An economy can be efficient on the basis of traditional activities.

However, a closer look at the European situation suggests different conclusions. For one thing, Europe has several important assets on the high-tech front. Many studies have shown that its strength lies in basic research, which can be seen in the proliferation of its scientific publications (see the European Commission Green Paper on innovation, 1996). Furthermore, the differences between the Member States in the technological field mean that for each specialization one or two major centres can usually be found somewhere in the Union. All this means that the Community as a whole is extremely well placed for future developments in the worldwide technology system.

The question therefore arises as to what factors constitute obstacles to the effective exploitation of the resources possessed by Europe? Purposefully targeted strategies and policies are needed to maintain, reinforce or create comparative advantages. Comparative advantages are never achieved once and for all, and they rely on well-thought out policies and strategies, including intensive human resource training and promoting innovations, as well as initiatives to facilitate the formation of a critical mass on the financing level. A first level of action is in the hands of the corporations.

It is true as it ever was that the main role is played by companies themselves. Looked at in this way, European research is not sufficiently translated into international competitive advantages. It is not because the quality is any lower than that of US research, as can be seen from the examples of Airbus, telecommunications, chemistry and Scandinavian robot technology. The problem is rather the failure to incorporate R&D and new breakthroughs into an overall strategy that would capitalize on them and give them direction. New breakthroughs do not automatically translate into effective production, let alone match up to consumer requirements and expectations. In other words, it is not up to R&D to plan the strategy, but the other way round. The ability of a company to do this will depend on the policy it has on products, the balanced development of marketing, production and management resources and the quality of its information systems and organization.

At the policy level, innovative capacity also depends on investments in research and technological development. In 1995, total R&D spending of the European Union amounted to 1.9 per cent of its Gross Domestic Product while it was 2.45 per cent in the US.

Other important factors that could be influenced by public policies are access to a broad and integrated market, a fast-moving industrial fabric that is regularly rejuvenated by the entry of new companies, in particular innovative SMEs, a supporting institutional environment, and the availability of research.[6] Europe is still handicapped by regulatory obstacles and rigidities but new efforts are made to improve its competitiveness. Several initiatives of the European Commission try to meet these challenges:

- strengthening the size and cooperative nature of precompetitive research efforts;
- promoting generic technologies, such as new materials, biotechnology, and information technology, whose characteristic is that they do not only concern specific firms or sectors but the whole industry;
- promoting rapid transfer of know-how from basic research to industrial application, and ensuring that small and medium-sized enterprises have access to this know-how and the ability to make best use of it;
- recognizing the positive effects on demand that can flow from introducing high product standards, from implementing technologically advanced trans-European networks (transport, energy, communication), and from opening public procurement to the most sophisticated technologies;
- strengthening training, through specialized centres of higher education, and improving the circulation of information and scientists, from both within and outside the Community.

These policies raise the question of global cooperation on research and technology beyond the boundaries of the Community. The huge costs associated with certain large-scale research work (such as the human genome and nuclear fusion), the growing shortage of technical staff and the global implications of environmental issues are just some of the factors that explain the globalization of corporate strategies, including R&D. This has been a feature of the scientific world and basic research for some time now.

However, there are two points which need to be considered here. First, rather few companies are truly global in the sense of not having a home country. Despite the 'techno-globalism' rhetoric, many firms maintain their national identity and corporate culture and subject their operations abroad to scrutiny by the parent company in the home country. One aspect is that leading-edge R&D on a company's 'core' technology is usually performed only at company's central labs in the home country.[7] Second, since governments launch national research programmes, often with the label 'strategic', off their own bat, cross-border cooperation is far from commonplace. On the contrary, foreign involvement is more often than not excluded, particularly when the research may have commercial applications. Although the costs, complexity and risk associated with the development of new technologies are a powerful source for greater international cooperation, friction could also increase. 'Burden-sharing, equitable technical and technological contributions, and effective intellectual property protection are all sources of disputes'.[8]

This points to the need for political action to draw up shared rules of the game to overcome the barriers to international cooperation.

Considerable progress was made in the 1990s on cooperation between the US and the EU. This process was given a particular boost by the activities promoted and coordinated by the Joint Consultative Group for S&T. Action taken has covered a range of different areas, including high-tech activities, information technology, prenormative research on biotechnology, energy and the environment, and large-scale scientific projects such as the human genome and thermonuclear fusion.

Recently the EU and the US have undertaken to negotiate a comprehensive science and technology cooperation agreement by 1997, as part of a 'New Transatlantic Agenda'. Negotiations are expected to be tough:

> The United States and the EU have different expectations from an agreement. Officials at the Commission would like European researchers to have better access to federally supported research programmes in the United States. Their US counterparts, on the other hand, want a narrower 'umbrella' agreement, primarily concerned with bringing patenting arrangement into line. (Macilwain, 1996)[9]

More generally, transatlantic relations have always been affected by a complex set of shaping factors.[10] Trade, investments and cooperation in R&T can be sustained or discouraged by political relations, security imperatives, macropolicy or relations with third countries.[11]

This means that a pragmatic, *ad hoc* approach is likely to be the most realistic. This could yield major benefits given the extent to which the two regions rely on and complement each other, and in view of the fact that together North America and Western Europe would be 'a leviathan, accounting for almost two thirds of world trade and about half of world income'.[12]

NOTES

Pierre Buigues is a Head of Unit in the European Commission's economic department (DG II). Alexis Jacquemin is a Chief Adviser to the European Commission and Professor of Economics at the Catholic University of Louvain.

This document reflects the authors' personal views, which are not necessarily those of the Commission.

The authors thank A. Sapir and C. Martínez for comments, and M. Berges and M. Van de Stadt for technical assistance.

1. NACE: general industrial classification of economic activities within the European Union.
2. As previously pointed out, the explanation lies in the fact that the Improvement in the relative productivity of these activities compared with the manufacturing sector in general has been markedly greater in the United States than in the Union. While productivity in the manufacturing sector increased at the same rate on both sides of the Atlantic (by 3.6 per cent and 3.7 per cent a year respectively on average between 1985 and 1994), such was not the case in the high-tech sectors (+5.3 per cent a year in the United States, as against 4.5 per cent in the European Union).
3. The import penetration ratio is the ratio of imports to total domestic demand (production + imports − exports).
4. The European Union is not about to correct the disparity in this area since the difference between the respective contributions of high-tech industries to total exports of manufactured goods is still 14.6 percentage points!
5. The example of human genome patents is symptomatic. According to *Nature* (4 April 1996), 40 per cent of human genome patents issued by the European Patent Office are held by Americans as against 24 per cent by Europeans. Most of the American-held patents are in the hands of SMEs, whereas there are virtually no European SMEs holding such patents.
6. In 1996, the EU had 4.7 scientists and engineers per 1000 inhabitants, compared to 7.4 in the US.
7. Office of Technology Assessment (1994). See also Patel and Pavitt (1991).
8. National Research Council, 'Friction and cooperation project', Washington, 1996. See also Rembser (1995).
9. Interestingly, the scientific cooperation agreement between Canada and the EU was ratified in February 1996 and is in force. It covers reciprocal involvement in research programmes, on a project by project basis, without transfer of funds.
10. Woolcock (1996) discusses various scenarios on EU-US relations.
11. An important distinction is between privately and publicly funded R&D. A 1996 report from the US National Academy of Engineering has recommended that Congress should avoid legislating restriction on foreign participation in privately funded US R&D, and strike reciprocity requirement from existing laws governing federal R&D spending. Meanwhile, the share of total domestic R&D spending by US affiliates of foreign-owned companies rose from 9.3 per cent in 1982 to 15.5 per cent in 1993; see *Nature*, 13 June 1996.
12. Baldwin and François (1996).

REFERENCES

D'Aspremont, Cl. and A. Jacquemin (1988), 'Cooperative and non-cooperative R&D in duopoly', *American Economic Review*, December.

Bail, Ch., W. Reinicke and R. Rummel (1996), *Perspectives on Transatlantic Relations*, The Brooking Institution, Stiftung Wissenschaft und Politik, Ebenhausen, and the Forward Studies Unit, European Commission, Brussels.

Baldwin, R. and J. François (1996), 'Transatlantic free trade: a quantitative assessment', mimeo.

Buigues, P. and A. Jacquemin (1994), 'Foreign direct investment and exports to the European Community', in M. Mason (ed.), *Japanese Multinationals in Europe*, Oxford: Clarendon Press.

Buigues, P. and A. Jacquemin (1995), 'Les échanges commerciaux entre les pays à bas salaires et l'Union Européenne', *Economie Internationale*, 64.

Buigues, P. and A. Jacquemin (1996), 'Low wages countries and trade with the European Union', in P.J. Buckley and J.-L. Mucchielli (eds), *Multinational Firms and International Relocation*, Cheltenham: Edward Elgar.

CE (1996), *Les investissements directs à l'étranger de l'Union européenne, 1984–1993*, EUROSTAT.

Coe, D. and E. Helpman (1995), 'International R&D spillovers', *European Economic Review*.

Communication from the Commission to the Council (1995), 'Europe and the US: the way forward', Brussels, 26 July.

Competitiveness Advisory Group (1996), 'Enhancing European competitiveness', Brussels, June.

Competitiveness Policy Council (1995), 'Saving more and investing better, a strategy for securing prosperity', fourth report to the President and Congress, Washington.

Council on Competitiveness (1995), 'Endless frontier, limited resources, US R&D policy for competitiveness'.

Davies, S. and Lyons, B. (1996), *Industrial Organization in the European Union*, Oxford University Press.

Duysters, G. and J. Hagedoorn (1996), 'Internationalization of corporate technology through strategic partnering: an empirical investigation', *Research Policy*, 25.

European Commission (1996), *Green Paper on Innovation*, Brussels.

Hagedoorn, J. and B. Sadowiski (1996), 'General trends in international technology partnering: the prospects for European economies in transition', in J.B. Sedaitis (ed.), *Commercializing High Technology: East and West*, Stanford, California: Rowman.

Hugues, K. (ed.) (1993), *European Competitiveness*, Cambridge University Press.

Macilwain, C. (1996), 'EU-US cooperation talks may hinge on access to research programmes', *Nature*, 4/1.

National Research Council (1996), 'Friction and cooperation project', Washington.

OECD (1987), 'Perspectives de la politique scientifique et technologique – diffusion de la technologie', Paris, June.

OECD (1995), 'Industry and technology: scoreboard of indicators', Paris.

OECD (1996), 'Technology, productivity and job creation', Paris.

Office of Technology Assessment (1994), 'Multinationals and the US technology base', Washington, DC.

Patel, P. and K. Pavitt (1991), 'Large firms in the production of the world's technology', *Journal of International Business Studies*, First Quarter.

Rembser, J. (1995), Intergovernmental and International Consultations/Agreements and Legal Cooperation Mechanism in Megascience, Paris: OECD.

Sachwald, F. (ed.) (1994), *European Integration and Competitiveness*, Aldershot: Edward Elgar.

Torre, A. (1990), 'Quand les économistes mesurent l'intangible', *Revue d'Economie Industrielle*, 53.

Woolcock, S. (1996), 'Strengthening EU-US Commercial Relations?', London School of Economics, mimeo.

4. North American sectoral profiles and corporate strategy in the automobile industry

Alan M. Rugman and Gavin Boyd

This chapter will focus on the nature of the North American automobile sector in Atlantic trade and investment. It does this against a background of the US manufacturing sector in general, especially the role of US multinational enterprises in foreign sales and production. Brief profiles of leading US manufacturing sectors are presented, followed by a review of the organizational structure and industrial organization of these leading sectors. In the second half of the chapter, the five partners/flagship framework of international competitiveness is applied to the Canadian-based but US-owned automobile sector in order to analyse its role in Atlantic trade and investment.

US MANUFACTURING SECTORS: GENERAL TRENDS

In Atlantic trade and investment US manufacturing industries have special significance. For the United States, reduction of its large overall current account deficits depends on improvements in the export of manufactures and on expanding its exports of services. For the European Union (EU) the competitiveness of US manufacturing exports is a major challenge because of the larger resources, relatively higher technological levels, and global market strengths of US firms. Linked with this challenge is the size and scale of the US manufacturing presence in the EU, which is not balanced by the smaller European manufacturing presence in the United States. The strengths of the US firms are based on established positions in their large home market, which is expanding under the North American Free Trade Agreement (NAFTA). In Europe, the persistence of informal national trade barriers restricts opportunities for economies of scale and scope in manufacturing, more to the detriment of European firms than to the disadvantage of US multinational enterprises, as these generally have more extensive international organizations that ensure efficiencies in dispersed operations.

The competitive strengths of American manufacturing industries are increasing, in the Atlantic context, because of relatively greater investments in new technology than those by most European firms, and because large shares in global manufacturing trade are being maintained through international production as well as through exports from the United States. The global market shares are being contested more forcefully by Japanese enterprises than by European firms. Japanese firms have made large gains in world markets, especially in the automobile and electronic and electrical equipment sectors. Shifts in relative degrees of US and European involvement in the global trading and production systems, however, reflect not only contrasts in sectoral and structural competitiveness but also the effects of differing uses of bargaining leverage on degrees of market openness, and, of course, changes in capacities for such leverage. European bargaining strength tends to be increased by deepening integration in the EU, and by its enlargement, while in NAFTA the consolidation of the central role of the United States results in some increases in potential leverage when interacting with the EU.

The United States has a recent history of large imbalances in manufacturing trade. These have been attributable to several factors operating at the policy and corporate levels. Large fiscal deficits have drawn in imports, while necessitating heavy government borrowing that has diverted investment from productive use, increasing the cost of capital and raising tax burdens. National firms have emphasized sales in external markets through foreign production, which has sustained profitability. Persistent US current account deficits have focused much attention on adverse balances in manufacturing trade. These became very large because of high currency appreciation in the first half of the 1980s, and have remained large despite subsequent depreciations of the US dollar. Prospects for improvement in the US current account depend to a considerable extent on increases in exports of vehicles. Japanese competition is strong in the US's own market and, increasingly, in Europe. The competitiveness of the US automobile sector has been reduced by the relatively high-cost steel sector in which innovation has been lagging. The steel sector's deficiencies have also affected production costs in industrial machinery and related sectors. The electronic and electrical equipment industry has links with the automobile sector at higher technological levels, and is more internationalized than that sector. The most highly internationalized sector is chemicals, which has the lowest major ranking in manufacturing trade, and which has more diffuse links with the automobile, industrial machinery, and electronic and electrical equipment industries.

PROFILES OF US MANUFACTURING SECTORS

Manufacturing accounts for about 17 per cent of the US Gross Domestic Product – slightly less than for services as defined for statistical purposes and considerably less if that definition is broadened to include finance, insurance, and retailing. The proportion for services, using the statistical definition, has been gradually increasing over the past two decades, while that for manufacturing has been declining slowly, due to adverse balances in manufacturing trade, shifts to foreign production by US firms, and overall processes of structural change, driven mainly by technological advances.[1]

The US manufacturing sectors have attributes with varying dimensions: size, technological level, degrees of concentration, overall efficiencies, domestic and external market interdependencies, and international involvement. The size of each sector has been determined primarily by the scope for operations in the domestic economy, but foreign production is becoming more significant for the service of external markets, especially for the chemicals and electronic and electrical equipment sectors. Technological levels, rising unevenly with investments in innovations necessitated by increasing international competition, have reflected contrasts in entrepreneurial dynamism, overall efficiencies, and differing degrees of interest in rent-seeking political action. Some sectors are highly oligopolistic, and their degree of concentration is related to patterns of domestic and foreign market sectoral interdependencies.

The Automobile Industry

The automobile industry is notable for its range of domestic market interdependencies, in which the steel sector is very prominent; it has lost external market shares over the past two decades, partly because of production cost factors associated with reliance on the steel sector, but more importantly because of lower efficiencies (especially due to high labour costs) than those in Japanese automobile firms. The principal manufacturing contributions to the US Gross Domestic Product are electronic and electrical equipment (1.9 per cent, increasing by 18.5 per cent annually, 1992–94) industrial machinery and equipment (1.7 per cent, increasing by 8.4 per cent annually, 1992–94) chemicals and allied products (1.9 per cent, increasing by 1.9 per cent annually, 1992-94) and motor vehicles and equipment (1.2 per cent, increasing by 17.3 per cent annually, 1992–94).[2] In US exports of manufactures the motor vehicle and equipment sector ranks higher than electronic and electrical equipment, and considerably higher than industrial machinery and equipment. About 10 per cent of the US exports of manufactures are automobiles; this sector however has the highest deficit in US manufacturing trade – it totalled $50.6 billion in 1995, and this was an increase of about $7 billion since 1990.[3] The deficit was attributable mainly to large imports of Japanese cars, and its reduction depended to a considerable extent on recoveries of domestic market shares by US firms, but internal demand had been slack. Sales of automobiles within the United States in 1994 were 600,000 less than the 15.7 million registered in 1988.[4] Competition in this market is encountered not only from Japanese imports but also from the substantial and growing Japanese automobile manufacturing presence in the United States. The intensity of the two types of competition motivates political action by US firms for US government leverage to open the rather closed Japanese market.[5]

Electronic and Electrical Equipment

Electronic and electrical equipment, a higher-technology sector, is much less concentrated, has smaller-scale domestic market interdependencies, and exhibits greater dynamism, but has experienced relatively larger trade deficits. There is a higher degree of internationalization, as US firms in this sector serve external markets much more through foreign production, and are relying increasingly on research and development at foreign locations. Numerous international alliances are contracted for that purpose and for collaborative production projects. The scale of foreign production, and the technological and market-seeking imperatives which tend to increase it, pose difficult structural policy issues for the US administration.[6]

Industrial Equipment

Industrial machinery and equipment, and a related sector, specialized industrial equipment, are medium-technology industries, much less internationalized, relatively more concentrated, and somewhat less dynamic. Like the automobile sector they have had production costs problems due to somewhat high domestic steel prices. Large trade deficits were experienced during the 1980s but modest surpluses were achieved by 1990. Export performance has been adversely affected by losses of international competitiveness and by reduced demand in the Middle East and Latin America.[7]

Steel

The US steel industry has a strong domestic orientation, having lost much international competitiveness over the past two decades, mainly because of low efficiencies. Excess domestic capacity, in a context of global overcapacity, has tended to force restructuring, but aggressively competitive intercorporate relations have made this difficult. More dynamic firms have tended to leave the sector in order to seek opportunities in other industries. Trade deficits for this sector are about 10 per cent of those for the automobile industry, and improvements in service of the domestic market, while hindered by substantial imports at competitive prices, are also hindered by shifts of automobile production to foreign locations, notably in Latin America.[8]

Chemicals

Chemicals and allied products is a medium-high-technology sector, more dynamic than the steel industry, less concentrated, and more internationalized. The level of international competitiveness, is fairly high, building on a record of substantial surpluses which reached $16 billion in 1990, when total exports of the industry were $39 billion.[9] The degree of internationalization is increasing, as US chemical firms rely more and more on foreign production to service external markets. In the Atlantic context the sector's external linkages are extensive, as chemicals trade each way is large. Competition in third country markets is mainly European, as Japan's role is severely limited by resource deficiencies.

US INDUSTRIAL ORGANIZATION: SECTORAL ISSUES

The manufacturing sectors in the United States are encountering stronger pressures to increase efficiencies and secure larger domestic and international market shares as competition intensifies in the global trading and production systems. The pressures operate in a context of corporate governance that tends to hinder collaborative adaptation, causing firms to implement more ambitious internalization strategies while nevertheless concentrating on the development of their core capabilities. Because of imperatives for high performance in short-term financial management, there can be a resort to diversification strategies that strain commitments to the enhancement of core capabilities. The pattern of corporate governance is evolving in a larger national context of macro and microeconomic policies, which interact with the policy mixes of other major states, mainly in the Atlantic and the Pacific.

US corporate structures are responding to their competitive challenges by increasing the international dimensions of their more active internalization strategies, which are raising levels of concentration in world markets. This is happening in a complex configuration with hierarchical features based on domestic sectoral market interdependencies. As the configuration assumes a stronger international orientation the automobile industry becomes especially prominent and its links with suppliers and distributors become even more significant as a major pattern of sectoral interactions. The structural competitiveness of the United States can be strengthened if that configuration becomes a more integrated and more dynamic system. The international expansion of that configuration through foreign production can be managed in ways compatible with its systemic evolution, but the functional balance which is required might not be achieved. Constant review of this extensive process, it can be argued, is a structural policy imperative for the US administration.

The internal structure of the major US automobile firms has been more hierarchical than those of their Japanese competitors. For the managerial synthesizing of complex judgements about technology and marketing factors in the industry, Japanese consultative practices and reliance on working-level autonomy have been sources of superior efficiencies. The Japanese system of corporate management has, moreover, enabled managements to function without pressure for short-term profits, yet with the support of organizational dynamism which has ensured rising long-term profitability. The major US automobile firms have been challenged to adapt more effectively to their organizational tasks, but they have also been attracted by the opportunities for political action to secure protection of their domestic market positions, increased access to the Japanese market, and preferential treatment of their foreign manufacturing operations by host countries.[10]

In the other major manufacturing sectors issues of internal structuring for leading and satellite firms are less complex. In the electronic and electric equipment industry, high degrees of internationalization and imperatives to access advances in frontier technology require management styles that rely to a large extent on consensual working-level expertise. Such requirements influence structures and management styles much less in the industrial machinery sectors, as their degrees of internationalization are lower and their technology is relatively less advanced. In the *steel* industry structures and management styles have been even less attuned to challenges for higher performance, and, it must be stressed, this sector has been distinguished by low levels of innovation. It has also been distinguished as an industry that has occasioned dysfunctional structural measures by US administrations – measures that have figured prominently in appraisals of US structural policy initiatives and that have discouraged business interest in such measures.[11]

The internal organization of chemical firms has been influenced by high degrees of internationalization and strong challenges of global technological competition: these appear to have induced levels of organizational dynamism like those in the electronic and electric equipment sector, although the rivalry encouraged has been European rather than Japanese. Because of a relatively narrow range of domestic market interdependencies the steel sector and the electronic and electrical equipment sector have been less vulnerable to externalities associated with weaker performance in other industries. Partly for this reason, moreover, issues of corporate governance have been less critical for these two sectors than for the automobile and steel industries.

The national system of corporate governance, inducing emphasis on short-term financial management for the retention of shifting shareholder preferences, is in effect a source of pressures to seize the advantages of extensive foreign production. These have to be sought with high-cost large-scale operations by the automobile firms, but can be secured with smaller and lower-cost ventures by electronic and electrical equipment companies. The very large-scale automobile production in the home economy is being changed with the formation of integrated international production systems, in which components for the home operations are sourced from foreign production. Oligopolistic strength in the home economy weakens the effects of restraints on collaboration imposed by the national system of corporate governance, but these restraints are strong enough to prevent the emergency of industry groups like those which benefit the Japanese automobile sector.[12] In particular, the restraints in the US system of corporate governance appear to prevent extensive acquisitions in the steel sector by US automobile firms – that is in conjunction with managerial imperatives to concentrate on improving efficiencies in core functions.

The interacting effects of macro and microeconomic policies tend to reinforce incentives to expand foreign production. At the macro level the costs of government and the potentially destabilizing effects of large fiscal deficits strengthen motivations to incorporate domestic manufacturing into a global production system with widely dispersed vulnerabilities. Trade policy provides limited protection of the internal market but does not leverage much widening of the small access to the Japanese market. Technology policy, supporting precompetitive research, focuses on the electronic and electrical equipment sector, and is of minor significance for the automobile industry. The sector's investment in new technology is at moderate levels, and is strongly influenced by needs to access Japanese advances in applied technology. Competition policy, in effect preventing further concentration of the automobile industry, is ineffective against tacit collusion between the major firms.[13] Their pricing strategies, however, have to contend with those of their Japanese rivals, whose production in the United States is a potent challenge.

In global competition against Japanese automobile producers, the main areas of contest are Europe and Latin America. A problem in the EU is its diminishing degree of protection against Japanese imports. In Latin America opportunities have been limited by economic stresses, notably in Mexico, and while recoveries from these are being made there are uncertainties regarding the formation and extension of regional trading systems. The US administration's interest in expanding NAFTA by drawing in Latin American members confronts the Mercosur states with issues that can encourage deepening integration in their own group. With a focus on that objective there could be emphasis on diversifying external economic relations through the development of stronger trade and investment links with Japan and the EU.[14]

A basic US microeconomic concern relating to the future of the automobile sector, and of other medium- and high-technology sectors that are prominent in foreign trade and production, is that the national technology base may be weakened by outward movements of industrial capacity, by large-scale entries of foreign industrial capacity with very limited technology transfers, and by technologically advanced imports which force domestic firms into declines. The extensive literature expressing this concern indicates that there is a basis for anxiety, and that there is a case for partially managed trade, as has been argued by Laura Tyson, but that basic characteristics of the US government tend to make this a highly politicized process.[15] The literature has also reflected general awareness that persistent fiscal laxity has had cumulative negative effects on the external trade of most of the major manufacturing sectors, posing problems which have been especially serious for the automobile industry because of the strength of demand for price-competitive imports.

FLAGSHIP FIRMS AND BUSINESS NETWORKS

In the principal US manufacturing sectors, firms seek to cope with information problems and with uncertainties in markets, and more particularly in arm's-length relations with suppliers and distributors, as well as with entrepreneurial coordination problems, by forming and operating through networks. These operate generally on an instrumental basis, without the solidarity of Japanese industry groups, but with significant degrees of trust that reduce transaction costs and risks. The operational benefits of networks become more significant as the internationalization of markets continues. The increasing scale and complexity of the linkages adds the uncertainties about supply and demand and the coordination problems limiting entrepreneurial decision making to the dimensions of information problems.

In the United States' manufacturing sectoral pattern the functional requirements for network building are greatest in the automobile industry, because of the wide range of components that have to be secured, the large numbers of distributors required for the marketing of at least minimal production volumes, and the imperatives for limited expedient cooperation with competitors, for example in precompetitive research and the experimental development of new models.[16] Network formation by electronic and electrical equipment firms is on a large scale, but mainly between technologically affinitive enterprises. This is also true of the chemical industry.

Network formation in the automobile sector has to be led by a major manufacturer acting as a flagship firm, enlisting the cooperation of suppliers and distributors and collaborating on a restricted basis with other flagship firms. While the flagship enterprise concentrates on its core capabilities, it benefits from the higher levels of reliability in dealings with suppliers and distributors, from the increased information flows, and the coordination opportunities provided through its networks. It can also benefit from the interpenetration of its networks with those of its competitors. Assessments of these benefits is of course highly judgmental, especially because reputational factors assume significance over medium and longer terms, advances in frontier technology are difficult to predict, and market trends remain overshadowed by the dangers of serious downturns, due to the accumulation of heavy government debt and the persistence of strains in the US financial sector.

Because the networks are managed instrumentally, although with varying degrees of trust, much effort has to be devoted to securing and reviewing the cooperation of the suppliers, distributors, and competitors, but also to the evaluation and cultivation of alternative partners. The emphasis on financial management which this industry shares with other US manufacturing sectors tends to introduce short-termism into network relationships, and while this can limit the development of trust, it can also reduce attentiveness to emerging technological advances which would draw more entrepreneurial interest in networks with higher levels of solidarity.

Network management requirements make entrepreneurial tasks exceptionally demanding in the automobile sector, and these can be sources of strain at top and middle management levels. Difficulties in the performance of managerial teams that are common in large international firms can be especially serious because of the complex diversified task orientations of high-level managerial groups in the automobile sector. The problems of multi-functional managerial teamwork become more evident when the structures and functions of flagship automobile firms are examined closely, for the assessment of internalization efficiencies and network efficiencies. These warrant comparative study, but within limitations because of the breadth of production functions which distinguishes the automobile sector.

AUTOMOBILE FLAGSHIP FIRMS

Internalization logic and the logic of concentration on core functions have special applications in the automobile industry because of the range of production operations that must be combined, the high volume of output necessary for economies of scale, and the requirements for extensive network activity related to the range of core production functions and the output volumes. In the United States the system of corporate governance and the mix of microeconomic policies influence the balance between internalization logic and core functional logic by setting upper limits to the scale of internalization, discouraging diversification, and obligating network management within restrictions imposed by a competition policy which in conjunction with an individualistic business culture hinders the formation of industry groups. The efficiencies of network functions managed by a US automobile flagship firm thus have to compete against the efficiencies of Japanese industry groups. Flagship-specific efficiencies meanwhile have to compensate for weaknesses in that regard, while seeking advantages from political action to retain degrees of protection in the home market. Political action for that purpose has limited long-term prospects because of the US administration's gradual loss of bargaining leverage against Japan, due to dependence on partial Japanese financing of American fiscal deficits, and to the persistence of strains in Atlantic relations that limit EU cooperation in support of market-opening leverage against Japan. The balance between internalization logic and core functional logic is evolving, however, as the US automobile sector undertakes more extensive foreign production; in the external operations, especially in Latin America, the scope for efficient internalization may become wider, under weaker policy-level constraints imposed by host governments.

THE FLAGSHIP MODEL AND THE AUTO SECTOR

The five partners flagship framework emphasizes two key features of a business network: the members that constitute the network and the nature of the

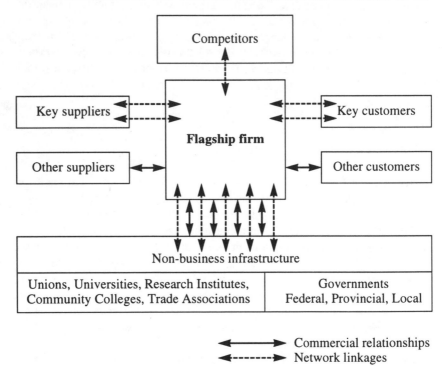

Figure 4.1   The five partners business network

relationship between them.[17] At the core of the network is the flagship firm which is usually a multinational enterprise, with key suppliers, key customers, selected competitors and the non-business infrastructure connecting to this central node. The strategic decisions and organizational considerations of the business network are led by the flagship firm. Figure 4.1 demonstrates conceptually these five partners in the flagship model as it applies to the North American, including the Canadian, auto sector.

The auto sector exhibits many of the characteristics of the five partners business network. The flagship firms amongst the vehicle assemblers are establishing the parameters of the relationship with key suppliers by specifying quality standards, product specifications and cost limitations to which those suppliers must adhere. They lead the relationship with their key customers, the franchised dealers. The Big Three (General Motors, Ford, and Chrysler) have also worked together in ways such as developing common quality standards. Finally, the sector is widely represented on government advisory committees, well served with numerous industry associations, and developing relationships with education and research institutions. We shall now discuss each of the five partners in the flagship model in detail and relate these to the US-owned Canadian automotive sector.

Flagship Firms

In the Canadian automotive sector, flagship firms are found primarily in the vehicle assembly industry. These consist of the wholly owned Canadian subsidiaries of the Big Three – General Motors of Canada Ltd (GM), Ford Motor Company of Canada Ltd, and Chrysler Canada Ltd.

Chrysler is a prime example among the vehicle assemblers of a flagship firm exerting leadership over the strategic interests of the broader business network. In 1994 Chrysler adopted the philosophy of 'extended enterprise' based on the Japanese concept of keiretsu. Under this approach, Chrysler views the roles, responsibilities and relationships of suppliers and others along the value chain as an extension of the company. The system demands a high level of mutual trust and builds on the teamwork developed through Supplier Cost Reduction Effort (SCORE) which was initiated in 1989. It includes joint research projects, participation in process redesign studies together, and joint management of second- and third-tier suppliers. At the same time as changing supplier management, Chrysler has been trying to institute cultural change with its dealer network though the Customer One programme. Customer One is an intensive dealer training programme that covers not only product knowledge but also customer relations and is aimed at improving customer (consumer) satisfaction. Overall, Chrysler's new culture is defined as 'new ways to research, create, test and build world-class trucks, minivans and cars and improved ways to provide world-class treatment of the people who buy and own them'.[18]

Key Suppliers

The relationship between the three Canadian vehicle assembly flagship firms and their suppliers, like their American counterparts, has undergone a fundamental transformation since the late 1980s. The traditional, vertically integrated organizational structure that had been based on the Fordist approach to corporate organization, i.e., the need for central control over all phases of production, has been replaced by a more deintegrated structure. As part of the shift to a lean production model, suppliers have been required to take on a larger role in designing, developing and testing components, becoming responsible for aspects of the production process that the vehicle assemblers had traditionally reserved for themselves. Tier One suppliers are expected to be system integrators that supply modules or systems to the auto makers, and to manage the supply chain. In return they may receive longer-term supply agreements.

Suppliers are also increasingly being asked to service an automaker worldwide. For example, Ford plans to single-source the majority of components for its common European/North American platform from multinational suppliers with production facilities in the United States and Europe.[19] As might be expected when developing key relationships, at the same time as the flagship firms are shifting greater responsibility to suppliers, they are reducing the total number of suppliers. Chrysler plans to reduce its North American supplier base from 1900 in 1992 to 750 in 1995 with an eventual reduction in Tier One suppliers from 1250 to 150. Similarly, Ford, plans to reduce the number of suppliers from 900 in 1992 to 750 in 1995; the majority of its components will be sourced from only 100 suppliers worldwide.[20]

In their drive to reduce costs, the flagship firms have opened the door to increased sourcing from independent producers, despite union protests. Consequently, the in-house producers' share of parts shipments in Canada has declined from 41 per cent in 1980 to 26 per cent in 1991. Of the Big Three, Chrysler outsources the most, purchasing 75 per cent of its components from independents; Ford outsources 50 to 55 per cent and General Motors 40 per cent.[21] Delphi Automotive Systems, a GM subsidiary, dominates the global parts suppliers with 1995 revenues of US $26.4 billion, almost twice as much as the next supplier.[22] Delphi's size is perhaps a reflection of GM's use of in-house suppliers.

The price of materials purchased from suppliers is the single largest cost component in the price of a car. Managing the cost of suppliers' materials is therefore an important strategy for the flagship firms, and each of the Big Three have set supplier cost reduction targets/requirements and established a process to accomplish these targets. For example, teams under General Motors' Purchase Input Concept Optimization System (PICOS) visit supplier plants and suggest/require improvements. Similarly, Chrysler's Supplier Cost Reduction Effort (SCORE) mandates cost savings from suppliers through efficiency improvements.

Chrysler pushes the collaborative relationship with its suppliers by using catalysts such as lean production workshops, classroom training and sharing of lessons learned at other suppliers. In the first phase of its Chrysler Lean Operating Supplier Enterprise (CLOSE) programme, Chrysler ensures that its top 150 suppliers understand lean manufacturing and apply its principles the way Chrysler does. In the second phase, Chrysler and its key suppliers co-host workshops for other suppliers, and finally the key suppliers introduce the workshops to their suppliers.[23] As an example, Chrysler and Eaton Corporation, the valve train system integrator for its new truck family, hosted a workshop at Eaton's Saginaw facility in which several non-competing suppliers learned common lean production techniques.

In other instances, automotive paint suppliers such as PPG and DuPont Canada are well integrated with their key customers, the vehicle assemblers. As discussed in the section on chemicals, the paint manufacturers are responsible for researching colour trends, new product development and technical support. They work closely with the vehicle assembler and may sit on OEM teams which create strategies for the global business. Hayes-Dana, the Canadian subsidiary of Dana Corporation which manufactures and distributes both original equipment and replacement parts for the automotive industry, asserts that close relationships with suppliers, customers and its parent are the key to the future. For example, a group of Hayes-Dana, Dana and General Motors personnel worked closely together to develop the equipment and tools necessary to build the frame sub-assembly for a new GM van.[24] The Woodbridge Group, which manufactures automotive polyurethane foam products and considers itself a speciality rather than Tier Two company, believes that it must develop sophisticated, innovative working relationships with customers and suppliers which will lead to greater interdependence.[25]

The development of long-term, collaborative relationships with their suppliers has been an important competitive strategy for the flagship firms. While aspects of the relationship between the Big Three and their suppliers are becoming more collaborative, at least from the flagship firm's perspective, there remain many elements of the power asymmetry typical of flagship firms with their partners. The vehicle assemblers establish the quality and design parameters. They require suppliers to invest in additional capital equipment and technology to meet the assemblers' deintegration policies at the same time as demanding cost reductions. The flagship firms bestow awards. They rate the suppliers according to performance. Chrysler, for example, qualifies suppliers on past performance and uses a rating system that considers technology, delivery, price and quality. Ford Tier One suppliers get individual report cards, including data on the supplier's role in recall campaigns, delivery performance and defects; Ford then meets with each supplier and charts a plan to improve its rating. In all these ways, the assembly flagship firms are exercising their power over the supplier network.

Key Customers

Close relationships with key customers play a vital role in the success of the network as a whole. According to Donald Fites,[26] Chairman and CEO of Caterpillar, the biggest reasons for Caterpillar's success in combating the cost advantage of Japanese manufacturers are its distribution network and close relations with its dealers. Local dealers can get closer to a customer than can a global company, but to benefit from their knowledge of the market, the dealers must be integrated into critical business systems. He writes: 'The quality of the relationship between a company and its dealers is much more important than the contractual agreements or the techniques and tactics that make the relationship work on the surface. What matters is mutual trust ....' This view echoes the findings that trust is the most important attribute in a long-term supply agreement between a supplier and a vehicle assembler. It is also an element that the five partners model requires for the network to be successful.

Each of the motor vehicle assemblers in North America has dealers which operate franchised retail outlets that carry the manufacturer's product lines. There are over 3700 manufacturers' dealers in Canada, 55 per cent of which are associated with the Big Three (Canadian Automobile Dealers Association). In most, if not all cases, new vehicles are sold only through franchised dealers; these effectively are the key customers. While the characteristics of a franchise relationship and a single supplier necessarily align the strategic interests of the manufacturer and the dealer, some flagship firms are extending the relationship into a more collaborative one.

Chrysler Corporation has intensified its efforts to incorporate the dealers into its competitive thinking. It has invested in the Customer One training programme, as described earlier, and established performance standards for its dealerships. Advanced level training to service and general managers includes methods for achieving Chrysler's strategic initiatives. Like Ford, it has a satellite system which broadcasts to both dealers and employees but which appears to be more of a one-way communication device than an interactive tool. In the United States, Chrysler's 1992 'Adopt-A-Dealer' programme provided for each assembly plant manager to adopt a specific dealership.[27] Small groups of assembly workers regularly met with the service manager, found out what problems had arisen, and solved those problems back at the plant. Typically, the group could solve the most difficult problem within two to three hours, compared to the two to three days it might take the dealer. At the plant, records are kept of the dealers visited and the types of problems encountered.

The dealers tend to think of themselves as entrepreneurs or independent businesses. However, the behaviours they can exhibit, the standards to which they must adhere, the performance appraisal measures applied by the manufacturer, and the limitations on products they can sell, particularly in exclusive franchises, point to an organizational form that has limited autonomy and is closely tied to the manufacturer. In terms of the five partners model, the flagship firms exert considerable influence over the strategic interests of the dealers, their key customers. While there has been some movement towards seeking a more collaborative relationship on a day-to-day level, the drive, initiatives and controls appear to remain with the vehicle assemblers.

Selected Competitors

Flagship firms within one industry often have multiple strategic objectives, some of which may be pursued in conjunction with other flagship firms without loss of competition. In the North American auto industry, the threat posed to the domestic vehicle assemblers by the Asian manufacturers has caused the Big Three to work together in a variety of ways that include common standards or precompetitive research.

In 1994, General Motors, Ford and Chrysler announced their long-awaited common quality system for their suppliers, QS 9000. The system is an adaptation of ISO 9000 standards and is specific to the auto industry. It combines the ISO 9000 quality assurance with industry-specific guidelines drawn from former auto industry programmes for quality – GM North American Operations Targets for Excellence, Ford's Q101 Quality System Standard and Chrysler's Supplier Quality Assurance Manual.[28]

The Big Three are determining a strategic element of the network, quality, by requiring Tier One suppliers to become QS 9000 certified (though in practice, mandatory certification has been delayed whilst issues around the training of registrars are resolved). In turn Tier One suppliers are expected to ask their suppliers for QS 9000 certification. Only third-party registrars trained by the Big Three will be able to issue QS 9000 certificates. Since QS 9000 certification is more stringent than ISO 9000 certification, the latter is not acceptable to the Big Three. Consequently suppliers will have to incur substantial additional costs in order to be eligible as a supplier, illustrating once again the ability of the flagship firms to affect the internal operations of network partners and indeed, the network itself.

Another area in which manufacturers and suppliers are becoming more integrated is in the electronic exchange of data. STEP (Standard for the Exchange of Product model data) is an international communications standard being developed to enable industrial engineers to exchange electronic data. Under an AutoSTEP pilot project initiated in 1995 by the Automotive Industry Action Group (which represents North American vehicle manufacturers and suppliers), the Big Three and six Tier One suppliers exchange product data and graphics using parts of the STEP program. An additional nine suppliers have since joined the project. Cost is a driving force behind the project since separate CAD systems can cost up to US $100000 each, not including training and maintenance.

Similarly, representatives from the Big Three joined with their suppliers and the Auto/Steel Partnership to standardize tooling within the auto industry. After three years' work, the team created a manual, 'North American Automotive Metric Standards (NAAMS): Forming and Stamping'; a similar team is addressing common assembly tooling standards. The manufacturers want the suppliers to follow the standards so that they can interchange the same component from multiple suppliers without retooling.

In the parts industry the changing nature of the business, in which a smaller number of Tier One suppliers are being asked to supply larger systems, means that a parts manufacturer may be the Tier One supplier for one contract but act as a Tier Two supplier to a Tier One competitor for another. In one estimate, only 25 per cent of the present global Tier One suppliers will exist by the end of the decade; of the remainder, 25 per cent will be acquired or enter partnerships with each other, 30 per cent will go out of business and 20 per cent will leave the auto industry altogether.[29] *Ward's Autoworld* reported nearly 100 globalization initiatives in 1995 among suppliers including acquisitions, joint ventures and strategic partnerships. One recent example of a partnership among competitors is the ABS Education Alliance formed in 1996 by Robert Bosch Corporation, Delphi Chassis Systems, ITT Automotive and Kelsey Hayes to promote a joint nationwide campaign that will educate drivers on how to use the new braking technology.[30] Thus there appear to be shifting alliances amongst the suppliers during a shakeout of the industry and it is not clear at this point whether any of these alliances will develop the characteristics of a key customer-key supplier relationship.

Overall, while there are some elements of collaboration amongst selected competitors in both assembly and parts industries, these relationships are often tentative and not strongly developed.

Non-business Infrastructure

Since the auto sector is such a significant component of the economy, it has long attracted attention from governments seeking to enhance the economic health of their constituencies. Assistance has traditionally taken the form of investment incentives, loans and subsidies, and the role between an organization and the government has primarily been of a lobbying rather than collaborative nature.

There have, however, been some opportunities for the industry to work with government on public policy issues. During the Free Trade Agreement negotiations, the ITAC and SAGIT were influential in maintaining key elements of the Auto Pact. The auto sector has also had the opportunity to work with the Canadian government through the Automotive Advisory Committee. This Committee, formed in 1989, is composed of a broad representation of manufacturers, importers, dealers and industry associations and gives sectoral policy advice to the Minister of Industry. Participation is at the CEO level. Industry Canada provides the organizational and co-ordinating services, and the Ontario and Quebec governments have observers on the Committee. The Executive Co-chairs are from the automotive parts and assembly industries, currently the President and Chief Executive Officers of Magna International and Chrysler Canada Ltd. Specific issues are dealt with at the sub-committee level. The Committee provides a forum for government/industry communication as well as cooperation amongst competitors on issues of mutual concern. Ultimately, however, it is an advisory not a decision-making committee.

Provincially, efforts at cooperation have been less successful. The Canadian Independent Automotive Components Council, which grew out of the Components sub-committee of the Automotive Advisory Committee, began work on a strategic action plan for the auto parts industry with the financial support of Ontario's Sector Partnership Fund, Industry Canada and Quebec's Ministry of Commerce, Science and Technology. However, the Council has not been able to complete its work, largely because it was unable to resolve strained relationships among its members. Hostility amongst the primarily non-unionized manufacturers to the inclusion of the Canadian Auto Workers union as a partner and competitive rivalries between the diverse parts manufacturers hindered any collaborative efforts. With the change in Ontario's government in 1995, the Sector Partnership Fund was cancelled, and the Council no longer exists. Given the Ontario government's policies of reduced involvement in the economy, it appears unlikely that further sectoral initiatives will be forthcoming.

One of the areas in which flagship firms can influence the non-business infrastructure is through collaborative ventures with universities and colleges in which the research and training is directed to the company's needs. Some of this occurs in the auto sector though perhaps not as much as its importance dictates.

Chrysler Canada is showing leadership with respect to research partnerships, as demonstrated by its collaboration with the University of Windsor. In May 1996, Chrysler and the University opened the first jointly operated automotive research facility in Canada, the University of Windsor/Chrysler Canada Automotive Research and Development Centre. This facility will allow Chrysler to pursue niche research in new automotive product technology with university facilities and at the same time enable the university to offer hands-on experience for its students. As an example, the road test simulation labs will allow Chrysler engineers to develop and evaluate structural characteristics of automotive products under laboratory conditions. Chrysler has also sponsored two industrial chairs in the engineering department, in conjunction with the Natural Sciences and Engineering Research Council of Canada; one chair is in design and one in alternative fuels, with potentially a third chair in acoustic imaging. The incumbents will not only carry out R&D based on Chrysler's needs but also teach students, thus helping to produce graduates with the skills sought by Chrysler. Chrysler is not the only flagship firm involved with academic institutions; Ford has also sponsored a chair in aluminium casting at the University of Windsor to promote R&D.

General Motors and Ford, as well as Honda, Toyota and Canadian Tire, have taken a different approach in their interactions with the education sector. Each has formed a partnership with Centennial College, a community college in Toronto, by which the college delivers a company-specific, modified apprenticeship programme to employees of each company. Each programme has courses ranging in length from a few hours to four days, may be offered at the college, the company site or through distance learning, and is intended to upgrade the mechanical skills of company's employees.

In summary, the flagship firms are beginning to develop some long-term, company-specific relationships with the research and education sectors. While interaction with government in the past has been effective in trade policy, the current relationships often show more form than substance.

CONCLUSIONS

The technical and operational changes made by the vehicle manufacturers, coming as they did after a period of insulation and stability, have transformed the North American auto industry. These structural changes have not only involved internal business processes and technological improvements, but have also restructured the relationships in the business network. The Big Three, typically the flagships in the network, have each sought competitive advantage by incorporating key suppliers and customers (dealers) into their strategic thinking. Where a network previously existed primarily between the parent company and its Canadian subsidiary, with in-house parts manufacturers supplying assemblers on either side of the border, now the network has been simultaneously extended (more out-sourcing) and constrained (long-term, global sourcing from fewer suppliers).

The changed supplier relationship stems in part from observing the effect of the relationship between Japanese suppliers and manufacturers. Helper has estimated that superior relations with suppliers gave the Japanese a $300 to $600 per car cost advantage in the 1980s.[31] Early supplier involvement in product design was the key to faster introduction of new models using fewer labour hours. In a more recent survey of 600 US and almost 500 Japanese automotive suppliers,[32] she and Sako (1995) found that a voice-based relationship, one where problems are resolved jointly, produced significant supplier cost reductions. Better performance was found among suppliers that provided detailed process information to their customers, saw their customer commitment as long-term, and expected to engage in joint problem solving with the customer. This voice-based relationship, however, only applied to 29 per cent of US and 32 per cent of Japanese suppliers. They concluded that the automotive industry in both countries reveals a tension between the automakers' desire to select the best supplier at any point in time while creating good suppliers by working with them over a long period of time.

The introduction of Japanese lean production management techniques has not been easy, and has required the flagship firms to hold fast to the strategic aims for the network. A flexible production system with integrated quality control, a leaner supply system and labour-management relations based on work teams has forced the suppliers and unions to reconsider their role in the network. According to Yanarella and Green,[33] much of organized American labour has moved from the more adversarial model towards a more cooperative approach, in contrast to the Canadian unions. While this statement may be directionally true, the Spring 1996 strike by workers protesting General Motors' proposal to make greater use of outsourcing affected production levels throughout North America and temporarily threatened the overall network. Similarly, the CAW strike against GM Canada in October 1996, and the issue of outsourcing, also affected production. A cooperative labour-management relationship in the Big Three is not strongly developed and this lack of collaboration represents a major weakness of the network. The unions' position is not surprising, since their perceived role is the protection and improvement of their current members' jobs, with less emphasis on future members' benefits. The challenge remains for the flagship firms that are unionized to manage that relationship in a way that recognizes the short- and long-term needs of both parties in order to improve the competitiveness of the network.

Since the auto industry is often the major if not sole customer for many of the suppliers and the dealers are franchisees of the assemblers, the success of these network partners is ultimately dependent on the success of the flagship firms. Consequently, the relationship between them is asymmetrical, a characteristic of the five partners model. Another key feature of the model, the development of long-term, collaborative relationships between and among the partners is also evident, albeit in a transitional stage between suppliers and OEMs. The increasing role of the flagships in ensuring that their education, research and development needs are met, and the initiatives of the numerous industry associations, both testify to the presence of an active network. Overall, the auto industry in Canada is well on the way to developing partnerships that align the strategic objectives of the partners.

NOTES

1. Robert F. Yuskavage, 'Improved estimates of gross product by industry, 1959–1994', *Survey of Current Business*, 76 (8), August 1996, 133–55.
2. *Ibid.*
3. Robert E. Scott, 'The western hemisphere motor vehicle industry: market structure, trade flows and integration prospects', Paper for Conference on Globalization and Regionalization, University of Paris I, Panthéon Sorbonne, 29–30 May 1996.
4. *Ibid.*
5. Dennis J. Encarnation, *Rivals beyond Trade: America versus Japan in Global Competition* (Ithaca: Cornell University Press, 1992).
6. These issues are discussed in *Multinationals and the US Technology Base* (US Congress: Office of Technology Assessment, 1994)
7. Allen J. Lenz, *Narrowing the US Current Account Deficit* (Washington, DC: Institute for International Economics, 1992). See Chapter 5.
8. *Ibid.*
9. Encarnation, *Rivals beyond Trade*. Also see Wyn Grant and William Paterson, 'The chemical industry: a study in internationalization', in J. Rogers Hollingsworth, Philippe C. Schmitter and Wolfgang Streeck (eds), *Governing Capitalist Economies* (New York: Oxford University Press, 1994), 129–55.
10. *Ibid.* at 5. Also see references to the automobile sector in Murray Smith, 'The North American Free Trade Agreement: Global Impacts', in Kym Anderson and Richard Blackhurst (eds), *Regional Integration and the Global Trading System* (New York: St. Martin's Press, 1993), 83–103.
11. Stefanie Lenway, Randall Morck and Bernard Yeung, 'Rent seeking, protectionism and innovation in the American steel industry', *The Economic Journal*, 106 (435), March 1996, 410–21.
12. Lawrence J. White, 'Competition policy in the United States: an overview', *Oxford Review of Economic Policy*, 9 (2), Summer 1993, 133–51.
13. *Ibid.*
14. See references to Mercosur in *Trade Liberalization in the Western Hemisphere* (Washington, DC: InterAmerican Development Bank and Economic Commission for Latin America and the Caribbean, 1995).
15. Laura D'Andrea Tyson, *Who's Bashing Whom: Trade Conflict in High Technology Industries* (Washington, DC: Institute for International Economics, 1992). Also see references to the United States in Samuel Kernell (ed.), *Parallel Politics: Economic Policymaking in Japan and the United States* (Washington, DC: Brookings Institution, 1991).
16. The complexities of network management thus require much cross-functional consultation. See observations on the automobile industry in Mark Casson, *The Organization and Evolution of the Multinational Enterprise: An Information Cost Approach*, University of Reading Department of Economics Discussion Paper no. 222, November 1996.
17. See Joseph R. D'Cruz and Alan M. Rugman, *New Compacts for Canadian Competitiveness* (Toronto: Kodak Canada Inc., 1992); Joseph R. D'Cruz and Alan M. Rugman, 'Developing international competitiveness: the five partners model', *Business Quarterly*, 58 (2) (Winter 1993), 101–7; and Joseph R. D'Cruz and Alan M. Rugman, 'Business Network Theory and the Canadian telecommunications industry', *International Business Review* 3 (3) (1994), 275–88.

18. Chrysler Canada, *1995 Annual Report* (Windsor: Chrysler Canada Ltd, 1995), and Chrysler Corporation, 'Supplier relations', *Annual Report 1994* (http://www.chrysler.com).
19. Industry Canada, Automotive Branch, *Automotive Strategic Framework* (Ottawa: The Department, 1995).
20. *Ibid.*
21. *Ibid.*
22. Robert Bosch GmbH, *Automotive News* (1996).
23. Chrysler Corporation, 'Valve train extended enterprise spreads lean manufacturing principles', *Supplier Newsletter* (May/June 1996), Chrysler Corporation (http://www.media).
24. Hayes-Dana Inc., *Annual Report 1994* (St. Catherine's, ON: Hayes-Dana).
25. *Ward's Autoworld* (December 1995), entire issue.
26. *Ibid.*
27. John McElroy, 'Crusade at Chrysler', *Automotive Industries*, June 1992, 24.
28. Amy Zuckerman, 'Ford, Chrysler, and GM introduce a common quality standard', *Iron Age/New Steel*, November 1994, 22.
29. Lindsay Chappell, 'Forecast: Fewer Suppliers', *Automotive News*, 8 July 1996, 1.
30. Ralph Kisiel, 'ABS ABSc', *Automotive News*, 26 February 1996, 24i.
31. Alex Taylor III, 'The auto industry meets the new economy', *Fortune*, 5 September 1994, 52–60.
32. Susan R. Helper and Mari Sako, 'Supplier relations in Japan and the United States', *Sloan Management Review*, 36 (3), 1995, 77–84.
33. Ernest J. Yanarella and William C. Green, 'The UAW and CAW confront lean production at Saturn, CAMI, and the Japanese automobile transplants, *Labor Studies Journal*, 1 January 1994, 52.

5. Atlantic systems of corporate finance and governance

Stephen Prowse

Dramatically different systems of corporate finance and governance have emerged among the major industrialized countries in the post-war period. Even the casual observer notices large differences between the way firms finance and govern themselves in the US and the UK on the one hand, and Germany on the other. In this chapter I describe how firms obtain external finance and how the primary mechanisms of corporate governance operate in these three countries. I analyse reasons for the dramatic differences observed in corporate finance and governance systems. I discuss some of the costs and benefits of each system. Finally, I evaluate the current pressures that each system is under to change, and make some prophecies as to how corporate finance markets will evolve in the future in each country.

These issues are of course fundamental to the theory of the firm, corporate finance and corporate governance that have exercised academics for many years. However, recently they have taken on a policy relevance that they have not enjoyed before. In the US and the UK there is an intense on-going debate about the most preferred methods of financing and governing firms.[1] And in the last few years, Germany has initiated substantial changes in its corporate finance markets.

Examination of the corporate finance systems in these countries is also relevant to the issue of strategic alliances between firms in the US, the UK, and Germany – or more generally, between firms that operate in financial and governance systems that approximate those of the US and the UK (such as Canada), and those that approximate those of Germany (such as a number of continental European countries). Clearly, managers of firms considering strategic alliances with firms in countries where the finance system is radically different would benefit from an understanding of those differences. And likewise, policy makers attempting to improve the environment for such strategic alliances would undoubtedly appreciate an understanding of the important differences in the corporate finance systems in the major industrialized countries, why such differences exist, the relative strengths and weaknesses of each system, and the pressures and prospects for change in these systems. This chapter attempts to provide insight on these issues.

One argument in this chapter is that the large differences we observe in corporate finance and governance between the industrialized countries are not just accidents of history or culture, but are the product of three aspects of the legal and regulatory environment under which each system has evolved. The first aspect relates to the legal and regulatory environment for universal banking and the ability of financial institutions in general to own large stakes in firms and play an active role in their governance (to be 'active investors' as Jensen (1989) puts it). Banks and other financial institutions in Germany have been allowed to be active investors in the firms to which they lend, whereas Anglo-Saxon financial institutions in general have not. The second aspect is the degree to which corporate securities markets[2] have been actively suppressed by regulatory fiat, taxation and/or cumbersome mandated issuance procedures. Relative to the Anglo-Saxon countries, Germany has had severe regulatory constraints on the development of their corporate securities markets. The third aspect is the degree to which securities markets have been 'passively' suppressed by the lack of any mandated standardized disclosure requirements for firms wishing to issue securities to public investors. Germany has lagged behind the Anglo-Saxon countries in mandating information disclosure by firms issuing securities. For this to influence securities market activity in these countries, there must be a public good aspect to the voluntary provision of information by firms to outside investors. I discuss some evidence on this issue.

I also look at the relative costs and benefits of each system of corporate finance and governance. While particular advantages are claimed for both systems, it is impossible to say from the evidence which is the more efficient system overall, or even whether any efficiency differences are important enough in magnitude to be of practical relevance.

I identify some of the emerging pressures for change in corporate finance markets and draw some implications for the future development of financial systems in the industrialized countries. Rapid changes in technology, market innovation, the globalization of financial markets and the increasing importance of small firms in the economy and of institutional investors in the financial markets all have put pressure on the German finance system to change. This pressure is already having an effect: Germany has substantially deregulated its securities markets in recent years and vastly increased firms' access to non-bank sources of finance.

These changes have also affected Anglo-Saxon finance markets, although somewhat less drastically, probably because their greater reliance on securities markets has proved to be more consistent with the emerging pressures for change. Corporate finance markets that cater to small and medium-sized firms are growing rapidly in the US. In addition, institutional investors are changing their view of their role in the corporate finance markets, and appear increasingly willing to take on a more active monitoring and governing role in the companies in which they invest.

Overall, these changes are moving the Anglo-Saxon and German financial systems closer together. However, the focal point of this convergence is not the German or US/UK systems as they currently exist but an environment where financial institutions are free to be active owners *and* where securities markets are unhindered by regulatory obstacles.

In the following section, I describe the generic information problems of external finance and governance that all corporate finance markets face regardless of their nationality. I then lay out a description of the corporate finance and governance systems in the US, the UK and Germany, explaining how each system addresses these problems and highlighting the major differences between countries, focusing on the major legal and regulatory factors I believe are the main determinants of these differences. Finally I look at the factors that are inducing change in corporate finance and governance systems in all countries, and that, taken together, appear to be moving such systems closer together.

GENERIC PROBLEMS OF CORPORATE FINANCE AND GOVERNANCE

Corporate finance markets in all countries must address two generic information problems facing firms attempting to raise funds from outsiders: sorting and incentive problems.

Sorting problems arise in the course of selecting investments: firm owners and managers typically know much more about the condition of their business than outsiders and it is in their interests to accent the positive while downplaying potential difficulties. Sorting problems and their implications for corporate finance were first analysed by Leland and Pyle (1977) and Ross (1977), who emphasized that the choice of a particular capital structure was important in minimizing such problems. More generally, sorting problems require that potential outside financiers conduct extensive information-gathering and verifying activities into the firm's operations in order to minimize such information asymmetries.

Incentive problems arise in the course of the firm's operations. Firm managers have many opportunities to take actions that benefit themselves at the expense of outside investors. Jensen and Meckling (1976) were the first to address these issues. They stressed that a combination of methods is usually needed to align the incentives of managers and investors, including the use of an appropriate capital structure, the use of collateral and security covenants and direct monitoring. Diamond (1991) stressed the role of reputation in mitigating incentive problems: managers of firms that have a stake in maintaining a good reputation with outside investors have strong incentives not to act opportunistically at the expense of such investors.

Problems of external finance thus cannot be separated from problems of governance. Both stem from very similar and related information problems. More importantly, outside investors will not extend external finance to firms without some assurance that mechanisms are in place to control the activities of the firm after funding. Indeed, the form of the governance mechanisms in place often will dictate the characteristics of the external financing.

It should also be clear that information problems are likely to vary with the size of the firm. In particular, they are likely to be worse for small firms. Smaller firms do not produce detailed information about themselves and are often too young to have a credible reputation. Larger public firms make available detailed information about their activities and usually have a clear stake in maintaining a good reputation among potential financiers. They suffer least from these problems. Methods of financing and governance are thus likely to vary between large and small firms. This has implications for how the structure of financial markets evolves in economies where small firms are becoming increasingly important.

The following section describes the structure of US, UK and German financial markets and how they address these financing and governance problems.

CORPORATE FINANCE SYSTEMS IN INTERNATIONAL PERSPECTIVE

Corporate finance and governance systems in the industrialized countries have two defining characteristics. The first is the degree to which securities markets compete with intermediaries (typically banks) to provide external finance to firms. The second is the degree to which intermediaries have tight ties to the firms to which they lend and use such ties to monitor and influence the firm's decisions on strategic matters. Based on these characteristics, the US and UK systems of corporate finance and governance are broadly similar and very different from those in Germany. Securities markets in the US and the UK have been much more important in the provision of funds to firms than in Germany. Second, US and UK banks generally have had arm's-length relationships with the firms to which they lend, in contrast to the much tighter ties between banks and firms in Germany where banks often take large equity stakes in the firms to which they lend, sit on the board of directors, and act as insiders with respect to the knowledge they have of the firm's operations and the influence they have over the firm's decisions.[3]

SECURITIES MARKETS AND EXTERNAL FINANCING

The relative importance of corporate securities markets across industrialized countries differs dramatically, both in terms of size and liquidity. Table 5.1 shows stock market capitalization as a proportion of GNP in 1994 for the US, the UK and Germany. Comparing stock market capitalization can be misleading if there is a high degree of inter-corporate shareholding in one country, because these shares are double counted. Table 5.1 adjusts for this bias by removing these shares from the calculation. Stock markets in the Anglo-Saxon countries are clearly larger than those in Germany even before a correction is made for the double counting associated with inter-corporate shareholding. This pattern is also revealed by data on public equity issues over the five years to 1995, shown in Table 5.2. Annual average public equity issuance (as a percentage of GDP) is much higher in the US and the UK than it is in Germany.

Table 5.1   Stock market capitalization, 1994

As percentage of GNP

	United States	**United Kingdom**	**Germany**
Unadjusted	75	112	24
Adjusted	70	95	11

Note: Adjusted figures are corrected for the double counting of shares associated with inter-corporate shareholdings.

Source: OECD (1995).

Corporate securities markets for *debt instruments* (bonds, debentures and commercial paper) also differ dramatically in size across countries. Table 5.3 illustrates that the corporate bond market is by far the most developed in the US, while the German market is almost non-existent. The US commercial paper

Table 5.2   Gross public issuance of equity

Annual average 1991–95, as percentage of 1993 GDP

	United States	**United Kingdom**	**Germany**
	1.2	2.1	0.04

Sources: US: Federal Reserve Board (1995); UK: Central Statistical Office (1995); Germany: Deutsche Bundesbank (1995).

Table 5.3   Corporate bond and commercial paper markets

Outstanding amounts of corporate bonds of non-financial corporations, 1993

Country	Percentage of GDP
United States	19.1
United Kingdom	2.7
Germany	0.1

Outstanding amounts of commercial paper, 1992

Country	Percentage of GDP	
	All firms	*Non-financial corporations*
United States	9.1	2
United Kingdom	0.7	n/a
Germany	0.6	n/a

Source: OECD (1995).

market is the most active, reflecting the fact that the US was among the first to allow its development.

The debt financing patterns of non-financial firms across countries is shown in Table 5.4, which indicates that in the US almost 50 per cent of non-financial firms' credit market debt was in the form of securities in 1994, compared to 10 per cent in Germany, and about 25 per cent in the UK.

Table 5.4   Composition of companies' credit market debt, 1994

As a percentage of total credit market debt

	United States	United Kingdom	Germany
Intermediated debt	51	76	90
of which, from banks	16	45	80
Securities	49	24	10

Note: Credit market debt excludes trade debt. Intermediated debt refers to loans from financial intermediaries. Securities includes commercial paper and long-term bonds and debentures.

Sources: OECD (1995); for the UK, Central Statistical Office (1995).

THE STRUCTURE OF CORPORATE OWNERSHIP

The ownership structure of the corporate sector also differs dramatically across the three countries under study, especially with respect to the importance of banks as shareholders of firms. These differences are partially illustrated by simple inspection of the aggregate statistics on the ownership of listed companies in Table 5.5. Table 5.5 reveals the heavier weight of banks in corporate ownership in Germany compared to the US and the UK. Unlike in Anglo-Saxon countries, banks are the most important large shareholders in firms in Germany. In Germany, they own 10 per cent of the outstanding stock of non-financial corporations, but under current law they have great flexibility to vote according to their own wishes the additional 14 per cent of common stock owned by individuals but held by banks in trust for them. In contrast, banks in Anglo-Saxon countries own negligible amounts of the stock in non-financial firms. Also notable is the greater importance of German non-financial firm holdings compared to the US and the UK.

Table 5.5   Ownership of common stock of listed companies

Percentage of outstanding shares owned

	United States	**United Kingdom**	**Germany**
All corporations	44.5	62.9	64.0
Financial institutions	30.4	52.8	22.0
Banks	0	4.3	10.0
Insurance companies	4.6	—	—
Pension funds	20.1	48.5	12.0
Other	5.7	—	—
Non-financial corporations	14.1	10.1	42.0
Individuals	50.2	28.0	17.0
Foreign	5.4	6.5	14.0
Government	0	2.5	5.0

Source: Prowse (1995a).

These aggregate figures, however, reveal nothing about the *concentration* of ownership, which is important from a corporate governance perspective. What is required is an analysis of the ownership patterns of a sample of firms in each country. This is illustrated in table 5.6, which presents data on ownership concentration in a sample of US, UK and German non-financial firms. Ownership concentration is significantly higher in Germany than in the US and the UK. The

Table 5.6   Summary statistics of ownership concentration of large non-financial corporations

Percentage of outstanding shares owned by the largest five shareholders

	United States	**United Kingdom**	**Germany**
Mean	25.4	20.9	41.5
Median	20.9	15.1	37.0
Standard deviation	16.0	16.0	14.5
Minimum	1.3	5.0	15.0
Maximum	87.1	87.7	89.6

Samples: United States: 457 nonfinancial corporations in 1980.
United Kingdom: 85 manufacturing corporations in 1970.
Germany: 41 nonfinancial corporations in 1990.

Sources: For the United States, Prowse (1995a); for the United Kingdom, author's estimates from data in Collett and Yarrow (1976); for Germany, Prowse (1993).

holdings of the largest five shareholders average over 40 per cent in Germany, 60 per cent more than in the US, and almost double the percentage in the UK.

MERGER AND ACQUISITION ACTIVITY

One of the starkest differences between the Anglo-Saxon and German financial systems is the frequency of corporate takeovers. Table 5.7 illustrates that the

Table 5.7   Average annual volume of completed domestic mergers and corporate transactions with disclosed values, 1985–89

	United States	**United Kingdom**	**Germany**
Volume (in billions of US$)	1070	107.6	4.2
As a percentage of total market capitalization	41.1	18.7	2.3

Dollar values calculated at current exchange rates for each of the five years covered. Market capitalization figures are for 1987.

Source: For the United States, the United Kingdom and Germany, Securities Data Corporation, Mergers and Corporate Transactions database.

market for corporate control appears much less active in Germany than in the Anglo-Saxon countries. Part of the reason for the much greater merger and acquisition activity in these countries is of course the larger number of companies listed on the stock market in the US and the UK. However, even normalizing the dollar value of mergers and acquisitions by stock market capitalization fails to alter the impression that the merger market is much more active in the US and the UK – twenty times more so in the US and almost ten times more so in the UK.

Table 5.8 shows the percentage of hostile offers (whether ultimately successful or not) made for firms as a percentage of all attempted transactions for the US, the UK and continental Europe. The data reveal the much lower incidence of hostile takeover activity in continental European countries compared to the US. The differences in *actual, completed* hostile takeovers are even more striking. Since the Second World War, for example, there have only been four successful hostile takeovers in Germany (see Franks and Mayer 1993). Conversely, in the US almost 10 per cent of the Fortune 500 in 1980 has since been acquired in a transaction that was hostile or started off as hostile.[4]

Table 5.8 Hostile takeovers and leveraged buyouts as a percentage of all attempted transactions, 1985–89

	United States	United Kingdom	Rest of Europe
Hostile takeovers	17.8	37.1	9.6
Leveraged buyouts	20.0	5.9	2.7

Note: Hostile offers are defined as those transactions in which the acquiring company proceeds with its offer against the wishes of the target company's management. Data include both completed and withdrawn transactions.

Source: Securities Data Corporation, Mergers and Corporate Transactions database.

CORPORATE FINANCE IN THE ANGLO-SAXON COUNTRIES

These dramatic differences are indicative of the different ways in which the US and UK financial systems on the one hand, and the German system on the other, have addressed the problems of corporate finance and governance. In the US and the UK, there are firstly a host of stock and bond analysts, ratings agencies, and other advisors which analyse the operations and reports of large firms and offer opinions about whether the firm is worthy of new capital. Second, liquid equity markets make credible the threat of a takeover of a poorly performing firm, helping to discipline management to act in shareholders' interests.

Third, American and British firms have a large number of potential sources of external finance from which to choose: banks and non-banks, intermediated sources and non-intermediated sources. Research on these markets in the US has demonstrated that, just as firms vary in the degree to which they suffer from sorting and incentive problems, US corporate finance markets differ in the extent to which they are designed to mitigate these problems.[5] This provides a natural selection mechanism as to which firms use which markets. Thus, small firms – which suffer most from the information problems related to external finance and governance – are forced to raise funds in markets that have developed the greatest safeguards to mitigate such problems, such as the markets for private equity and bank loans. Medium-sized firms may be able to tap the private bond market, while some of the larger or more promising middle-market firms may also be able to issue public equity. Large firms that suffer least from information problems gravitate towards markets that have the fewest safeguards and where capital is the cheapest, such as the public bond and commercial paper markets.

CORPORATE FINANCE IN GERMANY

German firms, regardless of their size or the severity of their information problems, have traditionally relied much more on bank financing than have Anglo-Saxon firms, while securities markets have been much less important.

Banks consequently have a potentially powerful position as active monitors in Germany. First, they have typically comprised the lion's share of external finance to firms and may therefore exercise influence through their control of the firm's access to external funds. Second, the loans they make are often short-term in nature. In normal times, they would be rolled over on an almost automatic basis, but should questions arise about management strategy or quality, the bank always has the option of not renewing the loan at a fairly frequent interval. Finally, their large shareholder status means that they have both the incentive and ability to directly monitor management through their presence on the board and the votes they can exercise at the shareholders' meeting.

Unlike in Anglo-Saxon countries, German banks act as insiders to firms. One aspect of this relationship is bank ownership of equity of non-financial firms. They typically have great access to information about the firm's operations, and have the ability to engage in monitoring and influencing management. Banks' dual role as important lenders and shareholders has given them a primary role in the financing and governing of firms.

LEGAL AND REGULATORY DETERMINANTS OF CORPORATE FINANCIAL SYSTEMS

Why should corporate finance and governance systems differ so dramatically across countries? This fact poses a problem for the theory of corporate finance and governance. According to theory, there is a best way to organize and finance large firms, and so we should observe similar mechanisms of finance and governance in the large industrialized countries. The fact that we do not suggests that we should either attribute differences simply to accidents of history or culture or look to other factors which theory ignores – such as the laws, rules and regulations which govern the financial systems of industrialized countries.

In fact there are large legal and regulatory differences between the countries under study that affect the corporate financial systems in place. The differences are essentially of three kinds. The first is the severity of the legal and regulatory restraints on large investors being 'active' investors in firms. These are affected by differences in the portfolio regulation of financial institutions, tax laws, insider trading laws, and anti-trust laws. Anglo-Saxon laws are much more hostile to investors taking large influential stakes in firms than in Germany.

Second, there are differences in the degree to which sources of non-bank finance are actively suppressed. For much of the post-war period there has been 'active' suppression of corporate securities markets in Germany, taking a variety of forms including discriminatory taxation, regulatory fiat and cumbersome mandated issuance procedures.

Finally, there are differences in the degree to which corporate securities markets have been 'passively' suppressed by the absence of any strong mandated, standardized disclosure requirements by firms wishing to issue securities to outside investors. There are large differences in the disclosure requirements of German firms on the one hand and Anglo-Saxon firms on the other. These differences may have been important in determining the relative speed of securities markets development in different countries if there is a large public good aspect to the production of information by firms seeking external finance that only the imposition of government-backed disclosure requirements can solve.

LEGAL AND REGULATORY RESTRAINTS ON OWNERSHIP OF CORPORATE EQUITY

As Table 5.9 documents, financial institutions in Germany are given more latitude to own shares in and exert control over firms than they are in Anglo-Saxon countries.

Table 5.9 Legal and regulatory constraints on corporate control

Institution	United States	United Kingdom	Germany
Banks	Stock ownership prohibited or requires prior approval of FRB and must be 'passive'. *Source*: Glass-Steagall and BHC Act.	Bank of England may discourage ownership on prudential grounds. Capital adequacy rules discourage larger stakes.	No restrictions, apart from some generous prudential rules.
Life insurance companies	Can hold up to 2% of assets in a single company's securities. Can hold up to 20% of assets in equities. *Source*: NY Insurance Law.	Self-imposed limits on fund assets invested in any one company stemming from fiduciary requirement of liquidity.	Can hold up to 20% of total assets in equities. *Source*: Insurance Law.
Other insurers	Control of non-insurance company prohibited. *Source*: NY Insurance Law.		No restrictions.
Mutual funds	Tax penalties and regulatory restrictions if ownership exceeds 10% of a firm's stock. *Source*: Investment Company Act, IRS.	Cannot take large stakes in firms. *Source*: Financial Services Act, 1986.	No restrictions.
Pension funds	Must diversify. *Source*: ERISA	Self-imposed limits on fund assets invested in one company stemming from fiduciary requirement of liquidity.	No restrictions.
General	SEC notification required for 5% ownership. Anti-trust laws prohibit vertical restraints. Insider trading laws discouraging active shareholding. Bankruptcy case law makes creditor in control of firm liable to subordination of its loans.	Insider trading laws discourage large stakeholders from exerting control. *Source*: Insider Dealing Act.	Regulatory notification required for 25% ownership.

Sources: For the United States, Roe (1990); for other countries, various national sources.

In the US, financial institutions face significant constraints on their ability to take large stock positions in firms and use them for control purposes.[6] Banks are simply prohibited from owning any stock on their own account. Bank holding companies cannot own more than 5 per cent of a firm and their holdings must be passive.[7] Bank trust departments are allowed to hold equity for beneficial owners, but they cannot invest more than 10 per cent of their trust funds in any one firm, and there are often other trustee laws that encourage further fragmentation of trust holdings.

Other financial institutions also face strict rules governing their equity investments. New York insurance law, which currently governs almost 60 per cent of total life insurance industry assets, places a limit of 20 per cent of a life insurer's assets, or half of its surplus, that can be invested in equity, and a limit of 2 per cent of its assets that can be invested in the equity of any one firm. Other states have similar rules. Property and casualty insurers are prohibited outright from owning a non-insurer. Mutual funds are subject to tax and regulatory penalties if they own more than 10 per cent of the stock of any one firm. Pension fund investments are governed by the Employment Retirement Income Securities Act of 1974 (ERISA). ERISA requires all pension funds to be diversified, allowing little room for an influential position in a company.

In addition to institution-specific constraints, US securities laws discourage concentrated, active shareholding by investors in general. First, all entities acquiring 5 per cent or more of a company are required to file with the SEC, outlining the group's plans and revealing its ownership and sources of finance. Second, any stockholder who exercises control over a firm may be liable for the acts of the firm. Third, insider trading rules restrict large active shareholders from short-term trading of stock they own. Thus, Bhide (1993) reports that pension fund managers are reluctant to own more than 10 per cent of a firm, because this would restrict the liquidity of their stake, which by law they have a fiduciary responsibility to protect. Fourth, SEC regulations have prohibited communication among large shareholders – until 1992 it was a violation of proxy rules for ten or more equity holders to speak together about a firm's policies or management. Finally, the legal doctrine of equitable subordination discourages all creditors from taking equity positions in the company, since their loans are subject to subordination should they exert control over the firm.

In the UK, there are fewer formal restrictions on agents' ability to hold concentrated shareholdings in firms, but those that exist still appear substantial. Banks are usually subject to explicit Bank of England approval before they acquire significant shareholdings in non-financial firms. Banks' links with non-financial firms have also been subject to strict prudential rules which appear severe enough to have effectively precluded significant equity investments by deposit banks in the UK (see Santomero and Langhor 1985). Insurance companies and pension funds in the UK typically operate according to self-imposed limits on their shareholdings in one company, for diversification reasons similar to those that have inspired US pension fund reluctance to take large stakes in individual firms (see Minns 1980). And as in the US, insider trading laws in the UK discourage investors from holding large equity stakes and using them for the purposes of corporate control since doing so makes them insiders and therefore vulnerable to prosecution under the Insider Dealing Act.

The institutional structure of the German financial system is based on the universal banking principle. Universal banks can hold whatever share of equity they like in any non-financial firm, limited only by a number of prudential rules which do not appear to be particularly binding and give banks wide latitude to own equity.[8] There are few other aspects of the legal and regulatory environment that restrict concentrated shareholdings. Anti-trust laws have not been used to discourage inter-corporate shareholdings as they have in the US. There has for a long time been no explicit legislation against insider trading: Germany has only recently adopted EC-mandated standards regarding minimum levels of shareholder protection.

SUPPRESSION OF SOURCES OF NON-BANK FINANCE IN GERMANY

Table 5.10 documents some of the legal and regulatory restraints on access to external non-bank finance by non-financial firms in Germany in the post-war period. Unlike in the Anglo-Saxon countries, there have been significant obstacles to German firms raising external finance from sources other than banks.

Restrictions on non-bank finance in Germany have been significant until recently. Issuance of commercial paper and longer-term bonds was hampered by requirements under the issue authorization procedure and the securities transfer tax (see Deutsche Bundesbank 1992). The issue authorization requirements included obtaining prior approval by the Federal Ministry of Economics. Approval was granted if the credit standing of the issuer was satisfactory and if the application was supported by a bank. While this was little more than a formality for the large German firms, it added to the effective cost of a bond issue relative to a bank loan because firms could not generally issue the bonds at a time of their own choosing but were forced to wait for approval from the Ministry. The securities transfer tax often imposed a considerable burden on the secondary market for corporate securities, particularly at its short end. Foreign issuance of corporate debt has been subject to similar restrictions. Equity issuance and secondary trading of equities have historically been subject to a variety of taxes that have generally made equity uncompetitive with bank loans as a form of external finance (see Döser and Brodersen 1990). Most

*Table 5.10   German legal and regulatory constraints on non-financial firms'
access to non-bank finance*

Instrument	German constraints
Commercial paper	Issuance discouraged until 1992 by issue authorization procedure and securities transfer taxes.
Domestic bonds	Issuance discouraged until 1992 by issue authorization procedure and securities transfer taxes.
Euro-bonds	Issuance abroad required prior notification of the authorities and was subject to maturity restrictions until 1989. Issuance of foreign currency bonds prohibited until 1990.
Equity	New share issues must be offered to existing shareholders first. Corporation tax of 1% on all equity issues until 1992. Secondary trading in equities subject to securities transfer tax until 1992, ranging from 0.1% to 0.25%. Annual net asset tax of 1% on corporate net assets, payable irrespective of net income position.

Source: International Financial Law Review (1990).

important has been the legal requirements for employee representation on boards of public companies. These have been very important in discouraging the only form of organization that is legally permitted to raise funds on the public markets (see Borio 1990). Overall, these restrictions have made non-bank finance 'not a viable alternative for most German businesses'.[9]

FOSTERING NON-BANK FINANCE THROUGH DISCLOSURE REQUIREMENTS

Quite apart from the active discrimination against non-bank finance for much of the post-war period in Germany, its lax disclosure requirements *may* have been an additional (passive) factor in discouraging non-bank sources of corporate finance.

Firms in Anglo-Saxon countries wishing to issue securities to the public have been required to disclose much more information than those in Germany. Results from a recent OECD survey illustrate this pattern.[10] In a study of multinational firms' consolidated financial statements, the OECD rated their disclosure relative to OECD guidelines as 'full', 'partial', or 'not implemented'. Table 5.11 illustrates the results for two areas of disclosure – operating results and sales. Two-thirds of the US firms and three-quarters of the UK firms surveyed had fully implemented the OECD disclosure guidelines for operating results; the rest had partially implemented them. In Germany none of the firms surveyed had fully implemented the guidelines. The results for the disclosure of sales (and other areas not reported here) reveal a similar pattern.

Table 5.11   Selected results from a survey of the implementation of the OECD guidelines on the disclosure of information by multinational enterprises

Number of firms

Country	Implementation of guidelines on disclosure of operating results			Implementation of guidelines on disclosure of sales		
	Full	Partial	Not implemented	Full	Partial	Not implemented
US	34	19	0	35	18	0
UK	19	6	0	18	7	0
Germany	0	19	0	11	8	0

Source: OECD, 1989.

There is a fairly intense academic debate as to the effects of mandated corporate disclosure requirements, with no conclusive answer. One hypothesis is that mandated disclosure rules help firms make credible commitments to outside investors to provide honest and timely disclosure and protection from market manipulation or insider trading. In this view, for strategic, competitive reasons firms may not have sufficient incentives voluntarily to provide the financial information outside investors would require to consider extending such finance (for example, they may be afraid that competitors could take advantage of such information). Thus, absent a regulatory and legal framework requiring adequate, standardized disclosure to outside investors, the development of a liquid market for corporate securities may be effectively impeded.[11] The alternative hypothesis is that regulation unduly constrains the choices of firms and investors and prevents efficient contracting. In this view, firms have sufficient incentives to provide the optimal amount of disclosure to obtain external financing and regulations mandating such disclosure are, at best, irrelevant, and at worst, burdensome on both firms and investors.[12]

Ultimately, the effect of mandated disclosure requirements is an empirical issue. Unfortunately there is only a limited amount of empirical work that bears on this topic. Stock price studies of firms before and after the US 1933 Securities Act suggest that mandated disclosure regulations impose costs on firms (see Bentson 1973 and Chow 1983). On the other hand, Sylla and Smith (1995) explain the differing speeds of development of stock markets in the US and the UK since 1800 on differences in mandated disclosure rules. They attribute the faster development of the stock market in the UK in the nineteenth century and the early twentieth century to the various Companies Acts between 1844 and 1900 which required substantial disclosure by firms wishing to issue equity. Disclosure requirements were significantly less onerous in the US until the 1930s, when the Securities Acts of 1933 and 1934 went beyond even what the British had put in place. Sylla and Smith claim these disclosure rules were responsible for putting the US ahead of the UK in terms of the size and depth of the stock market in the immediate post-war period.

While this debate is far from settled, it is nevertheless possible that the marked differences in disclosure requirements between countries may be in part responsible for the differences in the relative speeds of development of securities versus intermediated markets.

COSTS AND BENEFITS OF DIFFERENT SYSTEMS OF FINANCE AND GOVERNANCE

There is much debate about the efficiency of the different systems of corporate finance and governance in the industrialized countries, with no clear conclusion. While much of the academic and policy related literature finds particular advantages in the financing and governing systems in a particular country, this has not translated into overall demonstrably cheaper capital for firms, nor obviously superior mechanisms of corporate control in any one country.

Without going into the detail of the individual studies on this broad topic, the consensus of the academic literature to date appears to be as follows:

1. There are a number of advantages to a system that allows large equity and debt holders of the firm to be the same agents, that encourages the concentrated holding of debt and equity claims, and where ties between financial institutions (typically banks) and firms are relatively tight. Cable (1985) and Elston (1993) provide evidence suggesting that the concentrated holding of debt and equity claims by financial institutions (typically banks)

in Germany mitigates the information problems of external finance and governance to a greater extent than in the Anglo-Saxon countries where ties between banks and firms are less tight.

2. The German system *may* be vulnerable to the 'who monitors the monitor?' problem. In systems where reliance is on direct shareholder monitoring, the large shareholders (typically the banks) have a particularly important role to play. However if these institutions themselves are diffusely held there may be a problem in ensuring that they conduct the investment and monitoring function in an efficient manner. Although there is plenty of evidence that German banks are diffusely held institutions (see Prowse 1995a), there is to date no evidence on whether this has resulted in any problems of corporate control.

3. Takeovers are a costly and sometimes weak mechanism of corporate control. The cyclical nature of the takeover market means that there are periods when the takeover market literally shuts down, typically in recessions when finance is hard to obtain. In these periods the takeover threat may not be credible. In addition, takeovers are vulnerable to broad political and regulatory forces that have provided a large impediment to the market for corporate control in the US in the early 1990s. Finally, in industries where for regulatory reasons takeovers are precluded, the corporate control mechanism may be weak (see Prowse 1995b).

4. Countries where securities markets play an important financing role appear to embody some important strengths that the German system lacks. Porter (1992) and Sahlman (1990) provide evidence that the US system appears better at funding emerging companies and new (often high-technology) business activities than the German system. Franks and Mayer (1992) argue that such a comparative advantage is the reason for the predominance of high-technology firms in the fields of oil exploration, biotechnology, pharmaceuticals and computer software in the US. Porter (1992) claims that liquid US capital markets are able to reallocate capital from low to high growth sectors more efficiently than in Germany.

5. The particular advantages of each system do not appear to translate into overall measurable aggregate differences in either the cost of external financing or the effectiveness of the corporate control mechanism. Both systems appear to have the power to cure the most egregious cases of management indiscipline. Conversely, both systems also have their embarrassing examples of breakdowns in corporate control. Kaplan (1993) reports that top management turnover exhibits *similar* sensitivities to measures of poor firm performance in the US and Germany. Similarly, there are legions of cost-of-capital studies with no consensus as to which system delivers external finance to firms at the lowest cost.[13]

PRESSURES FOR CHANGE IN THE EXISTING SYSTEMS

Static comparisons of the financial systems as they existed in the early 1990s miss a crucial point: the systems are evolving over time in response to a variety of external pressures. Overall, the legal and regulatory environment of the different countries appears to be converging, but the focal point of this convergence is not one system or another as it currently exists, but a new legal and regulatory environment that allows financial institutions to be active investors in firms *and* allows unfettered access to securities markets by firms seeking external finance. This evolution appears to be occurring most rapidly in Germany, probably because its traditional systems of finance and governance – which have involved tightly regulated securities markets – are most inconsistent with the emerging pressures for change.

What are the forces behind this evolution? I consider four trends that I believe are common to the major industrialized countries and which I believe will dramatically change systems of corporate finance and governance over the long term. These forces are:

1. technology, particularly as it effects financial globalization and market innovation;
2. the changing nature of the firm;
3. the growth of the institutional investor;
4. the increasing incentives for institutional investors to be active investors.

TECHNOLOGY, FINANCIAL GLOBALIZATION, AND MARKET INNOVATION

The most profound change is probably technology: the rapid growth of computers and telecommunications. Their spread has lowered the cost and broadened the scope of financial services, making possible new product and market development that would have been inconceivable a short time ago, and in the process challenging the institutional and market boundaries that in an earlier day seemed so well defined. Technological innovation has markedly accelerated the process of financial globalization. Both developments have expanded cross-border asset holdings, trading and credit flows, and in response both securities firms and US and other banks have increased their cross-border locations. Market innovation has been as much of a reaction to technological change and globalization as an independent factor. Overall, these combined forces have led to the development of global markets for corporate securities (equities, bonds and commercial paper) and intermediated loans, to which the large firms of all the major industrialized countries potentially have access. In particular these developments have made many of the statutes governing German corporate finance form an increasingly inconsistent patchwork, and have increased the pressure to relax the longstanding restrictions on access to non-bank finance.

Indeed, recently the German legal and regulatory environment has shown signs of changing. As part of the attempt to compete with London as a centre of finance, the authorities have relaxed many of the restrictions on corporate finance in recent years (see Deutsche Bundesbank 1992). In addition, other aspects of the German legal and regulatory framework will have to change under the planned EU reforms. This is likely to increase the role of securities markets in the financing of German firms.

Technology, market innovation and globalization are also adding to the pressure on authorities in the Anglo-Saxon countries to reduce the regulatory restrictions on banks being active investors in firms, particularly in the US where these restrictions are probably the most severe. US commercial banks have been fierce lobbiers in favour of repealing the Glass-Steagall Act, which prohibits them from engaging in investment banking activities, including the underwriting of corporate securities, and the holding of them on their own account. They claim such restrictions preclude them from effectively competing internationally with foreign banks which do have such powers, and domestically with non-banks which are also able to offer one-stop shopping financial services (loans, underwriting services) to firms. While Glass-Steagall has survived predictions of its demise for almost two decades, it is very likely that it will indeed be repealed before the turn of the century.

THE CHANGING NATURE OF THE FIRM

Another force at work is the changing nature of the firm. Small and medium-sized firms have become increasingly important in the economies of many industrialized countries. Figure 5.1 shows the employment share of small businesses in the US, the UK and Germany from the early 1960s to recent years. While inconsistencies in the data caution against making comparisons across countries, the common trend over time for each country is rather more clear: small and medium-sized businesses have been becoming increasingly important in recent years. In Germany the trend does not seem as pronounced. This may be because small and medium-sized firms have historically always been a very important sector in the German economy.[14]

The reasons behind this phenomenon are not entirely clear, but are very likely to be at least partly related to the evolution of the developed economies to an information-based structure. This has contributed to small firm growth since many service- and technology-based firms tend to be small or medium-sized. The

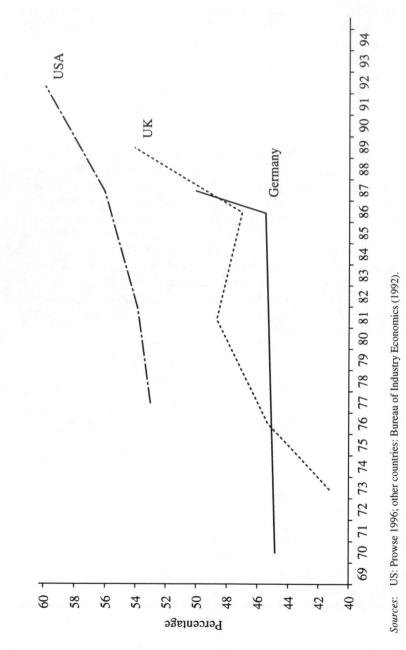

Sources: US: Prowse 1996; other countries: Bureau of Industry Economics (1992).

Figure 5.1 Percentage of salary and wage earners in small enterprises

increasing tendency for large firms to outsource many of their administrative functions (such as payroll, accounting and personnel) to smaller firms is also a factor in the growing importance of small firms in many countries.

The implications of this phenomenon for the corporate financial systems of these countries are somewhat more obvious: as small and medium-sized firms have increased in importance so has their demand for capital. Thus, there is pressure in many countries for an expansion of financial markets that can cater to the needs of smaller firms – in particular, those markets that can mitigate the information problems that smaller firms pose to investors. In the US this has manifested itself in the extremely rapid growth of the private placement and private equity markets – markets which cater primarily to small and medium-sized firms. For example, the private placement market – which caters to medium-sized firms with revenues between about $100 million and $500 million – has grown very rapidly over the last decade and is now quite large. Average annual issuance in recent years is almost five times greater than in the early 1980s and in some recent years issuance has actually exceeded that of public bonds, even though individual issue sizes are much smaller than those in the public market.[15] Similarly, the private equity market – which caters to start-up firms seeking venture capital and slower-growing medium-sized firms – has also expanded very rapidly. Indeed, although the private equity market is small compared to others, its growth since 1980 has been astronomic, much faster than other long-term finance markets. The private equity capital stock invested in small and medium-sized private companies in 1994 was about $40 billion, almost fifteen times larger than in 1980.[16]

In addition to market-based changes, there have been changes in the legal and regulatory environment designed to reduce the regulatory burden of raising capital for small and medium-sized firms. Of particular note is the SEC's endorsement of the Small Corporate Offering Registration, which, by simplifying disclosure requirements, allows small firms to raise equity publicly without incurring the large costs previously involved.

In Germany, the historical reliance on banks might seem tailor-made for the financing of small and medium-sized firms. But the banks have appeared to be more concerned with lending to their large customers and small firms have consequently been ignored. Combined with the undeveloped nature of securities markets, this has meant that smaller German firms have found it difficult to access growth capital. Many medium-sized European firms now find it easier to do IPOs on the US NASDAQ exchange rather than raise capital domestically. This small-firm finance problem has been an additional factor in the pressures on regulators in Germany to open up their securities markets to a greater number of firms.

INCREASING IMPORTANCE OF INSTITUTIONAL INVESTORS

An important development in many industrialized countries in recent decades has been the growing importance of long-term institutional investors such as life insurance companies and pension funds. In the Anglo-Saxon countries, these institutional investors have come to dominate the capital markets, and many of the implications of this domination are still playing themselves out in terms of how firms get financed and governed in these countries. Perhaps more important, if current trends continue, institutional investors will also come to dominate German capital markets. This would be a profound change for the German corporate finance system.

Table 5.12 illustrates the rapid growth of life insurance and pension fund assets in the three economies under study since 1970. Currently, these institutions are the most important institutional investors in the Anglo-Saxon countries, where their assets make up between 13 per cent and 27 per cent of total personal sector assets. In contrast, in Germany, they make up only 2 per cent of personal sector assets. Such differences in the importance of institutional investors are primarily accounted for by the scope and certainty of the state social security system and the way private pensions are structured in different countries. For example, in Germany relatively generous social security provisions have accompanied smaller private pension schemes. In addition, in Germany about two-thirds of the funds earmarked for the payment of private pensions is retained by the company as an unfunded liability. Only the remainder is invested outside the company via private pension funds. The funds retained by the company are used for general corporate purposes. The result is that there is less capital available for the capital markets and less demand for external financing than in Anglo-Saxon countries where the bulk of private pensions are channelled through private pension funds.[17]

Table 5.12   Life insurance and pension fund assets

Country	As a percentage of GDP		As a percentage of personal sector assets
	1970	**1990**	**1990**
United States	37	59	13
United Kingdom	43	97	27
Germany	10	22	2

Source: Davis 1992.

However, given the rapid ageing of the German population over the next few decades, the German government is likely to limit social security commitments and stimulate private saving for retirement. This is likely to stimulate rapid growth of private pension funds.

What are the implications of institutional investors being big players in the corporate capital markets? As Davis (1992) notes, what we observe is that countries with large pension fund sectors tend to have well-developed securities markets, and vice versa. The question is which is the causal factor? There are those who argue that other things being equal, the presence of large institutional investors in the market should encourage the development of securities markets, since their preferred investments traditionally have been in securities of various types rather than intermediated loans or real estate. However, Jensen (1989) argues that the investment philosophy of US public and private sector pension funds has been evolving recently. Whereas in the past a primary goal of pension funds was diversification, achieved by retaining many different investment managers each of whom traded an array of highly liquid public securities, recently such funds have increasingly participated in a select number of private illiquid investments and private pools of equity capital, making highly liquid public markets less essential to their operations. After all, since pension funds can project their cash needs well into the future based on predictable factors such as employee demographics, life expectancies and health trends, they do not have as much of an inherent need for liquidity as does the individual investor.

There is very likely some truth in both arguments. Proponents of the first argument can point to the considerable evidence that the presence of large institutional investors has improved the efficiency and degree of innovation in the public securities markets in the US and the UK (see Davis 1992). However, there are signs in the US that pension funds are beginning to turn to more illiquid investments. Indeed, regardless of their preferences for liquidity, there is considerable evidence that their holdings of public securities are becoming more illiquid simply because of their increasingly large holdings of such securities, and the trading costs involved with selling such holdings. This point is explored more fully in the next section.

INCREASING ATTRACTION OF ACTIVE OWNERSHIP FOR INSTITUTIONAL INVESTORS[18]

In recent years there have been signs that US and UK institutional investors are becoming more informed, active monitors of firms than has traditionally been the case. In the past, many institutional investors in the US and the UK were devotees of the 'Wall Street Walk', which involved selling the stakes of the companies in which the shareholder was unhappy with management behaviour. Recently, however, it appears there has been a significant change in the costs and benefits of becoming a more active investor in firms that has led to more and more institutional investors becoming informed, active monitors of firms rather than simply passive holders of shares. While they have a long way to go before their behaviour can be compared to that of the German banks, it does appear that the attractions of becoming active investors will continue to increase in the Anglo-Saxon countries.

The driving force behind this change in the cost-benefit calculus of active monitoring is the increasing concentration of corporate ownership in the hands of the institutional investors, along with (in the US) the relaxation of regulations that have made active investing by large shareholders difficult. Currently, the largest institutional investors in the US (mutual funds, pension funds, and life insurance companies) each own over 1 per cent of the largest 1000 companies listed on US stock exchanges. A 1 per cent investment might appear to be too small to give an institutional owner much incentive to monitor actively the management of the company, but in reality the opposite is the case: a 1 per cent ownership stake in a large US company is a huge investment that gives the institutional investor enormous incentives to act like an owner. For example, consider an institution that holds a 1 per cent stake in the common stock of GM. The market value of this holding is over \$450 million. Now consider the decision this owner faces when voting on a corporate issue. There may be the potential for the company's stock price to gain or lose 20 per cent depending on the initiative's outcome – which amounts to \$90 million of the 1 per cent owner's investment. Moreover, doing the Wall Street Walk and simply selling the stock could cost the 1 per cent owner as much as \$4 million in trading costs (brokerage fees and the fact that selling such a large stake would probably push the price down). To this extent, the sheer size of this stake and the trading costs associated with selling make the institution 'captive'. The 1 per cent owner of GM thus has an incentive to spend considerable resources if necessary, to analyse the issue and persuade management to follow the preferred course. In many cases it may be cheaper for the institutional investor to do just this rather than to sell.

A large number of institutional investors, all performing the same cost-benefit analysis, creates a large constituency with incentives to press a value-maximizing agenda on management. Thirty years ago, appealing to a majority of shareholders meant circulating material to tens or even hundreds of thousands of poorly informed individual owners. Owing to the increasing concentration of ownership in the hands of institutional investors, appealing to shareholders with sizeable voting power is much less costly: a dissident shareholder can reach a shareholder majority by contacting, say, 25 investment professionals all of whom understand the issues and can devote considerable expense to their analysis. This means a dissident investor should be able to press a serious counteragenda with a controlling fraction of shareholders for much less that the $4 million to $5 million typically associated with a full control proxy contest – in some cases for as little as $250,000 to $500,000.

In fact, US institutional investors are already using shadow management committees, independent director slates and outside experts to critique management policy. These mechanisms allow investors to exert pressure on management. The increasing motivation for activism has in turn led to institutional investors pressuring the SEC to allow them more freedom actively to monitor management. In recent years SEC regulations precluding large shareholders from communicating with each other have been relaxed. In addition, there is a fierce debate over the degree to which the current restrictions on the ability of financial institutions to be active investors in firms act as impediments to more efficient governance.

IMPLICATIONS OF CHANGING LEGAL AND REGULATORY ENVIRONMENTS

The preceding discussion suggests that current mechanisms of corporate finance and control in all countries may simply not be viable in the long run. There is clearly some long-term convergence going on in the legal and regulatory environments of these countries, and the focal point of this convergence is not the German or US/UK systems as they currently exist but an environment where financial institutions (including banks) are free to be active owners *and* where corporate securities markets are unhindered by regulatory and legal obstacles. What will be the primary mechanisms of corporate finance and control in such a system?

This is a difficult question to answer for a number of reasons. First, we do not have models among the developed industrialized countries we can look at where the legal and regulatory environment allows financial intermediaries to be active investors *and* allows firms easy access to securities markets. The closest thing to this model might arguably be the US in the early twentieth century. In the US in the 1920s firms had relatively free access to non-bank finance, securities markets were relatively active, and there were few restrictions on the ability of financial institutions to take equity and debt positions of a size to confer some control.[19] In this system, there might plausibly be some firms that would be able to solve their financing and governance problems better by using intermediated finance from intermediaries who would also take active equity positions in the firm, and conversely, some that might solve their problems better by relying on securities markets for external finance and an active takeover market for corporate control. Just how and why this 'mix' occurs is a subject worthy of further investigation in the form of a more detailed analysis of this period in US financial history.

The pressures for the German and US/UK finance and governance systems to converge have implications for the degree to which strategic alliances and other forms of corporate linkages become a viable option for firms on both sides of the Atlantic. The closer finance systems move together, the more likely it is that firms will become comfortable with the idea of fashioning alliances with firms in other countries. However, it is important to note that any convergence of financial systems in the future is unlikely to be complete. Why? Because where a system starts from may be important. In particular, a convergence of regulatory environments may not imply a convergence of economic outcomes because institutional history matters. That is why continuing research on the institutional and regulatory differences between financial systems is likely to remain important.

NOTES

Views expressed in this chapter are my own and not necessarily those of the Federal Reserve Bank of Dallas or the Federal Reserve System.

1. In the US, a recent manifestation of this is the Council on Competitiveness' 1992 report, *Capital Choices: Changing the Way America Invests in Industry*. In the UK, it is the Cadbury Committee's 1993 report, *The Financial Aspects of Corporate Governance*.
2. Throughout this paper, 'securities' refers to *any* traded corporate security, debt or equity.
3. This is not to say there are not differences between the US and UK financial systems, but merely that such differences are of second order importance when compared to the differences between the US and UK on the one hand and Germany on the other.
4. See Morck, Shliefer and Vishny 1989.
5. See Prowse 1996.
6. For a detailed description of these restrictions, see Roe 1990, Prowse 1995a.
7. See Carey *et al*. 1993.
8. The most onerous appears to be the requirement that total qualifying investments in equity and real estate should not exceed the bank's capital. A qualifying investment is one in which the bank takes a greater than 10 per cent share of the enterprise. See Deutsche Bundesbank 1991.
9. See Döser and Brodersen 1990.
10. See OECD 1989.
11. Proponents of this view include Dye (1990), Dye and Magee (1991) and Demski and Feltham (1994).
12. Proponents of this view include Bentson (1973), Leftwich (1980), Watts and Zimmerman (1986), and Phillips and Zecher (1981).
13. See for example Kester and Luehrman 1992.
14. Harm (1992) reports that small firms – the so-called 'Mittelstand' – have always been a large share of the economy in Germany. Figure 5.1 should not be taken to contradict this notion, since comparing levels of importance across countries is extremely problematic owing to different survey techniques and coverage.
15. See Carey *et al*. 1993.
16. See Fenn, Liang and Prowse 1995.
17. See Edwards and Fischer 1994.
18. Much of this section is taken from Pound 1992.
19. See for example De Long 1990.

REFERENCES

Bentson, G. (1973), 'Required disclosure and the stock market: an evaluation of the Securities Exchange Act of 1934', *American Economic Review,* 63, 132–55.

Bhide, A. (1993), 'The hidden costs of stock market liquidity', *Journal of Financial Economics,* 34, 1, 31–52.

Borio, C.E.V. (1990), *Leverage and Financing of Nonfinancial Companies: An International Perspective,* BIS Economic Papers, No. 27.

Bureau of Industry Economics (1992), *Small Business Review.*

Cable, J. (1985), 'Capital market information and industrial performance: the role of West German Banks', *The Economic Journal,* No. 95.

Cadbury Committee (1993), *The Financial Aspects of Corporate Governance,* London: HMSO.

Carey, M., S. Prowse, J. Rea and G.F. Udell (1993), *The Economics of the Private Placement Market,* Board of Governors of the Federal Reserve System Staff Study No. 166.

Central Statistical Office (1995), *Financial Statistics,* November.

Chow, C. (1983), 'The impacts of accounting regulation on bondholder and shareholder wealth: The case of the Securities Acts', *Accounting Review,* 58, 485–520.

Collett, D. and G.K. Yarrow (1976), 'The size distribution of large shareholdings in some leading British companies', *Oxford Bulletin of Economics and Statistics,* 38, 249–64.

Council on Competitiveness (1992), *Capital Choices: Changing the Way America Invests in Industry,* Boston, MA: Harvard Business School Press.

Davis, E.P. (1992), 'The structure, regulation and performance of pension funds in nine industrial countries', unpublished manuscript, Bank of England.

De Long, B. (1990), *Did J.P. Morgan's Men Add Value?,* NBER Working Paper No. 3461.

Demski, J.S. and G.A. Feltham (1994), 'Market response to financial reports', *Journal of Accounting and Economics,* 17 (1–2), 3–40.

Deutsche Bundesbank (1991), *Banking Act of the Federal Republic of Germany,* Frankfurt.

Deutsche Bundesbank (1992), 'Financial center Germany', *Monthly Report,* March.

Deutsche Bundesbank (1996), *Monthly Report,* April.

Diamond, D.W. (1991), 'Monitoring and reputation: the choice between bank loans and directly placed debt', *Journal of Political Economy* 99 (4), 689–721.

Döser, W. and Christian Broderson (1990), 'A guide to the law on issuing securities in Germany', *International Financial Law Review* Special Supplement.

Dye, R.A. (1990), 'Mandatory vs. voluntary disclosures: the cases of financial and real externalities', *Accounting Review,* 65 (1), 1–24.

Dye, R.A. and R.P. Magee (1991), 'Discretion in reporting managerial performance', *Economics Letters,* 35 (1), 359–63.

Edwards, J. and K. Fischer (1994), *Banks, Finance and Investment in Germany,* Cambridge University Press.

Elston, J.A. (1993), 'Firm ownership structure and investment: theory and evidence from German panel data', unpublished manuscript.

Federal Reserve Board (1996), *Flow of Funds Accounts.*

Fenn, G., N. Liang and S.D. Prowse (1995), 'The economics of the private equity market', Federal Reserve Board Staff Study No. 168.

Franks, J. and C. Mayer (1992), 'Corporate control: a synthesis of the international evidence', unpublished working paper, London Business School, London, England.

Franks, J. and C. Mayer (1993), 'German capital markets, corporate control and the obstacles to hostile takeovers: lessons from 3 case studies', London Business School Working Paper.

Fukao, M. (1995), *Financial Integration, Corporate Governance, and the Performance of Multinational Companies*, Washington, DC: The Brookings Institution.

Harm, C. (1992), 'The financing of small firms in Germany', World Bank Working Paper No. 889.

International Financial Law Review (1990), *A Guide to the Law on Issuing Securities*.

Jensen, M.C. (1989), 'The eclipse of the public corporation', *Harvard Business Review*, September.

Jensen, M.C. and W.H. Meckling (1976), 'Theory of the firm: managerial behavior, agency costs and ownership structure', *Journal of Financial Economics*, 3, 305–60.

Kaplan, S. (1993), 'Top executives, management turnover and firm performance in Germany', University of Chicago Working Paper.

Kester, W. Carl and T. Luehrman (1992), 'Cost of capital comparisons across countries', *Harvard Business Review*, May/June, 130–38.

Leftwich, R. (1980), 'Market failure fallacies and accounting information', *Journal of Accounting and Economics*, 2, 193–211.

Leland, H. and D. Pyle, (1977), 'Informational asymmetries, financial structure and financial intermediation', *Journal of Finance*, 32 (2), 371–87.

Minns, C. (1980), *Pension Funds and British Capitalism*, Heinemann.

Morck, R., A. Shleifer and R.W. Vishny (1989), 'Alternative methods for corporate control', *American Economic Review*, 79 (4), 842–52.

OECD (1989), *Disclosure of Information by Multinational Enterprises*, Working Document by the Working Group on Accounting Standards, No. 6, Paris.

OECD (1995), 'An assessment of financial reform in OECD countries', Working Paper No. 154.

Phillips, S. and J.R. Zecher (1981), *The SEC and the Public Interest: an Economic Perspective*, Cambridge, MA: MIT Press.

Porter, M. (1992), *Capital Changes: Changing the Way America Invests in Industry*, Boston, MA: Harvard Business School Press.

Pound, J. (1992), 'Beyond takeovers: politics comes to corporate control', *Harvard Business Review*, March–April, 83–93.

Prowse, S.D. (1991), 'The changing role of institutional investors in the financial and governance markets', in A. Sametz (ed.), *Institutional Investing: The Challenges and Responsibilities of the 21st Century*, NYU Salomon Center.

Prowse, S.D. (1993), 'The structure of corporate ownership in Germany', unpublished manuscript.

Prowse, S.D. (1995a), 'Corporate governance in an international perspective: A survey of corporate control mechanisms among large firms in the United States, United Kingdom, Japan and Germany', *Financial Markets, Institutions and Instruments*, 4 (1).

Prowse, S.D. (1995b), 'Alternative methods of corporate control in commercial banks', *Federal Reserve Bank of Dallas Economic Review*.

Prowse, S.D. (1996), 'A look at America's corporate finance markets', *The Southwest Economy*, 2, Federal Reserve Bank of Dallas.

Roe, M.J. (1990), 'Political and legal restraints on ownership and control of public companies', *Journal of Finance Economics*, 2 (1), 7–43.

Ross, S. (1977), 'The determination of financial structure: the incentive-signalling approach', *Bell Journal of Economics*, 8 (1), 23–40.

Sahlman, W. (1990), 'The structure and governance of venture capital organizations', *Journal of Financial Economics*, 27 (1), 473–521.

Santomero, A.M. and H. Langhor (1985), 'The extent of equity investment by European banks', *Journal of Money, Credit and Banking*, 17 (2), 243–52.

Sylla, R. and G.D. Smith (1995), 'Information and capital market regulation in Anglo-American finance', in Michael Bordo and Richard Sylla (eds), *Anglo-American Financial Systems*, Burr Ridge, IL: Irwin Publishers.

Watts, R. and J. Zimmerman (1986), *Positive Accounting Theory*, New Jersey: Prentice-Hall.

6. Atlantic sectoral linkage potentials

Maria Papadakis

Accelerating globalization of international markets has created a relatively new form of business cooperation, the international strategic alliance. Distinct from most international arrangements, strategic alliances represent *collaborative* efforts to gain or further the competitive advantage of their partners. Such alliances challenge the parochial nature of national regulatory structures and non-tariff barriers to trade, and signify, as Cowhey and Aronson (1993) put it, that the globalization of firms has changed in important ways.

This chapter assesses the potential for international strategic alliances between the European Union (EU) and North America Free Trade Area (NAFTA). Given the growing globalization of competition and associated changes in corporate strategy, international alliances may be keys to the on-going integration and well-being of EU and NAFTA markets. There is evidence that the business community has already recognized this linkage: transatlantic strategic alliances far exceed transpacific ones despite the preeminent role of the Pacific Rim in North American trade and foreign investment (Hergert and Morris 1988).

Four indicators of alliance potential are analysed here for 14 of the 18 countries in the EU and NAFTA. (Excluded for lack of data are Mexico, Ireland, Greece, and Luxembourg.) Alliance potential is assessed at the sectoral level: 32 three- and four-digit ISIC industries are evaluated in terms of national competitive patterns and capacity to engage in an alliance. The result is a profile of the most likely EU-NAFTA alliance partners within each sector and an overall assessment of alliance potential for each industry. Data are from the Organization for Economic Cooperation and Development Structural Analysis (STAN) database.[1]

Using a very different type of data and analysis, the research presented here confirms the findings of other scholars, namely that alliance potential is highly concentrated in some sectors, particularly high-growth and high-technology industries. Half of the manufacturing sectors examined here have little or no alliance potential. This is due to a variety of factors, including a lack of competitors on at least one side of the Atlantic, the global structure of the industry, the presence of non-tariff barriers to trade, and highly localized market preferences.

Allowing for both positive and negative impacts of transatlantic alliances, the most relevant spheres of government policy making are domestic competition policies, regulatory (health, safety, and environment) structures, and the promotion of small and medium-sized enterprises. These three areas capture the issue of greatest relevance in international trade, that of non-tariff barriers. While strategic alliances do prove to be viable competitive tools to firms, the transatlantic patterns of alliance potential identified here suggest that international benchmarking and technology transfer may also be attractive options within the scope of a firm's competitive strategy.

This chapter is organized into three sections. The first reviews the concept of strategic alliance and develops a framework for understanding the concept of alliance potential. The second section presents the empirical findings and interpretation of the data, and the third addresses the conclusions and policy implications. A description and formula for each indicator, together with all indices for each sector and nation, is provided in the Appendix.

THE POTENTIAL FOR TRANSATLANTIC ALLIANCES: A CONCEPTUAL OVERVIEW

The term 'strategic alliance' is used in this chapter to conform with the growing perception in business scholarship that alliance partners exist as independent agents engaged in on-going alliance transactions and relations (Hergert and Morris 1988, Yoshino and Rangan 1995, Cowhey and Aronson 1993). Excluded from this approach are many forms of equity arrangement (subsidiary joint ventures), most instances of single-contract licensing and franchise, and mergers and acquisitions.

What is of concern here is partnering that reflects mutual and voluntary commitment of corporate energy and resources *without* ownership or control of a partner (Business International 1990). Strategic alliances are distinctive in their arm's-length cooperative dynamics. For example, global restructuring via consolidation and elimination of business establishments is a form of strategic behaviour motivated by economic needs, industrial structures, and market constraints typically different from those of cooperative alliances. What remains in the pool of international alliance behaviours is still an impressive array of inter-firm collaborations: cooperative R&D and technology projects, joint production ventures, and marketing alliances, to name but a few.

While there is no single definition of strategic international alliance, core characteristics consistently emerge from the literature. These can be reduced to three broad types – capture motives, collaborative exchange, and risk-sharing. While other forms of international business arrangements may share one or even two of these characteristics, it is unlikely that they would reflect all of the three features.

Strategic alliances are firstly a means to an end, to either gain or further a firm's competitive advantage. The goal is to acquire, via the alliance, something another firm *already has* – their 'sets of competences' (Sachwald 1993). Gilroy expresses this acquisitiveness as an effort by firms to 'capture business assets' (1993, p. 17); Cowhey and Aronson as 'bringing external resources under their control' (1993, p. 43).

Such resources and assets are diverse and may include technical know-how, a particular channel of distribution, state-of-the-art production facilities, financial resources, a core technological competency, a foothold in a market, and so on.[2] To this extent strategic alliances are motivated by impulses similar to many licenses, mergers, acquisitions and foreign direct investments – to obtain a tangible or intangible asset of another firm to enhance one's own competitive strength.

What distinguishes strategic alliances from virtually all other forms of international business arrangement is the way in which they are executed. The second core characteristic of strategic alliances is therefore their *collaborative* nature. Capture of another firm's asset is not gained by a single purchase transaction, ownership, or indirect financial control, but through on-going mutual contributions of energy and resources (Hergert and Morris 1988, Yoshino and Rangan 1995). Assets flow both ways in the partnership through 'a specialized sharing of unique competitive resources' (Cowhey and Aronson 1993, p. 224). Strategic alliances thus function as a sort of 'economic détente' – the mutual advancement of competitive power.[3]

Third, strategic alliances involve risk-sharing in intent and are intrinsically risky in execution. In many instances cooperation is motivated by the need to spread risk among partners (Contractor and Lorange 1988); risks may emanate from large economies of scale, high capital costs, the uncertainty of R&D, the unpredictability of market behaviour, and so on. The success of the alliance depends fundamentally on how effectively the partners collaborate and are able to accomplish their strategic goals.

Because strategic alliances represent collaborative resource-sharing and risk-taking by independent firms, many conventional international business agreements and arrangements do not qualify as alliances. Traditional contracts – which reflect arm's-length buying, selling, licensing, or franchising – do not involve the on-going mutual exchange of resources. Foreign direct investment (in the form of subsidiary creation) and mergers and acquisitions do not involve separate business entities, but ownership, control, and exchange within the same corporate structure.

The key exceptions to the foreign direct investment[4] exclusions discussed here are joint production ventures. In these cases, alliances comprise partners with shared managerial control over the enterprise even if equity shareholdings are not perfectly balanced. To a lesser extent, minority equity investments are also direct investments that may constitute a strategic alliance under certain conditions.[5] Table 6.1 summarizes the types of international business arrangements that may be regarded as strategic alliances.

Table 6.1   International business arrangements that constitute strategic alliances

Collaborative agreements or contracts	Equity arrangements
Research and product development • Joint R&D • Joint product development • Standards setting • Research consortia	• Minority equity investments • Non-subsidiary joint ventures (equal or unequal equity)
Production • Long-term sourcing agreements • Joint manufacturing	
Marketing • Joint marketing • Shared distribution/service	

The Concept of Alliance Potential

Strategic alliances are an on-going process of inter-firm cooperation that falls between simple contractual agreements and direct ownership. They are inherently risky precisely because of their collaborative nature. In the absence of formal control or authority, successful alliance outcomes rely on the ability of partners to sacrifice autonomy and mutually serve each other's needs. Companies may possess any number of transparent and tacit assets strategically desirable to others. These include, but are not limited to, distribution networks, production capacity, brand name recognition, components or resources required for upstream manufacturing, market power, R&D capacity, and a wide range of knowledge and know-how (research, design, process, managerial).

Given the enthusiasm for strategic alliances, it would seem that their potential is unbounded. Alliances frequently occur between rivals, and do not even require that both firms be competitive in the conventional sense – alliances may involve catch-up or major restructuring for firms in follower or weak market positions (Lorange and Roos 1992). Limited data, however, suggest that the real world of alliances is not so universally promising.

Hergert and Morris (1988) find that the vast majority of alliances (71 per cent) occur between rivals with buyer-supplier and new market entry alliances equally accounting for the remaining share of partnerships. Lorange and Roos (1992) report Zajac's findings that there are four predominant motives for alliances, at least with respect to joint ventures: (1) acquiring means to distribution and preempting competitors, (2) gaining access to new technology and diversifying into new lines of business, (3) obtaining economies of scale and achieving vertical integration, and (4) overcoming legal and regulatory barriers. These motives are not entirely inconsistent with Hergert and Morris' findings that joint product development alone accounts for 38 per cent of agreements; if joint product *and* marketing arrangements are included, then product development accounts for nearly two-thirds of all strategic alliances.

While there are sector-specific variations to the above patterns (Hagedoorn 1995), relatively few industrial groupings account for the bulk of strategic alliances. Hergert and Morris identify the electrical, aerospace, telecommunications, computers, and auto industries; in a study of strategic technology alliances, Hagedoorn and Schakenraad (1993) identify a virtually identical set of sectors: information technology, new materials, aerospace (defence), chemicals, electrical machinery, and autos. What these sectors all share are high entry costs, globalization, scale economies, rapidly changing technology, and/or substantial operating risks (Hergert and Morris 1988).

Empirical evidence and business theory thus suggest that the potential for strategic alliances is at least a threefold consideration: the *opportunity* to collaborate through the use of desirable business assets and resources; the *incentive* to cooperate by virtue of product cycle dynamics, industrial organization, market structure, and so on; and the *propensity* to partner, either by managerial wherewithal or organizational culture. While opportunities may be boundless, incentives appear to be sector-specific and propensities are tied to the 'personalities' and outward-looking nature of individual firms.

With respect to international alliances, a fourth factor at play is the degree to which national or regional policies and practices act as facilitators or barriers to the formalization of an international alliance. Opportunities, structural incentives, and a willingness to partner may be thwarted or enhanced by public policies or 'cultural' practices. For example, anti-trust regulations, product standards, domestic content requirements, product liability laws, procurement practices, regulations (health, safety, environment), and fair trade principles all affect the opportunity and willingness of firms to partner in an alliance. 'Cultural' industrial practices – such as quality circles in Japan or ISO 9000 in Europe – may also limit alliance potential. Such practices may be intrinsic to national industries but do not necessarily translate into formal industrial or market structures; some business strategists suggest that a basic compatibility in business culture and practice is a fundamental prerequisite of an alliance (Houghton 1990).

In sum, alliance potential is a function of four relatively discrete factors: opportunity, incentive, propensity, and political-cultural contingency. Firms must possess competitively desirable assets (opportunity), a motive for partnering (incentive), and the willingness to collaborate (propensity) as the core preconditions of potential. Such potential may be enhanced or undermined by political and cultural features of the business environment. Alliance potential is not the same as alliance success. Once engaged, there is no certainty that a partnership will achieve its goals. Indeed, evidence suggests that alliance failure rates may be anywhere from 30 percent to 70 per cent (Killing 1983, Beamish 1985, Harrigan 1988).

THE POTENTIAL FOR TRANSATLANTIC ALLIANCES: AN EMPIRICAL OVERVIEW

Empirically evaluating EU-NAFTA strategic alliance potential is a challenging task. Not only must indicators highlight opportunities, incentives, and propensities to collaborate, but a substantial variety of political and industrial practices and conditions must be accounted for in ways that cannot be readily quantified. Additional complexities arise because of the cross-national character of the analysis; appropriately comparable and detailed data are frequently not available.

This research takes advantage of the OECD's Structural Analysis (STAN) database, which reports a variety of production, investment, employment, and trade data for OECD member states. The data series start in 1970 and continue until between 1990 and 1993, depending on the nation and indicator for which data are collected. Roughly 40 two-, three- and four-digit industries are reported on a comparable ISIC basis for all countries.[6] Data for all nations in the EU and NAFTA except for Mexico, Greece, Ireland, and Luxembourg are analysed; data for these countries either are not available or are sufficiently inconsistent that reliable indicators could not be calculated.

STAN data were used to construct four indicators of alliance potential: share of sector exports, revealed comparative advantage, import penetration, and exports-to-production. A description of each measure and its precise formula is provided in the Appendix to this chapter, as are all of the indices calculated for the EU and NAFTA.

Because of the nature of the data, empirical profiles of alliance capacity are limited to the 'opportunity' and 'propensity to collaborate' dimensions of alliance potential. Two measures – share of sector gross exports and import penetration ratios – are used to capture opportunity as it manifests itself as 'competitive presence'. In order to engage in a strategic alliance, a nation's industry must register a basic presence in overseas markets (hence share of sector exports) and/or in a capacity to assert itself in its home market (hence import penetration ratios). 'Competitive advantage', measured as revealed comparative advantage in trade, denotes a heightened potential to engage in an alliance by virtue of salient competitive skill relative to other countries. The fourth measure, exports-to-production, is used as a proxy for propensity to collaborate.

It is assumed for all three alliance opportunity measures that the business assets and strategically desirable resources of a firm must be manifested in some fashion as competitive ability. This assumption is certainly implicit, if not explicit, in the alliance literature (e.g., Yoshino and Rangan 1995, Sachwald 1993). The competitiveness measures used here have been repeatedly identified as appropriate for sectoral and national competitive analyses (Buckley, Pass and Prescott 1992; Sachwald 1993; Papadakis 1994, 1995).

These measures are clearly not perfect; they are quite crude as measures of alliance potential. They capture only a few dimensions of potential, and imperfectly so. They reflect intra-industry alliance potential and not cross-sectoral potential, which is often significant. The industry mix, and hence empirical 'noise', is still quite large even at the three-digit level. Qualitative information must be 'backed in' to the analysis: strategic alliances are fundamentally firm-based decisions emanating from the competitive psychology, assets, and calculus of the firm. In spite of these caveats, a broad-brush treatment of the alliance landscape does appear to adequately differentiate the alliance capacities of nations and industries. While the idiosyncratic potential of any given firm in any given industry (in any given country) is lost from view, the general potential is revealed.

Interpreting Strategic Alliance Potential

Interpreting the alliance potential of an industry or nation is complicated by a variety of factors. First, even though the three-digit level of aggregation is relatively specific, the industry mix within the sector may consist of anything from a half dozen (as with non-ferrous metals) to more than one hundred (as with food) discrete industries and product markets. Differentiating alliance performance and potential within the industry is generally not possible.

Second, the data indicate that every nation has indigenous production capacity and export activity in virtually every sector under review. This suggests that a fundamental capacity for strategic alliance is present in nearly every industry for each country under review. Assessing the overall strength and viability of this potential is, however, complicated by a third difficulty: the manufacturing import penetration ratios and export-to-production shares for EU members and Canada are quite large relative to the United States, reflecting the importance of exports and intra-industry trade in their economies (see Table 6.2). Distinguishing a broad competitive market presence from intense specialization within the three-digit industry mix is therefore a challenge. Relatedly, the low export-to-production ratios for the United States suggest that its propensity to engage in an alliance may be relatively low for most sectors, even when it accounts for a relatively large share of sector exports.

Table 6.2   Import penetration and export-to-production ratios for the manufacturing sector, EU and NAFTA

Country	Import penetration	Exports-to-production
NAFTA		
United States	12	15
Canada	37	36
EU		
Austria	40	38
Belgium	72	74
Denmark	52	54
Finland	30	35
France	30	30
Germany	27	30
Italy	22	24
Netherlands	66	68
Portugal	42	34
Spain	25	19
Sweden	37	40
United Kingdom	33	30

Fourth and finally, Canada is anomalous within the EU-NAFTA group.[7] Canadian manufacturing has been highly penetrated by foreign ownership; for the past few decades roughly 50 per cent of manufacturing output has been accounted for by foreign enterprises (OECD 1994); most of these are wholly owned or majority-owned enterprises. Nearly 80 per cent of this ownership is American, with foreign investment concentrated in the iron and steel, wood and paper, chemicals, non-ferrous metals, and food industries (Rugman 1990). Notably, the US-Canadian bilateral trade relationship is the most vigorous in the world; about 70 to 80 per cent of Canadian exports flow to the United States and about one-third of this is automotive products (Rugman 1990, Preston and Windsor 1992).

What we may infer from this is that for any given Canadian industry, the vast majority of its exports are destined for the US market and its competitive presence in all other foreign markets is accordingly circumscribed. The 'real' outward-orientedness of Canadian firms is thus hard to interpret; moreover, it is not clear to what extent foreign-owned firms would be receptive to alliances focused on the Canadian market. For example, major US subsidiaries in Canada invest significantly less in R&D than do their parent organizations (Rugman 1990), suggesting that these Canadian enterprises do not have a strategic orientation of their own.

As a way of dealing with these analytical complications, the following approach was used to profile the alliance potential between EU and NAFTA nations:

- The United States was considered a 'competitive presence' (a) in its domestic market if it had a lower than average import penetration ratio in the sector, and (b) in foreign markets if it had a 7 per cent or greater share of sector exports. US sectors were rated as having competitive advantage and a high propensity to engage in an alliance if the sector demonstrated a revealed comparative advantage index of .90 or greater and a 20 per cent or greater share of sector exports.
- Canada was considered a 'competitive presence' in its domestic market if it had a lower than average import penetration ratio in the sector. Canadian sectors had competitive advantage if they had a revealed comparative advantage index of .90 or above.
- EU countries were generally identified as 'core' or 'niche' competitors. If a nation accounted for 7 per cent or more of sector exports and had a revealed comparative advantage index of .90 or greater, it was considered a core competitor. If export shares were less than what would be predicted based on an equal distribution of exports across all fourteen EU-NAFTA nations (7 per cent), then it was considered a 'niche' or specialized competitor. In most instances large volume EU exporters also had a sizable revealed comparative advantage index; a .90 ratio simply reflects no appreciable disadvantage in trade.

The alliance capacity profile developed here is thus based on the assumption that Canada and the United States need only register a competitive presence in an industry, whereas EU members must demonstrate competitive advantage as either core or specialized competitors. This was done in part to control for the risk of underrepresenting Canada as a potential alliance partner (by virtue of its very low sector export shares) and overrepresenting EU members (by virtue of their generally heightened export activity).

Using the above criteria, the alliance potential indicators do in fact reveal distinctive patterns for Canada, the United States, and members of the EU (see Table 6A.1 in the Appendix). Not only do these indicators differentiate industries in terms of which sectors have greater or lesser alliance potential, but they also seem to capture niche/intra-industry trade specialization relatively well.

In the sections below, transatlantic sectoral alliance potential is assessed based on the above interpretations of the quantitative indicators. Interpretation of alliance potential was supplemented with detailed information about each industry; the empirical indicators alone suggest little about either incentives to engage in an alliance or political and cultural contingencies. Qualitative information about sectors was obtained from the *U.S. Industrial Outlook* (published annually by the US Department of Commerce) and the *Panorama of EC Industries 1991–92* (Commission of the European Communities 1991).

Sectors with Generally Limited Alliance Potential

Of the 32 three- and four-digit ISIC industries analysed here, half have limited alliance capacity. Five sectors were excluded entirely from the analysis of alliance potential: leather products (ISIC 323), footwear (ISIC 324), pottery and china (ISIC 361), shipbuilding (ISIC 3841), and motorcycles and bicycles (ISIC 3844). Import penetration rates, revealed comparative advantage indexes, and export shares in leather, footwear, and pottery and china generally indicated that for both Canada and the United States no meaningful competitive presence exists. An EU-NAFTA alliance would consequently be highly unlikely.

In the case of shipbuilding, global excess capacity still exists and alliance behaviour cannot be assessed independently of the on-going restructuring and associated industrial policies of this industry. With regard to motorcycles and bicycles, there appears to be competitive mismatch. Canada has no meaningful competitive presence in this sector; although the United States does, 69 per cent of 'motorcycle' consumption in the EU is mopeds. Hence the US and EU do not produce in any meaningful way what is consumed in the other's market. (It is not possible to extract bicycle market dynamics from that of the larger sector in the STAN data; admittedly there may be some alliance potential here because of the strength of both US and EU manufacturers.)

Another twelve sectors generally reflect either limited or weak alliance potential (see Table 6.3). In many instances, these are industries for which import penetration and export-to-production ratios are much lower than those for the manufacturing sector as a whole, suggesting that each country produces, by and large, for its own domestic market. Most of these industries satisfy consumption with strong localized preferences, needs, and tastes – food, beverages, tobacco, printing and publishing, fabricated metal products,[8] and furniture and fixtures.

Table 6.3   Sectors with limited transatlantic alliance potential

ISIC No.	Sector	Reasons for limited potential
311	Food	Localized tastes/regulatory barriers
313	Beverages	Localized tastes/regulatory barriers
314	Tobacco	Localized tastes
332	Furniture & fixtures	Localized tastes
342	Printing & publishing	Localized tastes
353	Petroleum refineries	Global market structure
354	Petroleum & coal products	Global market structure
355	Rubber	Global market structure
362	Glass & products	Localized tastes/extensive market access
371	Iron & steel	Voluntary export restraint system
372	Non-ferrous metals	Global market structure
381	Metal products	Localized tastes

Some of these sectors are also protected by longstanding non-tariff barriers. An elaborate bilateral network of voluntary restraint agreements has existed in the steel industry for decades; health, safety, and packaging regulations have historically acted as strong barriers to trade in the food and beverage industries. Indeed, the Cecchini Report identified 200 separate regulatory barriers to intra-EC food trade (Commission of the European Communities 1991, pp. 15–16). EU mergers and acquisitions have been most substantial in the food sector, reflecting efforts to circumvent barriers and gain market access. Regardless of cause, what the data suggest is that for these industries, countries produce largely for domestic consumption.

While there are notable international exporters in these sectors, the potential for transatlantic strategic alliances is limited. First, the nature of the tastes and demand that govern them are highly localized. Printing and publishing, for example, are characterized by cultural, intellectual, and educational preferences unique to each nation; fabricated metals are similarly tailored to domestic industries. Second, non-tariff barriers to trade may act as barriers to alliances.

Third, some of these sectors are already characterized by very high degrees of oligopolistic globalization – the non-ferrous metals and rubber industries are cases in point. Barriers to entry are high, producers have their markets very well staked out, markets are mature, product cycles are not characterized by rapid obsolescence, vertical integration has maximized corporate efficiency, manufacturing processes are highly standardized, and new product development is not R&D-intensive. There is no transparent incentive or competitive advantage to collaboration. Notably, two of Canada's most distinctively competitive industries fall into this group of sectors: the Canadian rubber and non-ferrous metals industries have distinctive competitive and comparative advantages in trade.

Finally, the glassware industries are also of limited consequence in terms of strategic alliances. Although the EU has a respectable presence in world production and export shares in this sector, the industry is a conglomerate of sub-sectors with clearly separate demand dynamics. Canada's competitive presence in this industry is extremely weak and the US competitive presence is weak and largely domestic. Again the question of incentive is significant: these are mature sectors with moderate growth rates and no meaningful market barriers in terms of either entry or distribution.

In sum, transatlantic alliance potential for many sectors is not significant (see Table 6.3). Markets reflect highly localized tastes and preferences requiring localized manufacturing knowledge. In some industries (e.g. steel), barriers to trade are meaningful and have real implications for strategic alliances; in others (e.g. food), regulatory or taste barriers exist and may be dealt with more effectively through direct investments. In still others, market structure suggests competitors have no particular incentive to collaborate (non-ferrous metals and rubber). Low value added or extensive market access may remove incentives to engage in alliances (glassware). The reasons are varied, but they all point to a lack of incentive; firms in these sectors do not appear to have much to gain competitively by engaging in a strategic alliance. A notable exception may be the printing and publishing industries, which are very advanced technologically; strategic technology alliances may provide a competitive advantage within the partners' home markets.

Sectors with Reasonably Good Alliance Potential

The remaining industries all have reasonably good prospects for alliances – opportunity, incentive, and a basic propensity to engage in a cooperative arrangement exist for many countries. These sectors are, by and large, ones that have already been identified in other research as areas of substantial alliance activity (Hergert and Morris 1988; Hagedoorn and Schakenraad 1993) and are generally characterized as high-technology or high- and medium-growth sectors (Sharp 1992). Table 6.4 presents a profile of the alliance potential in these sectors by denoting the industry, the US and Canadian competitive presence, and the core and niche EU competitors. Brief descriptive summaries of the sectors and identification of specific issues that may affect alliance potential are presented below. Note that EU and NAFTA firms may engage in a strategic alliance to enhance their position in their home/internal markets, in foreign/external markets, or as a defensive manoeuvre against Japanese firms (Nugent and O'Donnell 1994).

Table 6.4   Profile of industries with good transatlantic alliance potential

ISIC No.	Sector	NAFTA competitors	EU competitors	
			Core	Niche/Speciality
321	Textiles	US	Belgium, France	Austria (321),
322	Wearing apparel	Canada (322)	Germany, Italy,	Portugal (321)
			Netherlands,	Denmark (322)
			Portugal (322)	
331	Wood products	Canada[a]	Austria (331) Finland	Portugal
341	Paper & products	US	Germany[b] (341)	Denmark (331)
			France[b] (341)	
			Sweden	
351	Industrial chemicals	US[a] (351)	Belgium, France,	Denmark (352)
352	Other chemicals	Canada (352)	Germany,	Sweden (352)
		US (352)	Netherlands, UK	
3522	Drugs & medicines	Canada	Belgium, France,	Austria, Denmark,
		US	Germany, UK	Sweden
382	Non-electrical machinery	US[a]	Germany, France[b] Italy, UK	Austria, Denmark, Sweden
3825	Office & computing machines	US[a]	France, Germany, Netherlands, UK	
383	Electrical machinery	US[a]	France, Germany, UK, Italy[b]	Austria, Finland, Portugal, Sweden
3832	Radio, TV, & communications equipment	US[a]	France[b] Germany[b] UK	Austria, Finland, Netherlands, Sweden
3842	Railroad equipment	Canada[a] US	Austria, France, Germany, Italy[b] Spain	Spain, Sweden
3843	Motor vehicles	Canada[a] US[b]	Belgium, France, Germany, UK	
3845	Aircraft	US[a]	France, Germany, UK	
385	Professional goods	US[a]	France, Germany, Netherlands, UK	Sweden Denmark

Notes:
[a]   Competitive advantage and propensity to engage in an alliance (see text).
[b]   Competitive domestic presence but not competitive advantage (see text).

Textiles and clothing

Major restructuring of the means of production in the US and European textile industry occurred throughout the 1980s. Textile manufacturing technology is highly automated, and competitive skill has moved into the 'fashion' end of fabric as well as clothing markets. Competitive strategies are based on differentiation and highly specialized designs tied to local tastes; the market is somewhat dichotomous, with many small manufacturers and large, multinational corporations. Asian competition is fierce, but both the EU and NAFTA maintain a considerable competitive presence in the high end of this market. Strategic alliances would be a good way for both industries to manage the phase-out of the Multifibre Agreement.

Wood products, paper and products

Wood and paper products are two industries in which Canada is a world-class competitor. The US has a major domestic presence in these industries, as do several EU member states. The wood products industry is characterized (in the EU) by many small, rural, highly specialized family enterprises, not dissimilar to the industry in the US Pacific northwest. Product development alliances (e.g. in building materials) that provide market access and higher value added may be good strategies for the wood products sector.

Paper products is a leading EU sector – product development, quality, and production techniques are all highly advanced. Although the sector captures many diverse sub-markets (packaging materials, household and sanitary goods, stationery and office supplies), US and Canadian firms could gain substantial market advantage by linking with core EU competitors. Regulatory barriers could be a problem for packaging industries, although this is less of a problem as the EU institutes a policy of reciprocity among member states.

Industrial and other chemicals

The European chemical industry is the most advanced in the world, and this sector worldwide is characterized by both high levels of foreign direct investment and highly specialized intra-industry trade. Canada has a weak competitive position in this industry, the US a relatively strong one. As discussed in Sachwald (1993), the chemical industry is already engaged in a number of strategic alliances, particularly in refined and speciality chemical markets. Biotechnology alliances are a growth area in this industry; environmental regulations may constitute significant barriers to cooperation.

Drugs and medicines

The pharmaceutical industry is substantially enhanced by strategic alliances and one of the most alliance-intensive sectors (de Wolf 1993). The industry is characterized by extraordinary innovation costs, long product development lead times, and large economies of scale. Barriers to entry are generally high; this is in all respects a truly global industry. EU political constraints are somewhat more severe than in the US; patent protection is not extended (as in the US) to compensate for clinical regulatory review, and there is more state control over drug prices because of national health care systems. Price scrutiny is becoming more common in the US as it moves to managed care systems and because the federal government is the proprietor of many critical new compounds.[9]

Non-electrical and electrical machinery

In both machinery industries, five countries evidence considerable competitive advantage and propensity to engage in an alliance – the US, France, Germany, Italy, and the UK. These are highly diversified sectors with robust intra-industry trade, particularly between the EU and North America. The high degree of product specialization – including customized machinery – suggests that this is a prime industry for international strategic alliances, particularly product development and process technology alliances. Cooperative arrangements are already a common feature for the electrical machinery industry in the EU; of particular concern in electrical machinery are government procurement practices and standards, which may effectively act as non-tariff barriers to trade. Canada is not a significant international competitor in either sector; both have much higher than average import penetration ratios.

Office and computing machines

A problematic sector in terms of assessing alliance potential is that of office and computing machines. It has a highly diversified industry mix, and some countries have no meaningful production capacity in some product lines. For example, both the US and EU are weak in the computer peripherals market, and the EU has a limited capacity in PCs. Moreover, the EU industry is marked by extensive foreign ownership: the OECD reports that this sector is the most highly penetrated in Europe, with foreign affiliates accounting for 74 per cent of sector output in France, 60 per cent in Germany, and 99 per cent in Ireland (1994, p. 26). Nonetheless, the industry meets certain basic requirements for alliance potential; it is R&D-intensive and globalized, and high barriers to entry exist for many sub-sectors. Four EU countries dominate export markets (and production) – France, Germany, the Netherlands, and the UK. Because of highly integrated global production structures, alliances are most likely between manufacturers and component suppliers.

Radio, TV, and communications equipment

Information technologies currently reflect a considerable degree of alliance activity (Bloom 1993, Hobday 1993, Hergert and Morris 1988, Hagedoorn and Schakenraad 1993). The US is a significant global competitor in many sectors, together with the UK, Germany, and, to a lesser extent, France. The potential for niche and specialized competition is high; Austria, Finland, the Netherlands, and Sweden all reflect some degree of specialized trade (due to, for example, the presence of single multinational competitors such as Finland's Nokia). Large cyclical swings exist in these sectors and there is a rapid rate of product obsolescence, leading to the common use of mergers and acquisitions as a key production strategy and to R&D partnerships in product and component development. Information technology is one of the few sectors where Europe still represents an important share of world production; among the top fifteen suppliers in the EU market, only two are not European (Commission of the European Communities, section 12). Regulatory non-tariff barriers, particularly through licensing and procurement, are still common in this industry, but are also going through rapid change (Jacobson 1994).

Professional goods

Professional goods is a diversified sector including precision instruments, medical equipment and devices, watches, clocks, and cameras, unified by the use of micro-operations and devices. In the EU, small and medium-sized firms are highly specialized, and typically face competition only at the global level. As an R&D-intensive sector, product alliances may be particularly effective and enhance the position of small and medium manufacturers.

Motor vehicles

Motor vehicles is another sector characterized by intensive alliance activity, particularly through component and sourcing arrangements (Sachwald 1993; de Banville and Chanaron 1994). Foreign direct investment is extensive in both North America and Europe, although extra-EU auto trade is limited. Canada is a major competitor in the auto market, even though a sizable proportion of its output is destined for the US. Domestic content and environmental regulations may actually stimulate alliances, and channels of distribution will change considerably with the Single European Market initiatives.

Aircraft

Given the intense competition between Airbus and Boeing, the civil aircraft industry seems an unlikely place for strategic alliances. However, there are other dimensions to the aerospace industry for which alliances are not unusual and may be advantageous, such as in the small jet aircraft industry, engine design, and avionics. NATO induces a certain degree of cooperative arrangements as well. European competitors are few, however, and concentrated in France, Germany, and the UK.

Summary

In sum, there is considerable potential for strategic alliances between NAFTA and the EU. In some instances there is growth potential in sectors where alliances are already a common activity (machinery, autos, information technologies, pharmaceuticals). In other sectors it may be in anticipation of future market changes (such as textiles and wearing apparel) or to exploit current market dynamics and competitive advantages (wood and paper products). However, what we do see is a disproportionate representation of technology-intensive and high-growth sectors, suggesting that the motive for strategic alliances emanates directly from the technological, competitive, and industrial structures of these sectors. Almost all EU members evidence a capacity to engage in alliances as either comprehensive or specialized competitors; the US presence is widespread as well. Canadian potential is more limited, and most likely in wood and paper products, speciality chemicals, pharmaceuticals, and motor vehicle industries.[10]

CONCLUSIONS AND IMPLICATIONS FOR GOVERNMENT POLICY

We cannot assume, *a priori*, that strategic alliances are necessarily successful, beneficial, or harmful to consumers or the structural competitiveness of individual sectors and nations. The implications of strategic alliances – whether they should be left alone, stimulated, or managed in some way by the state – depends largely on what their actual outcomes are. At present this is uncertain, and some authors have raised doubt that alliances will even continue once many industrial markets mature or become more fully liberalized (Kay 1993; Cowhey and Aronson 1993).

What governments should actually do about alliances, if anything, is tied to the types of benefits and costs that alliances might create. What *is* apparent from current patterns of alliance behaviour, which may reduce concerns about their contribution to declining structural competitiveness, is that they typically arise between rivals and should ideally enhance the competitive power of all partners. In addition, they also typically occur in industries which, by virtue of characteristics intrinsic to the industry, might induce sub-optimal economic behaviour (underinvestment, monopoly pricing) in the absence of alliances. And in industries such as information technologies, it is clear that alliances may function to forestall a loss of structural advantage or reclaim advantage that was once lost.

There are clear potential benefits and costs to alliances. The perpetual risk is that they cross the fine line between collaboration and collusion, with all the associated harms that diminished market competition may bring. The EU is probably more at risk in this than the US, since Article 85 of the EU treaty provides that restrictive practices may be tolerated if a cooperative agreement contributes to technical progress or the enhanced competitive position of EU member states in extra-EU markets. Parallel exemptions are missing in the US Sherman Anti-trust Act, and even though research consortia have been 'legalized' in the US, firms are still liable for single damages.[11] Nations should accordingly be vigilant in their surveillance for anti-competitive practices, but the lack of harmonization between US and EU competition policies in this regard could be problematic. On the other end of the spectrum, alliances that stimulate too much competition in a sector may be harmful as well.

The potential large-scale benefits of alliances, in contrast, are considerable. First, there are the classic increased efficiencies that result from the greater rationalization and exposure to competition that many alliances stimulate. Second, product differentiation and diversification encourage net growth in many sectors. Third, alliances may elevate and prepare high-technology sectors for 'take-off' on the next long cycle of global economic development: integrated technological advance among the industrialized nations may be key to macroeconomic welfare in the long run. Fourth, alliances may help firms circumvent market failures in global industries, particularly information technologies and pharmaceuticals. Fifth, alliances have the capacity to enhance compliance with environmental, health, and safety regulations on a global scale – in spite of widespread market deregulation, the protective regulatory environment in many nations is intensifying, particularly in reaction to perceived technological risks.

Removing barriers to alliances, particularly procurement practices and standards, may enhance rationalization and exposure to competition. Relaxing 'national origin' requirements for industry-government R&D consortia may go far in stimulating the next long cycle and avoiding constricted growth in emerging sectors. Global harmonization of some environmental, health, and safety standards may eliminate the economic drag of redundant compliance costs and improve overall social welfare. The potential for public 'alliance' policy is considerable.

Businesses will no doubt continue to engage in strategic alliances as a rational response to their competitive environment, and in many instances direct investments and mergers and acquisitions may be viable alternatives. However, what the research here demonstrates is that the sectoral potential for EU-NAFTA strategic alliances may be a little more broad than current patterns of alliance indicate; the limited role that alliances presently play in some sectors may be a result of industry fragmentation, a lack of any kind of external orientation to the market, or business ignorance of overseas competitive skills ('imperfect information'). Expanded business horizons and a sharpened competitive strategy may be necessary in such sectors. Finally, the lack of alliance potential in many sectors does not mean that firms should be inattentive to their foreign counterparts; the competitive presence of many countries suggests that international technology transfer or comparative benchmarking may significantly enhance the competitive strength of firms in their domestic markets.

APPENDIX

Below is a brief description of each alliance potential indicator and its associated formula. The actual indices for all sectors and countries are provided in Table 6A.1. Notations are country (i), sector (j), exports (X), imports (I), and production (P).

Share of Sector Gross Exports

The first indicator reflects the competitive foreign market presence of a nation in a sector. If each country had an equal competitive presence in foreign markets, then the export share for each country in this study would be 7 per cent (100 percent divided by 14 countries). Thus any nation with a sector export share of 7 per cent or more would demonstrate some extra degree of foreign market presence. The formula for share of sector exports is:

$$X_{ij} / \Sigma X_{i \ldots n, j}$$

Revealed Comparative Advantage

Revealed comparative advantage indexes highlight countries with 'absolute' trade advantages. In this study, the indexes are used to identify countries with heightened competitive advantage or expertise in a sector. An index of 1.00 reflects no comparative advantage or disadvantage in trade. The formula for revealed comparative advantage is:

$$[X_{ij} \div \Sigma X_{i,j \ldots n}] / [X_{i \ldots n,j} \div \Sigma X_{i \ldots n,j \ldots n}]$$

Import Penetration Ratios

Import penetration ratios, or the share of apparent domestic consumption accounted for by imports, is a measure of the domestic market presence and competitive strength of a nation. The lower the import penetration ratio, the higher the competitive presence of a country in its home market. Typically net sales are used to calculate apparent consumption; production is used here so a modest amount of production may not actually go toward consumption, but inventory. The formula for sector import penetration is:

$$M_j / P_j + M_j - E_j$$

Exports-to-production

The share of domestic production which goes to export markets is used here as a proxy for willingness, or propensity to cooperate. Even though a country may account for a large share of total sector exports, this may reflect the economic size and production capacity of the country and not necessarily its outwardness or the significance of exports to firm well-being. The higher the exports-to-production ratio, the more significant foreign markets are to producers and the greater the propensity to cooperate. The formula for exports-to-production is:

$$E_j / P_j$$

Table 6.A1   Alliance potential indicators for the EU and NAFTA

ISIC number, sector, and indicator	Country						

311.2, Food

	Canada	*US*	*Austria*	*Belgium*	*Denmark*	*Finland*	*France*
Export share	4	17	1	9	7	0	14
RCA	.72	.86	.37	1.46	4.07	.29	1.26
Import penetration	12	5	12	22	29	6	16
Exports-to-production	13	5	8	28	55	4	16
	Germany	*Italy*	*Netherlands*	*Portugal*	*Spain*	*Sweden*	*UK*
Export share	15	5	17	1	3	1	6
RCA	.67	.65	2.70	.58	1.05	.26	.64
Import penetration	18	18	33	15	10	12	17
Exports-to-production	14	10	52	6	8	6	8

313, Beverages

	Canada	*US*	*Austria*	*Belgium*	*Denmark*	*Finland*	*France*
Export share	3	6	1	3	2	0	37
RCA	.65	.31	.45	.57	.85	.24	3.31
Import penetration	12	8	6	34	31	7	20
Exports-to-production	14	2	7	23	29	4	57
	Germany	*Italy*	*Netherlands*	*Portugal*	*Spain*	*Sweden*	*UK*
Export share	8	4	6	3	5	0	21
RCA	.37	.48	.98	2.88	1.59	.13	2.29
Import penetration	11	11	33	25	7	18	19
Exports-to-production	5	21	35	44	9	4	27

314, Tobacco

	Canada	*US*	*Austria*	*Belgium*	*Denmark*	*Finland*	*France*
Export share	3	47	0	3	1	0	2
RCA	.56	2.4	.12	.46	.56	.10	.15
Import penetration	1	2	2	17	40	18	33
Exports-to-production	6	17	1	2	51	7	7
	Germany	*Italy*	*Netherlands*	*Portugal*	*Spain*	*Sweden*	*UK*
Export share	11	1	18	0	0	0	13
RCA	.52	.13	2.75	.08	.10	.07	1.48
Import penetration	5	24	29	6	10	26	24
Exports-to-production	6	4	57	2	1	7	35

321, Textiles

	Canada	*US*	*Austria*	*Belgium*	*Denmark*	*Finland*	*France*
Export share	1	12	4	10	2	0	10
RCA	.19	.60	1.57	1.6	.85	.33	.93
Import penetration	37	15	64	90	66	61	41
Exports-to-production	10	9	62	94	60	35	34
	Germany	*Italy*	*Netherlands*	*Portugal*	*Spain*	*Sweden*	*UK*
Export share	20	20	7	4	3	1	7
RCA	.92	2.41	1.04	4.52	.84	.38	.77
Import penetration	53	15	*	33	23	77	44
Exports-to-production	44	25	*	39	17	47	30

*: Ratios exceed 1.00.
nsa: Not separately available.

Table 6.A1   Alliance potential indicators for the EU and NAFTA (cont.)

ISIC number, sector, and indicator	Country						

322, Wearing apparel

	Canada	US	Austria	Belgium	Denmark	Finland	France
Export share	1	9	2	6	2	1	13
RCA	.23	.46	1.02	1.01	1.28	.57	1.15
Import penetration	23	31	65	75	87	56	40
Exports-to-production	4	5	45	65	84	39	30
	Germany	Italy	Netherlands	Portugal	Spain	Sweden	UK
Export share	20	22	6	8	2	1	8
RCA	.90	2.67	.92	8.11	.50	.28	.85
Import penetration	63	11	*	*	18	89	47
Exports-to-production	37	26	*	*	7	56	29

323, Leather & products

	Canada	US	Austria	Belgium	Denmark	Finland	France
Export share	1	11	2	4	1	1	14
RCA	.13	.58	1.06	.60	.43	.49	1.22
Import penetration	62	46	70	*	*	61	57
Exports-to-production	22	20	64	*	*	49	56
	Germany	Italy	Netherlands	Portugal	Spain	Sweden	UK
Export share	14	34	4	1	6	1	7
RCA	.67	4.01	.68	.83	2.05	.28	.73
Import penetration	66	22	*	36	24	75	54
Exports-to-production	54	35	*	3	25	52	45

324, Footwear

	Canada	US	Austria	Belgium	Denmark	Finland	France
Export share	0	4	3	1	1	0	7
RCA	.07	.22	1.21	.16	.73	.31	.58
Import penetration	52	69	58	94	79	57	52
Exports-to-production	8	12	47	69	64	33	27
	Germany	Italy	Netherlands	Portugal	Spain	Sweden	UK
Export share	10	44	3	12	10	0	4
RCA	.44	5.25	.49	13.15	3.23	.13	.45
Import penetration	64	12	*	*	13	95	49
Exports-to-production	33	44	*	*	55	70	20

331, Wood products

	Canada	US	Austria	Belgium	Denmark	Finland	France
Export share	28	18	7	4	2	6	5
RCA	5.22	.89	2.91	.67	1.28	5.16	.47
Import penetration	11	7	28	18	43	10	17
Exports-to-production	45	5	53	14	60	38	11
	Germany	Italy	Netherlands	Portugal	Spain	Sweden	UK
Export share	8	3	3	4	2	10	1
RCA	.37	.39	.46	3.82	.54	3.37	.12
Import penetration	22	18	67	10	17	7	31
Exports-to-production	11	6	43	52	7	25	3

*: Ratios exceed 1.00.
nsa: Not separately available.

Table 6.A1   Alliance potential indicators for the EU and NAFTA (cont.)

ISIC number, sector, and indicator				Country		

332, Furniture & fixtures

	Canada	US	Austria	Belgium	Denmark	Finland	France
Export share	6	10	3	7	8	1	7
RCA	1.05	.50	1.18	1.10	4.23	.55	.64
Import penetration	23	10	16	25	32	19	26
Exports-to-production	26	4	10	23	75	15	15
	Germany	Italy	Netherlands	Portugal	Spain	Sweden	UK
Export share	19	26	4	1	3	4	4
RCA	.85	3.06	.64	.95	.82	1.31	.46
Import penetration	19	2	49	28	13	46	15
Exports-to-production	7	21	32	35	14	46	8

341, Paper & products

	Canada	US	Austria	Belgium	Denmark	Finland	France
Export share	18	15	4	3	1	11	7
RCA	3.39	.76	1.78	.53	.41	8.62	.63
Import penetration	19	8	41	64	60	12	32
Exports-to-production	63	7	59	55	35	72	23
	Germany	Italy	Netherlands	Portugal	Spain	Sweden	UK
Export share	14	4	5	1	2	12	4
RCA	.62	.43	.74	1.52	.64	4.06	.49
Import penetration	33	19	69	33	33	18	34
Exports-to-production	28	12	62	50	21	66	15

342, Printing & publishing

	Canada	US	Austria	Belgium	Denmark	Finland	France
Export share	3	23	2	6	2	1	11
RCA	.51	1.17	1.06	.99	1.04	.93	.96
Import penetration	13	1	19	26	7	4	7
Exports-to-production	3	2	10	25	8	5	6
	Germany	Italy	Netherlands	Portugal	Spain	Sweden	UK
Export share	21	6	7	0	3	1	13
RCA	.95	.74	1.06	.28	1.04	.50	1.48
Import penetration	7	2	10	14	5	7	6
Exports-to-production	14	5	11	6	6	3	8

351, Industrial chemicals

	Canada	US	Austria	Belgium	Denmark	Finland	France
Export share	4	20	2	8	1	1	11
RCA	.74	1.03	.75	1.34	.45	.69	1.01
Import penetration	61	14	55	93	78	52	66
Exports-to-production	63	21	51	94	63	47	65
	Germany	Italy	Netherlands	Portugal	Spain	Sweden	UK
Export share	24	5	10	0	2	1	10
RCA	1.12	.63	1.52	.37	.71	.48	1.00
Import Penetration	46	39	82	51	44	59	43
Exports-to-production	57	26	88	28	29	48	44

*: Ratios exceed 1.00.
nsa: Not separately available.

Table 6.A1   Alliance potential indicators for the EU and NAFTA (cont.)

**ISIC number,
sector, and indicator**   **Country**

352, Other chemicals

	Canada	US	Austria	Belgium	Denmark	Finland	France
Export share	1	17	2	8	3	0	16
RCA	.28	.89	.73	1.28	1.38	.24	1.42
Import penetration	23	7	45	*	86	48	27
Exports-to-production	8	10	31	*	89	21	35
	Germany	Italy	Netherlands	Portugal	Spain	Sweden	UK
Export share	21	5	8	0	2	3	13
RCA	.94	.65	1.30	.32	.60	1.12	1.47
Import penetration	22	31	*	43	17	51	29
Exports-to-production	30	19	*	18	9	51	38

3522, Drugs & medicines

	Canada	US	Austria	Belgium	Denmark	Finland	France
Export share	1	15	2	8	4	0	14
RCA	.16	.76	1.09	1.26	2.39	.26	1.25
Import penetration	20	5	44	82	99	47	21
Exports-to-production	6	7	36	84	100	19	26
	Germany	Italy	Netherlands	Portugal	Spain	Sweden	UK
Export share	20	7	5	0	2	6	15
RCA	.90	.86	.83	.21	.78	2.13	1.62
Import penetration	24	nsa	67	nsa	14	51	20
Exports-to-production	32	nsa	67	nsa	10	66	32

353, Petroleum refineries

	Canada	US	Austria	Belgium	Denmark	Finland	France
Export share	7	17	0	11	2	2	7
RCA	1.3	.85	.16	1.83	.96	1.74	.64
Import penetration	10	10	17	*	37	22	16
Exports-to-production	16	4	3	*	27	27	8
	Germany	Italy	Netherlands	Portugal	Spain	Sweden	UK
Export share	9	1	21	1	5	4	12
RCA	.42	.18	3.23	1.49	1.66	1.51	1.29
Import penetration	15	24	28	25	20	38	20
Exports-to-production	5	17	56	21	27	35	24

354, Petroleum & coal products

	Canada	US	Austria	Belgium	Denmark	Finland	France
Export share	6	15	1	8	1	0	7
RCA	1.18	.78	.64	1.31	.41	.33	.66
Import penetration	78	4	53	*	13	27	nsa
Exports-to-production	89	5	26	*	8	5	nsa
	Germany	Italy	Netherlands	Portugal	Spain	Sweden	UK
Export share	29	5	14	1	4	1	6
RCA	1.32	.60	2.18	1.24	1.35	.52	.65
Import penetration	14	9	*	nsa	14	21	13
Exports-to-production	21	6	*	nsa	15	12	14

*: Ratios exceed 1.00.
nsa: Not separately available.

Table 6.A1   Alliance potential indicators for the EU and NAFTA (cont.)

**ISIC number,
sector, and indicator**   **Country**

355, Rubber products

	Canada	US	Austria	Belgium	Denmark	Finland	France
Export share	6	14	3	6	1	0	18
RCA	1.11	.71	1.44	1.03	.28	.39	1.55
Import penetration	46	14	40	*	75	61	33
Exports-to-production	35	10	43	*	50	40	45
	Germany	Italy	Netherlands	Portugal	Spain	Sweden	UK
Export share	21	7	6	0	6	2	9
RCA	.98	.80	.90	.34	2.08	.76	1.02
Import penetration	31	22	*	57	27	50	29
Exports-to-production	31	25	*	33	33	25	29

361, Pottery, china, etc.

	Canada	US	Austria	Belgium	Denmark	Finland	France
Export share	0	8	2	5	2	1	10
RCA	.06	.43	.88	.88	.97	.53	.88
Import penetration	56	41	53	64	76	37	18
Exports-to-production	6	12	38	60	70	28	16
	Germany	Italy	Netherlands	Portugal	Spain	Sweden	UK
Export share	25	14	3	8	5	2	15
RCA	1.13	1.67	.51	8.14	1.57	.65	1.71
Import penetration	31	3	50	21	19	55	18
Exports-to-production	35	5	35	61	21	34	32

362, Glass & products

	Canada	US	Austria	Belgium	Denmark	Finland	France
Export share	2	14	4	12	1	1	18
RCA	.47	.71	1.65	2.05	.60	1.07	1.57
Import penetration	52	11	35	63	62	38	33
Exports-to-production	28	10	44	82	47	47	40
	Germany	Italy	Netherlands	Portugal	Spain	Sweden	UK
Export share	20	11	3	1	3	2	6
RCA	.91	1.28	.75	1.31	1.00	.69	.64
Import penetration	20	13	76	30	18	50	29
Exports-to-production	22	16	72	32	13	41	22

371, Iron & steel

	Canada	US	Austria	Belgium	Denmark	Finland	France
Export share	4	6	4	12	1	3	14
RCA	.70	.33	1.69	2.07	.53	2.05	1.28
Import penetration	26	11	40	*	*	36	28
Exports-to-production	24	5	55	*	*	52	33
	Germany	Italy	Netherlands	Portugal	Spain	Sweden	UK
Export share	23	8	5	0	4	5	9
RCA	1.06	1.09	.81	.22	1.44	1.78	.96
Import penetration	21	16	72	41	18	38	26
Exports-to-production	24	15	69	11	19	51	28

*: Ratios exceed 1.00.
nsa: Not separately available.

Table 6.A1   Alliance potential indicators for the EU and NAFTA (cont.)

**ISIC number,
sector, and indicator**   **Country**

372, Non-ferrous metals

	Canada	US	Austria	Belgium	Denmark	Finland	France
Export share	17	15	3	9	0	2	10
RCA	3.18	.76	1.12	1.47	.25	1.67	.92
Import penetration	28	15	44	80	89	29	36
Exports-to-production	51	10	40	80	73	41	27
	Germany	Italy	Netherlands	Portugal	Spain	Sweden	UK
Export share	20	5	5	0	3	3	9
RCA	.90	.55	.80	.13	1.04	.90	.96
Import penetration	29	35	61	67	22	46	50
Exports-to-production	23	17	63	22	17	42	41

381, Metal products

	Canada	US	Austria	Belgium	Denmark	Finland	France
Export share	3	13	4	5	3	1	11
RCA	.59	.66	1.64	.91	1.44	.88	1.01
Import penetration	28	7	30	56	34	25	21
Exports-to-production	19	5	30	55	41	24	19
	Germany	Italy	Netherlands	Portugal	Spain	Sweden	UK
Export share	26	14	6	1	3	3	7
RCA	1.17	1.66	.96	.72	.97	1.13	.78
Import penetration	15	15	42	35	18	21	19
Exports-to-production	20	31	41	25	16	22	18

382, Non-electrical machinery

	Canada	US	Austria	Belgium	Denmark	Finland	France
Export share	3	25	2	3	2	1	8
RCA	.50	1.28	1.09	.44	.95	.80	.74
Import penetration	65	24	62	90	63	47	42
Exports-to-production	42	47	60	86	65	42	37
	Germany	Italy	Netherlands	Portugal	Spain	Sweden	UK
Export share	25	10	5	0	2	3	10
RCA	1.17	1.20	.76	.26	.62	1.09	1.16
Import penetration	31	28	*	92	58	56	46
Exports-to-production	42	41	*	67	35	60	47

3825, Office & computing machinery

	Canada	US	Austria	Belgium	Denmark	Finland	France
Export share	4	38	1	2	1	1	9
RCA	.75	1.94	.45	.28	.49	.66	.79
Import penetration	87	45	nsa	nsa	*	77	51
Exports-to-production	76	42	nsa	nsa	*	60	40
	Germany	Italy	Netherlands	Portugal	Spain	Sweden	UK
Export share	13	4	8	0	2	2	16
RCA	.59	.43	1.28	.11	.59	.61	1.79
Import penetration	66	61	*	nsa	*	99	78
Exports-to-production	53	54	*	nsa	*	98	76

*: Ratios exceed 1.00.
nsa: Not separately available.

Table 6.A1   Alliance potential indicators for the EU and NAFTA (cont.)

ISIC number, sector, and indicator				Country		

383, Electrical machinery

	Canada	US	Austria	Belgium	Denmark	Finland	France
Export share	4	27	3	3	1	1	11
RCA	.68	1.35	1.2	.5	.77	.92	.94
Import penetration	60	30	41	75	84	63	34
Exports-to-production	41	23	41	72	84	58	33
	Germany	Italy	Netherlands	Portugal	Spain	Sweden	UK
Export share	23	7	5	1	2	3	10
RCA	1.05	.82	.78	1.03	.75	1.07	1.10
Import penetration	25	26	70	70	41	60	42
Exports-to-production	28	24	66	59	21	59	38

3832, Radio, TV, & communications equipment

	Canada	US	Austria	Belgium	Denmark	Finland	France
Export share	5	32	3	3	1	1	9
RCA	.96	1.66	1.12	.46	.75	1.01	.79
Import penetration	65	34	81	nsa	88	77	31
Exports-to-production	51	25	81	nsa	87	74	25
	Germany	Italy	Netherlands	Portugal	Spain	Sweden	UK
Export share	18	4	6	1	2	4	12
RCA	.83	.49	.89	.78	.50	1.23	1.32
Import penetration	31	48	nsa	nsa	47	77	48
Exports-to-production	28	30	nsa	nsa	16	80	45

3841, Shipbuilding

	Canada	US	Austria	Belgium	Denmark	Finland	France
Export share	1	14	1	1	10	5	13
RCA	.21	.73	.35	.14	5.24	4.41	1.15
Import penetration	21	4	24	nsa	37	24	15
Exports-to-production	9	10	47	nsa	38	46	20
	Germany	Italy	Netherlands	Portugal	Spain	Sweden	UK
Export share	24	4	6	1	9	5	5
RCA	1.11	.53	.93	1.36	3.09	1.64	.55
Import penetration	25	27	13	nsa	34	48	15
Exports-to-production	45	23	26	nsa	16	43	16

3842, Railroad equipment

	Canada	US	Austria	Belgium	Denmark	Finland	France
Export share	12	14	6	3	2	0	14
RCA	2.21	.53	2.47	.45	.93	.15	1.21
Import penetration	25	13	19	nsa	4	12	12
Exports-to-production	49	12	41	nsa	4	16	23
	Germany	Italy	Netherlands	Portugal	Spain	Sweden	UK
Export share	38	7	6	1	9	5	5
RCA	1.73	.86	.19	.02	.97	.65	.33
Import penetration	69	7	nsa	nsa	8	10	11
Exports-to-production	90	9	nsa	nsa	5	11	13

*: Ratios exceed 1.00.
nsa: Not separately available.

Table 6.A1   Alliance potential indicators for the EU and NAFTA (cont.)

ISIC number,
sector, and indicator   **Country**

3843, Motor vehicles

	Canada	US	Austria	Belgium	Denmark	Finland	France
Export share	11	15	2	7	0	0	11
RCA	2.12	.78	.83	1.21	.20	.36	1.01
Import penetration	72	30	92	NSA	NSA	96	39
Exports-to-production	75	16	88			95	45
	Germany	Italy	Netherlands	Portugal	Spain	Sweden	UK
Export share	29	5	2	0	0	3	7
RCA	1.34	.59	.30	.51	1.96	1.04	.74
Import penetration	27	39	100	NSA	38	48	48
Exports-to-production	38	31	100		41	59	46

3844, Motorcycles and Bicycles

	Canada	US	Austria	Belgium	Denmark	Finland	France
Export share	1	19	2	3	1	0	14
RCA	.13	.95	.68	.51	.63	.13	1.24
Import penetration	nsa	54	nsa	nsa	nsa	50	63
Exports-to-production	nsa	35	nsa	nsa	nsa	10	46
	Germany	Italy	Netherlands	Portugal	Spain	Sweden	UK
Export share	13	27	9	1	3	2	6
RCA	.60	3.27	1.35	1.20	1.12	.55	.62
Import penetration	60	34	88	nsa	43	70	81
Exports-to-production	35	44	80	nsa	10	48	59

3845, Aircraft

	Canada	US	Austria	Belgium	Denmark	Finland	France
Export share	4	45	0	1	0	0	15
RCA	.70	2.31	.04	.17	.24	.02	1.53
Import penetration	59	12	nsa	nsa	nsa	56	45
Exports-to-production	64	31	nsa	nsa	nsa	7	56
	Germany	Italy	Netherlands	Portugal	Spain	Sweden	UK
Export share	13	4	3	0	1	1	12
RCA	.60	.46	.48	.09	.41	.31	1.36
Import penetration	88	50	92	nsa	*	61	47
Exports-to-production	98	55	92	nsa	*	52	59

385, Professional Goods

	Canada	US	Austria	Belgium	Denmark	Finland	France
Export share	2	29	2	2	2	1	9
RCA	.36	1.50	.71	.31	1.08	.50	.83
Import penetration	nsa	13	*	*	*	76	78
Exports-to-production	nsa	14	*	*	*	66	73
	Germany	Italy	Netherlands	Portugal	Spain	Sweden	UK
Export share	25	5	7	0	1	3	12
RCA	1.15	.63	1.13	.25	.38	.95	1.28
Import penetration	83	35	*	*	94	72	*
Exports-to-Production	87	22	*	*	70	69	*

*: Ratios exceed 1.00.
nsa: Not separately available.

NOTES

1. The OECD publishes annually the Structural Analysis (STAN) database. Data are reported at the two- and three-digit ISIC level for most of the OECD countries. STAN reports seven variables of industrial activity (production, value added, gross fixed capital formation, employees engaged, labour compensation, exports, and imports).
2. See Business International (1990) and Teece 1986 for a fuller elaboration of business and 'complementary' assets.
3. Détente, as it is used in diplomacy and national security analysis, means the mutual restraint of military power. It was the basis for stabilizing US-Soviet nuclear relations during the 1970s.
4. See Organization for Economic Cooperation and Development (1994) for detailed definitions of types of foreign direct investment.
5. Minority equity investments constitute direct investments if they are greater than 10 per cent. Otherwise, they are considered to be portfolio investments without an ability to influence managerial decision making. See OECD (1994).
6. The comparability of international industrial and trade data is problematic. Each nation typically collects and reports industrial output and employment data on the basis of its own industrial classification system, which is different from the system for international trade (the standard international trade classification, SITC). The European Community has harmonized its industrial data into the NACE system, which is nonetheless not comparable to the individual SICs of other nations. The OECD has concorded a limited number of national output, trade, and expenditure data series into a comparable framework, the international standard industrial classification (ISIC) established by the United Nations.
7. Ireland also reflects similar levels of foreign direct investment; it is not clear if the Irish export structure is comparably bilateral.
8. This industry produces both consumer and industrial goods. Fabricated metal products for household use include cutlery, hand tools, hardware, metal furniture and fixtures; industrial products include fasteners, tools, and structural metal products.
9. For example, Bristol-Meyers-Squibb came under Congressional review because of its prices for the anti-cancer drug, Taxol. The Taxol patent is owned by the US Cancer Research Institute and was licensed exclusively to Bristol-Meyers for a period of five years.
10. Note that Canada is a case in which the aggregate data *do* mask idiosyncratic alliance behaviour. For example, the empirical indicators suggest that Canada is essentially non-competitive in the aircraft industry. However, Bombardier Aerospace Group is a Canadian multinational engaged in multiple strategic alliances; it is also one of the world's largest producers of small jet aircraft.
11. Prior to the mid 1980s, research consortia were illegal in the United States – they violated anti-trust law. Prohibitions have since been eliminated, but firms may still be liable for single damages via unfair competition lawsuits.

REFERENCES

Beamish, P.W. (1985), 'The characteristics of joint ventures in developed and developing countries', *Columbia Journal of World Business*, Winter, 13–19.

Bloom, Martin (1993), 'The consumer electronic industry', in Frédérique Sachwald (ed.), *European Integration and Competitiveness: Acquisitions and Alliances in Industry*, Aldershot: Edward Elgar.

Buckley, Peter J., C.L. Pass and Kate Prescott (1992), *Servicing International Markets: Competitive Strategies of Firms*. Cambridge, MA: Blackwell Business.

Business International (1990), *Making Alliances Work: Lessons from Companies' Successes and Mistakes*, London: Business International, Inc.

Cairns, Walter (1994), 'The legal environment', in Neill Nugent and Rory O'Donnell (eds), *The European Business Environment*, Macmillan Press.

Commission of the European Communities (1991), *Panorama of EC Industries 1991–92*, Brussels: Office for Official Publications of the European Communities.

Contractor, Farok and Peter Lorange (1988), 'Why should firms cooperate? The strategy and economic basis for cooperative ventures', in Farok Contractor and Peter Lorange (eds), *Cooperative Strategies in International Business*, Lexington, MA: Lexington Books.

Cowhey, Peter F. and Jonathan D. Aronson (1993), *Managing the World Economy: The Consequences of Corporate Alliances*, NY: Council on Foreign Relations Press.

de Banville, Etienne and Jean-Jacques Chanaron (1994), 'The automobile industry' in Frédérique Sachwald (ed.), *European Integration and Competitiveness*, Aldershot: Edward Elgar, pp. 101–44.

de Wolf, Peter (1993), 'The pharmaceutical industry', in Frédérique Sachwald (ed.), *European Integration and Competitiveness: Acquisitions and Alliances in Industry*, Aldershot: Edward Elgar.

Gilroy, Bernard (1993), *Networking in Multinational Enterprises: The Importance of Strategic Alliances*, Columbia, SC: University of South Carolina Press.

Hagedoorn, John (ed.) (1995), *Technical Change and the World Economy*, Aldershot: Edward Elgar.

Hagedoorn, John and Jos Schakenraad (1993), 'Strategic technology partnering and international corporate strategies', in Kirsty S. Hughes (ed.) *European Competitiveness*, Cambridge: Cambridge University Press.

Harrigan, Kathryn (1988), 'Strategic alliances and partner asymmetries', in Farok Contractor and Peter Lorange (eds), *Cooperative Strategies in International Business*, Lexington, MA: Lexington Books.

Hayward, Jack (1995), *Industrial Enterprise and European Integration*, Oxford University Press.

Hergert, Michael and Deigan Morris (1988), 'Trends in international collaborative agreements', in Farok Contractor and Peter Lorange (eds), *Cooperative Strategies in International Business*, Lexington, MA: Lexington Books.

Hobday, Michael (1993), 'The semiconductor industry', in Frédérique Sachwald (ed.), *European Integration and Competitiveness: Acquisitions and Alliances in Industry*, Aldershot: Edward Elgar.

Houghton, J.R. (1990), 'Corning cultivates joint ventures that endure', *Planning Review*, 18, 5, 15–17.

Jacquemin, Alexis (1994), 'Comments', in F.M. Scherer, *Competition Policies for an Integrated World Economy*, Washington, DC: The Brookings Institution.

Jacobson, David (1994), 'The technical and infrastructural environment', in Neill Nugent and Rory O'Donnell (eds), *The European Business Environment*, Macmillan Press.

James, Harvey S. Jr and Murray Weidenbaum (1993), *When Businesses Cross International Borders*, Westport, CT: Praeger Publishers.

Kay, Neil (1993), 'Mergers, acquisitions, and the completion of the internal market', in Kirsty S. Hughes (ed.), *European Competitiveness*, Cambridge: Cambridge University Press.

Killing, P. (1983), *Strategies for Joint Venture Success*, NY: Praeger.

Litvak, I.A. and C.J. Maule (1981), *The Canadian Multinationals*, Toronto: Butterworth.

Lorange, Peter and Johan Roos (1992), *Strategic Alliances: Formation. Implementation, and Evolution*, Cambridge, MA Blackwell Business.

Makridakis, Spyros *et al.* (1991), *Single Market Europe*, San Francisco: Jossey-Bass.
Mytelka, Lynn (1995), 'Dancing with wolves: global oligopolies and strategic partnerships', in John Hagedoorn (ed.), *Technical Change and the World Economy*, Aldershot: Edward Elgar.
Nugent, Neill and Rory O'Donnell (eds) (1994), *The European Business Environment*, Macmillan Press.
Organization for Economic Cooperation and Development (1994), *The Performance of Foreign Affiliates in OECD Countries*, Paris: OECD.
Papadakis, Maria (1994), 'Did (or does) the United States have a competitiveness crisis?', *Journal of Policy Analysis and Management*, 13, 1, 1–20.
Papadakis, Maria (1995), 'Confounding productivity and competitiveness: a comment on "How well is America competing"', *Journal of Policy Analysis and Management*, 15, 1, 82–8.
Preston, Lee and Duane Windsor (1992), *The Rules of the Game in the Global Economy: Policy Regimes for International Business*, Boston: Kluwer Academic Publishers.
Rugman, Alan M. (1990), *Multinationals and Canada-United States Free Trade*, Columbia, SC: University of South Carolina Press.
Sachwald, Frédérique (ed.) (1993), *European Integration and Competitiveness: Acquisitions and Alliances in Industry*, Aldershot: Edward Elgar.
Scherer, F.M. (1994), *Competition Policies for an Integrated World Economy*, Washington, DC: The Brookings Institution.
Sharp, M. (1992), 'Changing Industrial Structures in Western Europe', in D. Dyker (ed.), *The European Economy*, London: Longman.
Teece, J. David (1986), 'Profiting from technological innovation: implications for integration, collaboration, licensing, and public policy', *Research Policy*, 15, 285–305.
Tsoukalis, L. (1993), *The New European Economy: The Politics and Economics of Integration*, 2nd edn, Oxford: Oxford University Press.
Yoshino, Michael and U. Srinivasa Rangan (1995), *Strategic Alliances: An Entrepreneurial Approach to Globalization*, Boston, MA: Harvard Business School Press.

7. Atlantic high-technology complementarities

Jorge Niosi and Benoit Godin

On the basis of different historical paths of industrial development and resources, North America and Western Europe have followed diverging industrial trajectories (Pierre 1987). Several studies have, in the past, tried to assess the cross-national patterns of industrial technology development, either by measuring innovations (Chakrabarti *et al.* 1982), patents (Cantwell 1992, Kelly 1993, Pavitt and Patel 1990), or international investment flows (Dunning 1992). These studies have put the accent on industrial differences and the comparative advantages of each region. Other studies have focussed on more recent patterns of industrial cooperation between firms in North America and the European Union (Fusfeld 1987, Mowery 1992, Niosi 1995).

This chapter will analyse the relative industrial strengths of North America and Western Europe, together with some aspects of inter-regional industrial cooperation, using both the existing (secondary) literature and recent aggregate data on direct investment flows, patents and expatriate R&D. The theoretical framework is based on the concept of national systems of innovation, a concept developed in the last decade to account for national differences in industrial innovation. It also draws from the evolutionary framework in economics and management. We display some empirical evidence on national and regional (Western Europe versus North America) industrial capabilities, on the basis of cross-flows of foreign direct investment, patenting, and expatriate R&D as well as North Atlantic technological alliances. We conclude that there are important national differences in industrial capabilities in both regions, and that these are the basis for investment cross-flows and international alliances.

NATIONAL SYSTEMS OF INNOVATION

Innovation is concentrated in a few industrial nations: in 1994, 78 per cent of all world patents were claimed by firms based in only twenty market economies, including fourteen Western European nations, the US and Canada in North America, Japan, Korea, Australia and Israel (WIPO 1996).

Industrial nations differ in the way they conduct innovation. National differences are based on several determinants, including relative factor endowment, the size of the economy, specific cultural and institutional characteristics, and the given historical setting of industrialization (pioneers versus latecomers, colonial versus non-colonial powers). A few examples may illustrate this point. Industrial countries with a large endowment of natural resources (the USA, Canada, Sweden) have usually developed technologies for the refining and transformation of those resources, like minerals or forest. Nations with large markets (for example, the USA and Japan) have understandably contributed to the development of a much wider range of technologies than smaller industrial countries (like Switzerland or the Netherlands). Countries with a cultural model based on market competition (the UK, the USA) have developed institutions for the management and support of technological development different from those of nations where consensus and cooperation are important (Japan, Korea). Also, the state has played a larger role in the industrialization of latecomers (for example, Korea, Japan, Canada or Italy) than in the development of industrial pioneers (Britain, Switzerland and the Netherlands) (Lundvall 1992, Nelson 1993); the NSI of these industrial followers shows important differences from those of first industrializers. Last, but not least, governments promote innovation in the pursuit of different specific missions of national importance, be they military, health, environment or national unity. Therefore, countries usually show areas of technological strength that correspond to those missions that governments have historically supported.

National systems of innovation are sets of institutions participating in the development of new and improved products, processes and materials. The institutions involved are private firms (specially those with R&D capabilities), public laboratories and research universities, together with the governmental institutions that financially support, regulate and protect invention and innovation (Niosi *et al.* 1993). National systems of innovation also include the flows between these economic agents, be they information, personnel or funds. Industrial nations vary in the relative importance of these institutions, the intensity and quality of flows among them and the degree of coordination among these institutions.

At the roots of industrial and technological competition and cooperation between firms based in different nations, there are different models of innovation, and different determinants of national advantage (Porter 1990). Thus, the German supremacy in many areas of the world chemical industry (such as synthetic dyes, resins and paints) dates back to the 1860s, when that country had to compete with Britain and France in the textile industry. Germany needed synthetic dyes to replace the natural ones that Britain and France could obtain from their colonies. In the nineteenth century, German chemical firms introduced, for that purpose, a major organizational innovation, the in-house industrial R&D laboratory, a novelty that later spread to other Western countries and industries. Similarly, in the 1920s, German firms developed synthetic rubber to compete with British natural rubber produced in the colonies. Conversely, the abundance of oil and gas in the United States, and efficient industry-university collaboration in that country, created the technological innovations that nurtured the American petrochemical industry (Spitz 1988, Rosenberg and Nelson 1994).

NATIONAL SYSTEMS OF INNOVATION IN AN EVOLUTIONARY FRAMEWORK

The concept of national systems of innovation in Lundvall, Freeman and Nelson, like Porter's concept of national competitive advantage, were developed to account for the fact that innovation was concentrated in a few countries, but also to emphasize that national factor endowment was not the sole determinant of industrial and technological capabilities. History matters to explain what industries and technologies are developed in each industrial country and region (Arthur 1994). Once a few corporate pioneers innovate in an appropriate setting, economies of scale and cumulative learning processes usually create technological and organizational trajectories that tend to renew themselves and maintain that original advantage. Late industrializers have to overcome major barriers in order to catch up with pioneers and eventually take the lead in existing industries.

Evolutionary concepts thus help in explaining long-term competitive advantages of nations and leading firms, that often subsist for decades and sometimes for over a century. However, company and country strategies, and market characteristics, may help latecomers to attain industrial leadership and rapid catch-up. These strategies include government policies for inward technology transfer, adaptive R&D and technological cooperation (Porter 1983). Industries with rapid market growth and low barriers to entry (computers and semiconductors) display a higher turnover rate among leaders, and offer larger catching-up opportunities to newcomers. Conversely, industries with low growth (aluminium), and those in which patents or trade marks can be used as effective deterrents to entry (pharmaceutical products) are those where newcomers may experience the most difficulties in catching up. From a company point of view, the establishment of in-house R&D capabilities seems almost a condition for newcomers effectively to catch up with industrial leaders.

EMPIRICAL EVIDENCE OF NATIONAL AND REGIONAL INDUSTRIAL CAPABILITIES

Some countries and regions enjoy continuous leadership in specific industries. The United States leads the world in industries where R&D was originally funded and supported with a view to defence technology, such as aircraft, semiconductors, advanced materials, software and telecommunications equipment. Through continuous government support of university and public research, it has also created competitive advantages in science-based industries such as biotechnology and chemical engineering. In the post-war period, however, Western Europe has persistently caught up in a few of these industries, such as aircraft or nuclear technology, while maintaining the lead in others such as fine chemicals and building materials.

Conversely, one can find in several countries and regions evidence of continuous backwardness in other industries. Europe's electronic industries are a case in point. Except for a few firms, European computer, semiconductor and consumer electronics industries are second or third to North American and Japanese competitors. Similarly, Canadian pharmaceutical and advanced material industries are underdeveloped compared to those of any other large or medium-sized industrial country, in spite of the quality and quantity of Canadian university research and scientific publication in these areas.

The concept of revealed technological advantage (RTA) was developed by Keith Pavitt and Pari Patel to measure these national capabilities on the basis of patents granted by the US Patent Office. A number of national studies was produced that showed country capabilities and their evolution through time. Canada shows RTAs in biotechnology, telecommunications equipment, basic metallurgy, aircraft and mass transportation equipment, but it is technologically disadvantaged in areas such as semiconductors, computers and robotics (see Table 7.1). France shows RTAs in chemicals, telecommunications equipment, nuclear reactors and aircraft, while Germany is strong in industrial machinery, chemical products and fabricated metals. The UK shows decreasing technological advantages across the industrial spectrum, but it still shows some advantages in aircraft, nuclear reactors and telecommunications equipment (Pavitt and Patel 1990).

International Direct Investment Flows

Foreign direct investment (FDI) is considered a good indicator of national industrial advantages. FDI between North America and Western Europe is large and experiences a fast growth rate.

The United States and Europe are now roughly balanced in terms of cross-flows of FDI. By the end of 1995, US corporations had a total FDI in Europe evaluated at 363.5 US$ billion; 38 per cent of that amount was in finance and 36 per cent in manufacturing. Meanwhile European corporations had invested some 360.8 US$ billion in the United States; 44 per cent of that amount was in manufacturing and 24 per cent in finance.

American FDI in Europe was geographically concentrated in five countries: the United Kingdom, Germany, the Netherlands, Switzerland and France; these five nations represented nearly three-quarters of US FDI in Europe (see Table 7.2).

Table 7.1   *Revealed technological advantages of Canadian firms, 1988–91 (selected industries)*

Industry	RTA
Aircraft. aerospace	1.02
Biotechnology	1.44
Computers	0.41
Food, beverages	1.27
Inorganic chemicals	1.51
Metallurgy	1.18
Non-ferrous metal composites	0.71
Nuclear reactors and systems	0.52
Organic chemicals	1.51
Paper and cellulose	2.09
Pharmaceutical products	0.77
Rail transportation	2.14
Robotics	0.69
Semiconductors	0.26
Telecommunications equipment	1.03
Textiles	0.35

Note: A value over 1.00 indicates a revealed technological advantage of the country over the rest of the world in a given industry; conversely, a value under 1.00 indicates a revealed technological disadvantage.

Source: Kelly, 1993.

American foreign direct investment in finance was most conspicuous in Europe. Britain was the preferred destination of US investment in most areas: manufacturing, finance (both in banking and insurance), services and other industries. Within manufacturing, the US automobile industry occupies a major position in Western Europe, mainly in England and Germany, but US pharmaceutical, telecommunications equipment, computers and other corporations are also important in several European countries.

European FDI in the United States is mostly made by the same five countries that represent the preferred destinations of US direct investment abroad (see Table 7.3). The UK, the Netherlands, Germany, France and Switzerland constitute 52 per cent of all European direct investment in the US. In manufacturing the same countries represent 87 per cent of EFDI in the United States. British investments accounted for a large proportion of foreign-owned production in ten of the twenty SIC two-digit manufacturing industries; among these, British corporations were most important in tobacco products, petroleum and coal products, food and kindred products and instruments and related products (US DoC, 1994). German, Swiss, Dutch, British and French companies

Table 7.2   US FDI in Europe, 1995

US$ billions at year end, historical cost basis

Industry **Country**	All	Finance	Mftg	Whole. trade	Oil	Services	Other ind.
U K	120	60	28	7	14	6	5
Germany	43	11	24	3	2	1	2
Netherlands	37	18	10	4	2	1	1
Switzerland	36	21	4	9	1	1	n
France	33	7	17	4	1	2	1
All others	95	22	48	10	6	8	3
Totals	364	139	131	37	26	19	12

Note: n: negligible (under 1 billion US$).

Source: US Department of Commerce, *Survey of Current Business*, July 1996.

were overwhelming in the chemical industry; in 1990, foreign corporations
(mostly European) accounted for 32 per cent of total US chemical production.
In the petroleum and coal industries, British and Dutch corporations also
occupied an important position.

Table 7.3   European FDI in the United States, 1995

US$ billions at year end, historical cost basis

Industry **Country**	All	Mftg	Finance	Trade	Oil	Real estate	Other ind.
UK	132	57	28	8	11	4	24
Netherlands	68	21	15	7	13	5	7
Germany	48	24	8	9	n	1	ND
France	38	21	9	2	ND	n	ND
Switzerland	33	14	ND	1	n	n	2
All other	42	21	ND	9	ND	2	ND
Totals	361	158	87	36	27	12	42

Notes: ND: suppressed to avoid disclosure on individual companies.
            n: negligible (under 1 billion US$).

Source: US Department of Commerce, *Survey of Current Business*, July 1996.

Table 7.4 *Patents granted in the USA in 1993 in selected countries and industries (total numbers)*

Industry	*Computers*	*Radio/ TV*	*Industrial machines*	*Commun. technol.*	*Transp. equipm.*	*Aerospace*	*Chemical products*	*Drugs*
Country								
USA	2568	475	2506	6978	840	522	4312	3670
Japan	1689	535	763	4517	484	232	1586	989
Germany	145	45	435	481	252	113	846	588
France	90	30	165	409	49	45	244	294
UK	85	33	104	258	42	36	252	307
Canada	37	15	104	161	45	11	146	93

Sources: National Science Foundation, *Science and Engineering Indicators 1996*, Washington, DC; European Union, *Le rapport européen sur les indicateurs scientifiques et technologiques 1994*, Brussels.

Table 7.5 *Patents granted in the USA in 1993 in selected countries and industries (averaged by population)*

Industry	*Computers*	*Radio/ TV*	*Industrial machines*	*Commun. technol.*	*Transp. equipm.*	*Aerospace*	*Chemical products*	*Drugs*
Country								
USA	10	2	10	27	3	2	17	14
Japan	14	4	6	36	4	2	13	8
Germany	2	0.6	5	6	3	1	10	7
France	2	0.5	3	7	0.8	0.8	4	5
UK	1	0.6	2	4	0.7	0.6	4	5
Canada	1	0.5	4	6	2	n	5	3

Sources: National Science Foundation, *Science and Engineering Indicators 1996*, Washington, DC; European Union, *Le rapport européen sur les indicateurs scientifiques et technologiques 1994*, Brussels.

147

International Patenting

The analysis of patenting activities reveals important patterns in the competitive advantages of nations and the dynamics of innovation (Pavitt and Patel 1990, Godin 1996). Three of those results deserve mention here (see Tables 7.4 and 7.5). Firstly, the volume of patents flows directly from the volume of R&D investments; therefore, countries differ considerably in terms of inventiveness. In fact, countries with larger R&D investments in a particular technology also lead the same technological field in the area of patenting. This is obviously the case for the United States in petrochemicals or Japan in computers and communication technology. Other, smaller countries have developed specific core competencies, as revealed by their patenting activity, for example Switzerland in pharmaceuticals and heavy electrical equipment.

Secondly, and national specificities notwithstanding, patent data show that industrial sectors tend to behave similarly, regardless of the country origin. Indeed, high-technology sectors and science-based industries in all countries show a high tendency to invest in R&D and to patent accordingly: pharmaceuticals, computers and communication technology, industrial instrumentation and industrial processes are well known cases of this type of industries. At the opposite, low-R&D sectors are those which request less patents, including most natural resources industries.

Finally, the role of large firms, mainly multinational corporations, is crucial in the inventive activity of all industrial countries. They still are the major players in the NSIs, as they are responsible for a majority of patents, despite increasing participation by small and medium-sized enterprises in patenting.

International Technological Alliances

In the 1980s, a massive movement of technological alliances began both in Western Europe and North America. Companies of all sizes, across the industrial spectrum, are now collaborating in research and development to create new and improved processes and products and to make compatible existing electronic equipment. These alliances are long-term (typically over at least six months and usually over several years) cooperative undertakings, sometimes including university research centres and public laboratories. Alliances are agreements that maintain the economic independence of the partners and are, thus, alternatives to outright mergers and acquisitions. Partners are most usually chosen on the basis of complementary technical assets. The reasons for alliances include accelerating innovation, solving complex technical and scientific problems, reducing risk and uncertainty often associated with complex R&D projects, searching for standards, coping with the reduced life cycles of products, organization learning, realizing economies of scale in R&D and responding to government incentives.

In both Western Europe and North America, public policy has incorporated an increasing number of programmes supporting inter-firm collaboration. These include the ESPRIT, BRITE, EURAM, EUREKA, JESSI and other collaborative programmes in Europe, and similar ones in North America. The goal of governments is to reduce the rate of increase in public expenditures for R&D, avoid duplication, enhance technology diffusion and increase the chances of getting results from collaboration instead of individual efforts by particular companies. Most governments support technological collaboration among national firms, but an increasing number of alliances has been registered between firms based in different countries. Effective global competition increasingly requires access to technological competencies which are not based within the same nation. Thus some tensions have developed between national policies and the internationalization of technological cooperation, tensions that appeared time and again when American (or Japanese) firms requested access to some European consortia or when European (and Japanese) corporations knocked at the door of publicly funded US consortia.

The pattern is similar in both continents. Local and national alliances most often have precompetitive goals: increasing basic knowledge in an area of mutual interest (Fusfeld 1987, Mowery 1992, Niosi 1995). International alliances are almost always directed towards the development of products and processes, that is, towards the downstream end of the R&D process. Typical of these international alliances are collaborations between large pharmaceutical corporations and small and medium-sized specialized biotechnology firms. Also, international technological collaboration has soared in all areas of electronics, and has increased in the production of transportation equipment.

North Atlantic collaboration includes today hundreds of alliances between Western European and North American firms. These alliances follow the lines of revealed national technological advantages. European pharmaceutical firms have developed alliances with North American biotechnology firms. Typical of these alliances, and one of the more publicized, is the Glaxo Plc alliance with Montreal's Biochem Pharma in order first to develop, then to manufacture and later to commercialize 3TC, a successful compound that slows the progression of AIDS in patients who are HIV-positive. North American telecommunication equipment firms have developed alliances with European producers in order to adapt their more advanced hardware and software for the EU market. The Northern Telecom/Matra alliance illustrates this pattern. Similarly, US computer firms have developed alliances with EU computer manufacturers. Conversely, more advanced European Union mass transportation equipment manufacturers have developed alliances with North American producers to adapt their high-speed trains to US and Canadian markets.

Some of these alliances have evolved into outright mergers and acquisitions. The 1982 NorTel partnership with STC Plc of Britain was transformed into NorTel's acquisition of the telecommunication assets of STC. Similarly, Swiss Roche acquired US biotechnology leader Genentech Corporation, after several years of successful alliances, and Institut Mérieux of France acquired Canada's biotechnology leader, Connaught Laboratories from Toronto. The technologically and/or financially stronger partners have tended to acquire the weaker allies. A few other North Atlantic collaborations dissolved due to different goals and the inability of some partners to keep up with the terms of the agreement. One much publicized case was the Olivetti/AT&T alliance in the area of personal computers.

Most international partnerships have taken place among industrial nations. North Atlantic alliances are prominent among them, but US/Japan alliances (and more generally North American partnerships with south-east Asian corporations) are also very important and growing. In 1985–89, for instance, there were not less than 586 US-EU alliances, and 307 US/Japan alliances (NSF 1993). Also, Canada/EU alliances outnumbered Canada/Japan alliances and even Canada/US alliances (Niosi 1995). Canadian-European alliances were most prominent in transportation and telecommunication equipment, but they also encompassed advanced materials and biotechnology.

Expatriate R&D

The internationalization of R&D has also grown very rapidly in the 1980s and 1990s. This trend reflects, and is explained by, the internationalization of manufacturing firms. North Atlantic cross-investments in R&D have been more frequent than North Atlantic/Japan FDI in R&D.

Within the North Atlantic, the US and Canada are more often the recipients of foreign investments in R&D. By 1993, the US was the host of hundreds of expatriate laboratories of European firms. These include British, German, French, Dutch and Swiss R&D facilities among the most active (see Table 7.6). In the United States, European corporations own dozens of R&D laboratories in drugs and biotechnology (British, German, Swiss and French), chemicals (mostly German, British and French), instrumentation and controls (British) and food industries (British).

Conversely, North American firms have increased their participation in Western European industrial research and development. Firms based in the US and Canada are among the most active in Britain, Switzerland, Germany and France. The UK is the second most important location for expatriate R&D of both Canada and the US. American corporations are active most noticeably in European automobile R&D (Ford and GM in Germany, Ford in the UK), computers (IBM in Switzerland, Hewlett Packard in the UK), petrochemicals and pharmaceuticals (see Table 7.7).

Table 7.6   *R&D expenditure and employment by affiliates of foreign companies in the US, 1993*

Country	Expenditure (US$ million)	Employment
Switzerland	2524	14700
Germany	2321	19200
UK	2295	20000
Canada	2190	10300
Japan	1781	11800
France	1204	9300
Netherlands	691	6300
All other countries	3802	13600
Total, all countries	14618	105200

Source: Dalton and Serapio, 1995.

Table 7.7   *US expenditure for R&D abroad, by country, 1993*

Country of destination	Expenditures (US$ million)
Germany	2568
UK	1639
Canada	1030
France	942
Japan	862
Ireland	669
Belgium	460
Netherlands	392
Spain	321
Singapore	312
Italy	304
Brazil	220
Australia	176
Switzerland	109
Mexico	76
Hong Kong	74
Sweden	48
Total all countries	10 954

Source: Dalton and Serapio, 1995.

Canadian corporations conduct R&D in Europe in telecommunications equipment, food and beverages, metallurgy, pulp and paper and transportation equipment. Conversely among Canadian corporations conducting R&D within the Canadian borders, some 10 per cent were foreign-owned. Most of these were US firms, like IBM Canada and Pratt & Whitney. However, some of the larger R&D performers in Canada included several large Western European electronic firms like Canadian Marconi (a subsidiary of Marconi Plc) and Ericsson Telecommunications, but also some pharmaceutical corporations based in Germany, Switzerland, France, Italy and Sweden.

The industrial distribution of North Atlantic expatriate R&D investments thus reflects national revealed technological advantages and market considerations. US firms have acquired or created R&D laboratories in Europe in order to design entirely new automobiles (in the UK and Germany) better adapted to the European market, but there are no equivalent European car technology centres in the US. Both Canadian and US firms have invested in the European electronics industries.

Also, large pharmaceutical and chemical Western European firms, together with cement and industrial machinery manufacturers, are investing in North American R&D. In order to better grasp the nature of national technological advantages, one needs to get more into the detailed nature of the industrial activities involved. US chemical firms in Europe are mostly petrochemical and petroleum refining corporations. Conversely, European chemical firms active in US are involved in pharmaceutical R&D and in finer chemical products such as coatings, thermoplastics, resins, dyes, and organic pigments.

Market motivations predominate in foreign R&D, both within European and North American firms: most companies buy or establish foreign labs in order to support local manufacturing in the host country, collaborate with local users and/or design products better adapted to host markets. Technology and knowledge-absorption factors come second. A few large European electronic firms are investing in North America in order to absorb new ideas from a more innovative environment. Similarly, a few transportation equipment and fine chemical North American firms acquire European R&D facilities in order to gain new technical knowledge.

CONCLUSION

North America and Western Europe show divergent patterns of innovation and industrial strengths. The United States shows technological advantages in software, biotechnology and pharmaceuticals, aerospace (including aircraft), telecommunications equipment and services, advanced materials, computers, semiconductors, basic petrochemicals and all areas of defence technology.

Canada is strong in telecommunications equipment, aircraft, software (an area not shown by patent statistics) and several traditional resource-based industries, such as forest products and metallurgy. In other areas, like biotechnology, Canada is strong mostly in basic and advanced research, as shown by the patent record, but this strength is not always translated into commercial products.

Western Europe is lagging in most areas of advanced technology, including semiconductors, computers, consumer electronics, advanced materials and software. Its strengths are in more traditional industries, including food, apparel, furniture, building materials, leather products and textiles. However, Western European corporations display technological advantages in specific high-technology industries, for example mobile telecommunications equipment (the Swedish Ericsson), nuclear reactors (the French Superphénix), machinery, including heavy electrical equipment (Siemens in Germany) pharmaceuticals and fine chemicals (mainly through several German, British and Swiss corporations) and mass transportation equipment (the French TGV). But these remain isolated cases. Europe's largest manufacturing industry, automobiles, is still lagging behind the Japanese and American competitors. And in the more dynamic electronic and other high-technology industries, Europe suffers from a large technology gap, trailing behind both North America and Japan (Stevens 1990).

International technology gaps offer major opportunities for international direct investment as well as technological collaboration between North American and Western European firms. Many large corporations and a few small and medium-sized firms have built a dense web of networks of FDI, R&D and technological alliances over the North Atlantic. We can only suggest that these networks will increase and develop in the years to come as transnational activities grow and assume new organizational forms.

REFERENCES

Arthur, W. Brian (1994), *Increasing Returns and Path Dependency in the Economy*, Ann Arbor: University of Michigan Press.

Cantwell, John (1992), 'The internationalization of technological activity and its implications for competitiveness', in Ove Granstrand *et al.* (eds), *Technology Management and International Business*, New York: Wiley, pp. 75–95.

Chakrabarti, A.K., S. Feinman and W. Fuentevilla (1982), 'The cross national patterns of industrial innovations', *Columbia Journal of World Business*, 17, 3, 33–9.

Dalton, Donald and M.J. Serapio (1995), *Globalizing Industrial R&D*, Washington, DC: Office of Technology Policy, US Department of Commerce.

Dunning, John (1992), 'MNEs and the globalization of innovatory capacity', in Ove Granstrand *et al.* (eds), *Technology Management and International Business*, New York: Wiley.

Fusfeld, Herbert (1987), *The Technical Enterprise*, Boston: Ballinger.

Godin, Benoit (1996), 'Research and the practice of publication in industry', *Research Policy*, 25, 587–606.

Kelly, Guillaume (1993), *Les avantages technologiques révélés du Canada*, Montreal, MBA Thesis, UQAM.

Lundvall, Bengt-A. (ed.) (1992), *National Systems of Innovation*, London: Pinter.

Mowery, David C. (1992), 'International collaborative ventures and the commercialization of new technologies', in N. Rosenberg *et al.* (eds), *Technology and the Wealth of Nations*, Stanford: Stanford University Press, pp. 345–80.

National Science Foundation (1993), *Science and Engineering Indicators*, Washington, DC.

Nelson, Richard R. (1993), *National Innovation Systems*, New York: Oxford University Press.

Niosi, Jorge (1995), *Flexible Innovation: Technological Alliances in Canadian Industry*, Montreal and Kingston: McGill-Queen's University Press.

Niosi, Jorge and B. Bellon (1994), 'The global interdependence of national innovation systems: evidence, limits and implications', *Technology in Society*, New York, 16 (2), 173–97.

Niosi, Jorge *et al.* (1993), 'National systems of innovation: In search of a workable concept', *Technology in Society*, 15 (2), 207–27.

Pavitt, Keith and P. Patel (1990), 'L'accumulation technologique en France: ce que les statistiques de brevets tendent à démontrer', *Revue d'économie industrielle*, 51, 10–32.

Pierre, Andrew J. (ed.) (1987), *A High Technology Gap? Europe America and Japan*, New York: Council on Foreign Relations.

Porter, Michael (1983), 'The technological dimension of competitive strategy', in R.S. Rosenbloom (ed.), *Research on Technological Innovation. Management and Policy*, vol. 1, Greenwich, CO: Jai Press, pp. 1–33.

Porter, Michael (1990), *The Competitive Advantage of Nations*, New York: Free Press.

Rosenberg, Nathan and R.R. Nelson (1994), 'American universities and technical advance in industry', *Research Policy*, 23, 323–48.

Spitz, Peter H. (1988), *Petrochemicals: The Rise of an Industry*, New York: Wiley.

Statistics Canada (annual), *Canadian Balance of International Payments*, Ottawa.

Stevens, Candice (1990), '1992: the European technology challenge', *Research Technology Management*, 33 (1), Jan.–Feb., 17–23.

US Department of Commerce (1994), 'Characteristics of foreign-owned US manufacturing establishments', *Survey of Current Business*, January.

World Intellectual Property Organization (WIPO) (1996), *World Intellectual Property Report*, Geneva.

8. Atlantic foreign direct investment flows

Peter J. Buckley and Jeremy Clegg

This chapter examines the empirical evidence on Atlantic Foreign Direct Investment (AFDI) flows against the background of the theory of foreign direct investment (FDI). It also examines the function of international alliances and joint ventures in AFDI. We first examine the theory of FDI and then pick out special issues relating to Atlantic FDI. (We confine ourselves to the North Atlantic, taking essentially flows between the European Union (EU) and the members of the North America Free Trade Area (NAFTA)). We then examine the empirical evidence and provide an extensive discussion which relates the evidence to the theoretical perspectives.

THE THEORY OF FOREIGN DIRECT INVESTMENT

Foreign direct investment is defined as the acquisition or creation of income-generating assets in a foreign country which entails the control of the organization or operation in which these assets are embodied (see Buckley 1990a for a collection of key works). The key issue of FDI is that of control, indeed, control is the defining characteristic which separates FDI from foreign portfolio investment, where ownership of part of the assets is transferred abroad (through a transfer of equity shares, for example) but without this conferring control. Control is not always easy to define. If a foreign company owns 51 per cent of the voting shares, then most would agree that it has control. However, if it owns 25 per cent or 10 per cent, with the rest of the share ownership widely dispersed, then it may retain control (Buckley and Roberts 1982). Similarly control may be exercised by control of technology, or of management, as by the supply of crucial inputs. Arbitrary definitions are used in order to avoid marginal cases.

The connection between FDI and foreign joint ventures is evident. Foreign firms may take a majority stake or a minority stake with a local firm and if this stake is substantial, they will be defined as foreign direct investments.

The connection with international strategic alliances is not so clear-cut. Alliances may be defined as 'inter-firm collaboration over a given economic space and time for the attainment of corporate goals' (following Buckley 1992). Such a definition specifies that alliances must be inter-firm but there is no implication that the input of resources to the alliance from the partners need be in any way equal, nor that the alliance partners share the same goals. The definition of the alliance over space can mean local, national, regional or global cooperation. Its time span will rarely be indefinite but could be in terms of a fixed period of time (e.g. five years) or until certain goals are reached (e.g. the development of a new product, manufacture of a certain amount of output, achievement of a given market share). Alliances are thus essentially temporary (or at least not indefinite) and their very flexibility is a major source of strength. It is clear from this description that we can regard alliances as the general case of collaboration between firms and joint ventures as a special case which exists when the alliance is cemented by an exchange of equity. Joint ventures are thus equity-based alliances. We thus arrive at a key, if self-evident, issue – FDI is carried out almost entirely by multinational firms[1] and it is to the multinational firm that we must turn for the key to explaining the theory of FDI.

The multinational enterprise is generally explained as a special case of the theory of the firm although it is rather better to see it as the general case and the purely national firm as a special sub-set. It is best explained by the theory of internalization (or transactions costs) which states that firms grow until the cost of organizing the marginal transaction within the firm is greater than that of using the market. Thus, firms exist because they are superior means of organizing a core set of transactions and markets bound this range (Buckley and Casson 1976, Buckley 1990b, 1988). To this we need to add a theory of location which is simply that firms attempt to minimize the cost of their production by seeking to locate activities so that overall costs are minimized. Consequently, the multinational firm may be viewed as an internally coordinated network where activities are located so as to reduce overall costs, linked by internalized flows of information and physical production (see Casson 1990). The incentive to internalize (and therefore to internationalize) depends on the interplay of industry-specific, firm-specific, region-specific and nation-specific factors (Buckley and Casson 1976).

Within this framework, three key motives can be identified for FDI. The first is market-oriented FDI, where firms choose to invest in a market rather than use alternative forms of foreign market servicing such as export or licensing. The second is input-oriented FDI, where investment abroad is chosen as the best means of gaining access to key inputs (raw materials, management skills, R&D facilities and workers for example). The third is cost-oriented FDI where an investment abroad is chosen to reduce the overall cost of production. This will often be targeted on cheaper labour, but tax reduction could also be a reason. Glaister and Buckley (1996) found these key motives directly replicated in UK international strategic alliances.

In addition to the motives for FDI, its form is also important. Two key issues over the form of FDI are the ownership strategy and the choice between takeovers and greenfield entry. The ownership strategy (joint ventures or wholly owned subsidiaries) may boil down to the ability of the firm to secure all the necessary resources on its own versus the ability to recruit them only in partnership with others. The choice between greenfield entry or takeover may rest on the importance of packaged assets. Assets such as brand names, distribution networks. management teams and research facilities can often only be secured by takeover because these assets are embodied in firms and can only be accessed by purchasing the whole firm (although in certain cases they can also be accessed via alliances).

When we examine empirical data on FDI, it is important to look at the role which acquisition plays and also the role of reinvestment. In advanced host countries in particular these elements of total FDI are major components of the total.

SPECIAL ISSUES OF THEORY RELATING TO ATLANTIC FDI

Several key features of Atlantic FDI impinge on the application of theory to its empirics. First. the cultural similarity (of sections) of the flows are striking. These similarities in terms of language, colonial inheritance and culture reduce the transaction costs and make FDI easier because the investor faces lower costs of 'psychic distance' (Hallen and Wiedersheim-Paul 1979, Buckley and Ghauri 1993). This is true between the UK and Canada and the US, France and Quebec and Spain and Mexico. Two-way flows between these regions can be expected to be higher than in the presence of cultural barriers.

Second, AFDI flows take place between countries at similar, and high, levels of economic development. This has several potential consequences. First, we would expect there to be a high proportion of intraindustry FDI rather than inter-industry FDI. Second, it is likely that alliances will be an important mode of conducting international business. Glaister and Buckley (1994, 1996) have found that the motives for alliances are very similar to those of FDI. Third, the market size defined at national and regional (EU and NAFTA) level is large and this will encourage marketing seeking FDI in both directions. We should not, however, forget the differences between the two sides of the Atlantic and, in particular, difference in resource endowments, with Canada and the USA in particular being particularly resource-rich.

Third, AFDI takes place in an environment of increasing integration on both sides of the pond (Buckley, Pass and Prescott 1994, 1995a, 1995b, 1996;

Rugman 1994). The EU has taken enormous steps in creating the single European Market (SEM) amongst other integrationist actions and moves are well underway to accelerate the economic integration of the NAFTA members. This bi-focal integration has profound consequences for the economic structures of the two areas and will impact further on AFDI. For an analysis of the impact of the development of the European internal market on the incidence of joint ventures see Kay, Ramsay and Hennart (1996). This paper also suggests a growing preference for majority acquisition in the EU.

The long tradition of examining AFDI (from Dunning (1958) onwards) has frequently pointed to the importance of market structure relationships (following Hymer 1976). In particular it has been suggested that 'exchange of threat' or rivalry across the Atlantic has produced cross-investment to secure world market share (Knickerbocker 1973, Flowers 1975, Graham 1978, 1990). This is now seen more in the context of competitive games where strategic moves are predicated on the strategy of rivals. It may be argued that the closeness of market structures across the Atlantic fosters such strategies.

EMPIRICAL ANALYSIS

The data employed in this chapter are based on the FDI stock statistics of the USA and Canada. These are among the most accurate in the world. The decision was made early on to use information from the North American side in preference to the European side. The more variable level of accuracy in the different countries of Europe was a factor, as were the problems of consolidation and coherence, which escalate as the number of countries rises. Mexico produces no adequate stock figures, so the discussion of the transatlantic profile of this country is curtailed, and limited to an analysis of the available FDI flow statistics.

Canadian and US Outward FDI by European Host Country

There are two immediate contrasts between the outward FDI profile of Canada and the USA as presented in Table 8.1. The first concerns the share of Europe in the outward FDI of both countries: this share is considerably lower for Canada (21 per cent in 1995) compared with the USA (51 per cent). This observation can be explained by the pull of the US market on Canadian FDI. The second observation is that Canada has a higher percentage of FDI in the EU(12) relative to the percentage in all of Europe than the USA; however, the USA allocation to the EU(12) has been climbing faster. This acceleration in the attractiveness of the EU market relative to the rest of Europe is exactly what one would expect to follow from the SEM programme of the EU. The EU(12) share of Canadian FDI has risen since 1985 (roughly when the SEM programme

Table 8.1   Outward foreign direct investment stock of Canada and the USA into Europe, percentage distribution, 1985–95

	Canada			USA		
	1985	*1990*	*1995*	*1985*	*1990*	*1995*
Europe	**14.43**	**21.70**	**21.42**	**45.68**	**49.88**	**51.08**
EU	**13.21**	**20.10**	**19.46**	**36.44**	**41.92**	**42.19**
Belgium and Luxembourg	0.24	0.61	1.72	2.49	2.59	3.58
Denmark	0.08	0.05	0.02	0.56	0.40	0.32
France	0.34	1.91	1.35	3.32	4.45	4.59
Germany	1.12	0.96	1.66	7.28	6.41	6.04
Greece	0.50	0.10	0.07	0.09	0.07	0.06
Ireland	1.47	1.09	3.11	1.60	1.37	1.54
Italy	0.34	0.42	0.59	2.57	3.27	2.35
Netherlands	0.93	1.46	1.07	3.10	4.44	5.26
Portugal	0.01	0.13	0.05	0.10	0.21	0.24
Spain	0.49	0.59	0.13	0.99	1.83	1.36
UK	7.69	12.80	9.67	14.34	16.89	16.85
Other Europe	**1.22**	**1.61**	**1.96**	**9.24**	**7.96**	**8.90**
Austria	0.05	0.01	0.13	0.21	0.26	0.29
Norway	0.10	0.06	0.02	1.40	0.98	0.69
Sweden	0.02	0.03	0.04	0.41	0.42	1.72
Switzerland	1.02	1.38	0.97	6.85	5.83	5 11
Other	0.04	0.12	0.79	0.38	0.47	1.09
Rest of world	**85.57**	**78.30**	**78.58**	**54.32**	**50.12**	**48.92**
Total	**100.00**	**100.00**	**100.00**	**100.00**	**100.00**	**100.00**
Value in US$ m (current prices)	**41 916**	**78 387**	**103 706**	**230 250**	**430 521**	**711 621**

Source: Statistics Canada (1996) and United States Department of Commerce (various years).

was announced) from 13 per cent to around 20 per cent, while the EU's US share has risen from 36 to 42 per cent. To this extent. it does appear that Canada and the USA have increasingly favoured the EU over the rest of Europe, which is consistent with the hypothesis that market integration has behaved as an attractant to FDI.

The observation that the UK is by far the single largest recipient of both Canadian and US FDI throughout 1985–95 is unsurprising. The UK has set out its stall as a primary location for inward FDI into the EU, supported by grants, incentives and lower social overhead costs (the Social Chapter opt-out). It also benefits from the attraction of the English language, and in the case of Canada and the USA, from cultural affinities and similar systems of corporate governance However, while the UK share of US FDI has risen, its share of Canadian FDI has shown no clear trend, first increasing then falling. These developments apart, the primacy of the UK in the outward investment pattern in Europe of both Canada and the USA speaks not simply of political ties between Canada and the UK. It also testifies to cultural and economic links (based on a history of trade), cemented by FDI. Of the other leading European hosts the top 5 are identical between Canada and the USA with the exception of Ireland (number 2 for Canada), and the Netherlands (number 3 for the USA). The leading shared hosts are Germany, France and Belgium-Luxembourg, for which standard explanations of FDI based on market size and growth are tenable. The importance of Ireland for Canada seems likely to be a reflection of cultural affinity – Ireland's share has been disproportionately large over the ten-year period reviewed here. It also reflects Ireland's favourable tax regime as a base for serving EU markets.

The most remarkable thing about the countries of Europe outside the EU(12) is that they collectively add so little in terms of FDI share. The expansion of the EU to fifteen members would therefore not greatly increase the EU's share. Only Switzerland, which remains outside the EU, has a substantial share of US FDI, at just over 5 per cent in 1995.

Canadian FDI into the UK and EU by Industry

The precise geographical focus of the discussion of FDI patterns in Europe is dictated by the breakdown in the data. In the case of Canada, country by industry data are available only for the EU and the UK within Europe. However, as we know that the EU accounts for the preponderance of Canadian FDI in Europe, this is not too great a handicap. The definition of the EU shifts from EU(12) in 1985 and 1990 to EU(15) in 1995; however, from the data shown in Table 8.1, we know that this will not materially affect the discussion. The industrial analysis must rely on the industry categories given. Generally, these are adequate; however, the category 'Consumer goods and services' clearly mixes manufacturing and services, but probably refers mainly to those goods which are provided jointly with services.

Table 8.2 focuses on the Canadian outward industrial pattern of FDI in the EU, with some data on the World for comparison and to provide a benchmark as to the overall World pattern and trends. The movement away from manufacturing industry and towards services is a clear discernible trend, and this is reflected in the industrial countries of the EU, which have amongst the highest concentrations of manufacturing FDI. The UK in 1985 had a higher concentration of manufacturing FDI than the rest of the EU. However, the UK's percentage of manufacturing FDI fell from 77 per cent in 1985 to reach a low

Table 8.2   Outward foreign direct investment stock of Canada into the UK, other EU, and the world, percentage distribution, 1985–95

Industry group	UK			Other EU[a]			World		
	1985	1990	1995	1985	1990	1995	1985	1990	1995
Manufacturing	**77.24**	**43.62**	**52.19**	**75.52**	**65.21**	**61.46**	**59.03**	**50.84**	**48.99**
Food, beverages and tobacco	28.05	9.56	9.00	12.52	23.67	16.70	9.06	8.31	6.75
Wood and paper	13.03	5.29	2.16	5.89	8.94	7.12	3.68	3.84	3.35
Energy	8.23	7.39	11.69	12.55	3.31	1.14	14.22	7.70	8.54
Chemicals, chemical products and textiles	2.11	0.44	0.64	9.34	7.61	9.26	8.17	7.60	4.67
Metallic minerals and metal products	19.16	9.48	11.52	38.77	17.49	20.18	17.89	14.38	16.22
Machinery and equipment	2.82	2.43	1.04	-5.30	1.48	1.65	0.16	1.20	0.81
Transportation equipment	1.09	2.92	3.11	-0.10	0.16	3.66	1.13	2.32	2.72
Electrical and electronic products	2.75	6.11	13.02	1.85	2.55	1.76	4.71	5.48	5.93
Services	**22.76**	**56.36**	**47.82**	**19.28**	**32.43**	**34.40**	**40.97**	**49.16**	**51.01**
Construction and related activities	1.25	17.50	0.91	..	..	..	9.94	7.48	3.28
Transportation services	1.11	1.32	0.33	..	..	..	3.66	4.97	3.47
Communications	3.46	6.89	29.61	3.07	3.70	1.81	5.54	8.21	10.00
Finance and insurance	14.34	22.24	11.85	12.13	25.65	33.45	16.61	23.80	23.67
Accommodation, restaurants, recreation services and food retailing	0.77	3.90	0.94	4.08	3.08	-0.86	0.63	2.02	6.23
Consumer goods and services	1.50	0.35	1.11	..	..	..	4.09	1.50	3.44
Other[b]	0.32	4.15	3.07	..	..	..	0.51	1.18	0.92
Total	**100.00**	**99.98**	**100.01**	**94.80**	**97.65**	**95.86**	**100.00**	**100.00**	**100.00**
Value in US$ m (current prices)	**3 222**	**10033**	**10025**	**2101**	**5723**	**10307**	**41916**	**78387**	**103706**

Notes:

Figures may not sum precisely to 100 due to rounding and data suppression.

.. denotes data are not available.

[a] Other EU is defined as other EU(12) before 1995 and as other EU(15) in 1995.

[b] Other includes general services to business, government services, education, health and social services, and includes some suppressed data.

Source: Statistics Canada (1996).

in 1990 (of 44 per cent) rising again to 52 per cent in 1995. In the rest of the EU the trend has been consistently downwards, but the distribution proportion of manufacturing stands at 62 per cent in 1995 (i.e. greater than in the UK).

The shifting pattern from manufacturing to services is encapsulated by the UK, in particular by the impact of the liberalization of service industries. In 1985 Canadian FDI in the UK was dominated by the traditional food, beverages and tobacco sector, largely based on historical links with a tail of less important industries in the shape of metal manufactures (metallic mineral products), finance, and wood and paper. By 1995 communications services had become the leading industry, followed by electrical and electronic products. Both of these sectors are industries in which firm strategy has been a direct response to the liberalization in the UK of the telecommunications market, and of Canadian operators, particularly cable franchise firms (Bell Cable Media, Videotron) and equipment manufacturers (notably Nortel). As we will see again later, the UK has become a highly attractive market to inward FDI because of its leadership in liberalization in telecommunications within Europe.

The figures for the share of telecommunications FDI within the rest of the EU remain stagnant, and will continue to be so until liberalization makes material progress, scheduled for 1998 according to the EU timetable for the telecommunications industry. Within the rest of the EU, the finance and insurance industry is the leading industry for Canadian FDI, with a spectacular rate of growth (from 12 to 33 per cent over the period); but for the growth of telecoms specific to the UK, the trajectory of this industry's share would be the same in the UK. The growth and liberalization of financial markets largely accounts for this acceleration. The share of Canadian FDI in the energy industry in Europe has declined, while shares of food etc. and chemicals have more or less held up, again continuing existing well-established patterns.

US FDI into the EU and Selected European Countries by Industry

The industrial pattern of US FDI in Europe has a long and distinguished history in catalysing theory and innovative empirical work on international business and the multinational enterprise. Here we can see the vestiges of the historical cross-industry patterns observed in the manufacturing and extractive sectors, and at the same time similar underlying secular shifts to those that have characterized the Canadian FDI position in Europe.

The manufacturing sector was the basis for much of the innovatory work on the multinational enterprise in the last forty years. On the current pattern of US FDI in Europe, the theory of the multinational enterprise would have to be re-engineered to give prominence to service industries (Buckley, Pass and Prescott 1992). This rebalancing of FDI profiles is partly due to the relative decline of extractive industries, here characterized by the petroleum industry, which has declined from over 20 per cent in US FDI in Europe to just 7 per cent (see Table 8.3). These secular trends are not exclusive to US FDI in Europe, but they are more marked within Europe than elsewhere, because of the keenness of competition in the European market.

Table 8.3   Outward foreign direct investment stock of the USA into Europe and the world, percentage distribution, 1985–95

	Europe			World		
	1985	*1990*	*1995*	*1985*	*1990*	*1995*
Industry group						
Petroleum	**20.67**	**9.93**	**7.26**	**25.06**	**12.27**	**9.79**
Manufacturing	**43.14**	**39.60**	**36.06**	**41.13**	**39.53**	**36.20**
Food and kindred products	4.42	3.65	4.28	4.02	3.62	4.37
Chemicals and allied products	7.95	9.36	12.12	8.80	8.82	9.57
Primary and fabricated metals	1.79	2.29	1.64	2.18	2.44	1.83
Machinery, except electrical	11.70	9.11	5.05	8.25	7.17	4.71
Electric and electronic equipment	3.54	2.72	3.16	3.70	3.61	3.59
Transportation equipment	3.66	3.95	3.26	5.09	5.00	4.55
Other manufacturing	10.08	8.51	6.56	9.10	8.86	7.58
Services	**34.59**	**48.56**	**53.42**	**27.98**	**43.54**	**48.02**
Wholesale	11.20	12.02	10.05	9.90	10.15	10.03
Banking	5.96	4.25	3.96	6.28	4.80	4.28
Finance (except banking), insurance and real estate	15.02	28.24	34.24	9.77	25.47	29.80
Other services	2.41	4.05	5.17	2.03	3.12	3.91
Other industries	**1.60**	**1.91**	**3.26**	**5.83**	**4.66**	**6.00**
Total	**100.00**	**100.00**	**100.00**	**100.00**	**100.00**	**100.00**
Value in US$ m (current prices)	**105 171**	**214 739**	**363 527**	**230 250**	**430 521**	**711 621**

Source: United States Department of Commerce (various years).

The single biggest development is the supplanting of the dominance of the manufacturing sector by the services sector. US FDI in Europe has shifted from 35 per cent in services in 1985 to over 50 per cent in 1995. The leading service industry is clearly finance. The other leading industries are wholesale distribution and the familiar manufacturing industries of chemicals (which includes pharmaceuticals) and non-electrical machinery.

The calculation of a definitive aggregate FDI position for the EU alone is made difficult by the changing membership of the EU and data suppression. Therefore the discussion will concentrate on the four leading EU hosts which collectively dominate inward US FDI, plus Switzerland – the prime non-EU host within Europe. Table 8.4 traces the industrial patterns in these five countries that account for the lion's share of US FDI in Europe. Within the UK and Switzerland,

Table 8.4 Outward foreign direct investment stock of the USA into the UK, France, Germany, the Netherlands and Switzerland, percentage distribution, 1985–95

Industry group	UK 1985	UK 1990	UK 1995	France 1985	France 1990	France 1995	Germany 1985	Germany 1990	Germany 1995	Netherlands 1985	Netherlands 1990	Netherlands 1995	Switzerland 1985	Switzerland 1990	Switzerland 1995
Petroleum	**28.03**	**14.23**	**11.70**	**..**	**..**	**3.56**	**15.48**	**..**	**5.16**	**25.81**	**7.47**	**5.21**	**..**	**2.48**	**2.86**
Manufacturing	**38.64**	**31.91**	**23.23**	**64.74**	**60.31**	**50.71**	**63.93**	**58.46**	**55.05**	**49.03**	**34.24**	**27.93**	**7.15**	**5.34**	**10.57**
Food and kindred products	5.44	3.77	2.75	4.59	1.82	9.27	3.63	3.89	5.00	8.77	4.27	3.71	..	..	..
Chemicals and allied products	6.60	5.39	4.95	10.39	16 21	18.54	6.75	10.29	11.14	16.26	14.78	10.96	1.45	0.59	2.34
Primary and fabricated metals	1.60	2.21	1.50	1.90	2.64	1.99	3.77	4.75	3.70	3.38	2.77	1.67	..	0.34	0.47
Machinery, except electrical	8.05	6.40	4.74	25.40	19.05	7.13	19.61	13.20	10.43	8.89	5.76	3.28	0.49	0.83	1.09
Electric and electronic equipment	2.53	2.41	2.70	3.96	2.26	1.87	5.39	3.46	3.83	1.80	3.31	2.32	0.70	0.65	1.19
Transportation equipment	1.94	3.16	1.38	6.25	3.20	2.72	..	13.11	13.22	0.50	0.32	0.32	0.00	0.02	..
Other manufacturing	12.47	8.57	5.20	12.27	15.12	9.19	..	9.75	7.72	9.43	3.04	5.66	3.75	..	2.35
Services	**31.98**	**51.79**	**60.69**	**25.70**	**32.02**	**42.64**	**18.07**	**30.79**	**34.76**	**21.59**	**56.92**	**63.09**	**77.17**	**91.90**	**86.14**
Wholesale	4.37	5.36	5.53	15.71	17.22	13.50	3.78	8.09	7.73	9.31	8.40	11.90	29.12	30.78	25.61
Banking	5.68	3.89	4.33	4.79	1.54	1.11	7.95	5.72	5.41	1.78	0.73	0.37	8.16	5.62	6.20
Finance (except banking), insurance and real estate	19.75	38.47	46.03	2.97	9.34	20.85	6.08	13.73	19.40	2.47	39.01	48.04	36.41	52.68	50.36
Other services	2.18	4.06	4.81	2.22	3.92	7.12	0.27	3.25	2.22	8.02	8.78	2.78	3.48	2.83	3.96
Other industries	**1.36**	**2.08**	**4.37**	**2.00**	**..**	**3.09**	**2.52**	**..**	**5.03**	**3.56**	**1.37**	**3.77**	**..**	**0.27**	**0.42**
Total	**100.00**	**100.00**	**100.00**	**100.01**	**100.00**	**100.00**	**100.00**	**100.00**	**100.00**	**99.99**	**100.01**	**100.00**	**100.00**	**100.00**	**100.00**
Value in US$ m (current prices)	**33024**	**72707**	**119938**	**7643**	**19164**	**32645**	**16764**	**27609**	**43001**	**7129**	**19120**	**37421**	**15766**	**25099**	**36342**

Notes:
Figures may not sum precisely to 100 due to rounding.
.. denotes data are not available.

Source: United States Department of Commerce (various years).

finance has been the first-ranking industry since 1985, but the share has mushroomed in the UK (from just under 20 per cent to 46 per cent in 1995) and peaked at 53 per cent in Switzerland in 1990. In France, Germany and the Netherlands the share of finance has increased from single-digit levels to 20 per cent, and to almost 50 per cent in the Netherlands. This globalization of US FDI in finance is a worldwide phenomenon, but the growth has spread from the existing financial centres to elsewhere in Europe.

The chemicals industry is a strong attractant to US FDI, particularly in continental Europe (unfortunately, data are suppressed for Switzerland). The distribution of US FDI in this industry. which includes the pharmaceutical sector, has risen most in France, and slightly in Germany. The importance of US FDI in the old staple transportation equipment industry has stagnated in the UK (at a low share of around 2–3 per cent) to be supplemented by Japanese and Korean inward FDI, and in Germany (at around 13 per cent), and declined in France to just 3 per cent. The machinery and electrical industries equally have a very low prominence in what would have been their natural domain since the 1950s. Switzerland, which stands outside the EU, has the most static profile of the selected European hosts, with the US inward FDI structure loaded towards the services. Apart from finance, banking and the wholesale trade are the leading industries, and there appears to be little pressure for this pattern to change.

The impact of European market integration is difficult to discern in the industry pattern of US FDI in Europe, probably because US MNEs have taken a pan-European strategic perspective for a considerable time before the advent of the SEM (Clegg 1996). Unlike other countries investing in Europe, US MNEs had already adjusted to serving the European market on a regional basis.

European Foreign Direct Investment into North America

The countries of Europe play a proportionately greater role in the inward FDI of the USA than they do in Canada. This is again quite simply because of the importance of intra-North American FDI, into Canada from the USA. By 1995, 24 per cent of Canadian FDI was of European origin while for the USA the figure was 64 per cent (Table 8.5). Over the period 1985 to 1995 there was no clear trend in these shares, although they temporarily dipped in 1990 in the USA and peaked in Canada. This result may have been brought about by the impact of European integration and North American economic integration, and a preference for European investors to locate in the USA compared with Canada.

To a large extent the inward profiles mirror the outward pattern of North American FDI to Europe. The leading foreign investing nations in both Canada and the USA are the usual group of European countries: the UK, which is in both

Table 8.5   Inward foreign direct investment stock of Canada and the USA from Europe, percentage distribution, 1985–95

	Canada			USA		
	1985	*1990*	*1995*	*1985*	*1990*	*1995*
Europe	**19.55**	**27.65**	**24.02**	**65.77**	**62.63**	**64.41**
EU	**17.08**	**23.91**	**20.53**	**57.86**	**55.93**	**55.23**
Belgium and Luxembourg	0.41	0.51	1.64	1.43	1.54	1.48
Denmark	0.04	0.01	0.11	0.31	0.21	0.54
France	1.68	2.92	3.15	3.61	4.72	6.83
Germany	2.89	3.87	2.96	8.03	7.15	8.55
Greece	0.01	0.01	0.02	..	..	..
Ireland	0.21	0.06	0.12	..	0.34	1.28
Italy	0.04	0.24	0.15	0.67	0.39	0.40
Netherlands	2.21	2.41	2.56	20.07	16.38	12.08
Portugal	..	..	..	..	0.00	..
Spain	0.02	0.03	0.02	0.15	0.20	0.46
United Kingdom	9.57	13.85	9.80	23.59	24.99	23.62
Other Europe	**2.48**	**3.74**	**3.49**	**7.90**	**6.70**	**9.18**
Austria	0.06	0.19	0.05	0.07	0.16	0.29
Norway	0.05	0.46	0.32	0.21	0.20	0.34
Sweden	0.42	0.48	0.65	1.28	1.39	2.10
Switzerland	1.71	2.20	2.03	5.72	4.48	5.90
Rest of world	**80.45**	**72.35**	**75.98**	**34.23**	**37.37**	**35.59**
Total	**100.00**	**100.00**	**100.00**	**100.00**	**100.00**	**100.00**
Value in US$ m (current prices)	**66187**	**112385**	**122452**	**184615**	**394911**	**560088**

Notes:
Figures may not sum precisely to 100 due to rounding.
.. denotes data are not available.

Source: Statistics Canada (1996) and United States Department of Commerce (various years).

cases in premier position throughout, followed by France, Germany, the Netherlands and Switzerland, in a variety of rankings. The UK accounts for almost a quarter of US total inward FDI, and just under 10 per cent in Canada. France has risen from fourth place in Canada to second, but remained at fourth in the USA, which may reflect increased FDI bolstered on cultural and linguistic ties in Canada. Switzerland remains throughout the fifth most important investor in North America, and the only leading investor of non-EU origin from Europe. The questions that these aggregate positions raise can only satisfactorily be addressed at by inspecting the industrial profile for strengths and weaknesses (see Tables 8.6, 8.7 and 8.8).

Table 8.6 Inward foreign direct investment stock of Canada from the UK, other EU, and the world, percentage distribution, 1985–95

Industry group	UK			Other EU^a			World		
	1985	1990	1995	1985	1990	1995	1985	1990	1995
Manufacturing	**47.77**	**56.53**	**50.94**	**57.28**	**55.99**	**61.04**	**69.54**	**66.62**	**64.86**
Food, beverages and tobacco	14.07	17.16	20.70	0.77	0.08	12.43	6.63	7.03	9.49
Wood and paper	4.15	1.26	1.51	3.56	0.67	1.20	3.94	5.81	4.70
Energy	16.56	17.18	11.37	30.12	18.82	13.09	23.67	16.42	11.68
Chemicals, chemical products and textiles	5.02	9.11	8.68	4.92	16.73	15.11	8.97	10.36	10.90
Metallic minerals and metal products	2.34	5.58	2.80	4.40	7.34	6.33	4.80	7.44	6.07
Machinery and equipment	1.09	1.39	2.16	2.41	2.88	2.76	4.18	3.98	4.20
Transportation equipment	3.00	3.10	2.03	8.31	6.00	4.68	10.93	10.02	10.72
Electrical and electronic products	1.55	1.74	1.69	2.80	3.47	5.44	6.42	5.56	7.10
Services	**52.24**	**43.46**	**49.06**	**42.74**	**44.03**	**38.96**	**30.46**	**33.38**	**35.14**
Construction and related activities	8.09	5.79	6.80	18.57	10.95	6.72	5.53	5.36	6.49
Transportation services and communications	0.65	1.73	1.27	0.44	0.95	0.57	1.30	2.47	3.02
Finance and insurance	34.91	29.56	33.79	20.17	28.48	24.25	15.46	18.87	18.04
Consumer goods and services	7.36	2.91	4.36	2.01	2.30	2.92	5.18	3.86	4.64
Other^b	1.24	3.06	2.84	1.55	1.36	4.50	2.99	2.83	2.95
Total	**100.01**	**99.99**	**100.00**	**100.01**	**100.02**	**100.01**	**100.00**	**100.00**	**100.00**
Value in US$ m (current prices)	**6331**	**15562**	**12004**	**4962**	**11314**	**14343**	**66187**	**112385**	**122452**

Notes:
Figures may not sum precisely to 100 due to rounding.
^a Other EU is defined as other EU(12) before 1995 and as other EU(15) in 1995.
^b Other includes general services to business, government services, education, health and social services, accommodation, restaurants and recreation services, and food retailing.

Source: Statistics Canada (1996).

167

Table 8.7 Inward foreign direct investment stock in the USA by Europe and the world, percentage distribution, 1985–95

	Europe			World		
	1985	*1990*	*1995*	*1985*	*1990*	*1995*
Industry group						
Mining	**1.01**	..	..	**2.19**	..	..
Petroleum	**21.11**	**13.86**	**7.44**	**15.31**	**10.86**	**6.36**
Manufacturing	**37.76**	**46.83**	**43.70**	**32.27**	**38.69**	**37.55**
Food and kindred products	8.36	8.05	4.86	5.80	5.71	4.65
Chemicals and allied products	13.67	15.97	19.01	10.20	11.58	13.66
Primary and fabricated metals	2.17	3.41	2.57	3.77	3.47	2.72
Machinery	5.20	7.85	7.01	5.00	7.00	6.54
Other manufacturing	8.35	11.55	10.26	7.50	10.93	9.97
Services	**36.96**	**34.10**	**42.96**	**44.80**	**45.48**	**51.17**
Wholesale trade	11.35	8.49	7.91	15.74	12.89	12.79
Retail trade	4.25	2.69	2.00	3.70	2.34	2.40
Banking	4.73	3.16	5.84	6.16	4.67	7.47
Finance, except banking	2.06	0.24	8.22	2.30	2.12	8.56
Insurance	7.23	8.38	10.19	6.39	6.87	8.44
Real estate	7.35	4.38	3.20	10.51	8.85	4.73
Other services	..	6.76	5.60	..	7.75	6.77
Other industries	**3.16**	**5.21**	**5.90**	**5.43**	**4.97**	**4.92**
Total	**100.00**	**100.00**	**100.00**	**100.00**	**100.00**	**100.00**
Value in US$ m						
(current prices)	**121413**	**247320**	**360762**	**184615**	**394911**	**560088**

Notes:
Figures may not sum precisely to 100 due to rounding.
.. denotes data are not available or not separately available

Source: United States Department of Commerce (various years).

The conclusions on the geographical pattern of aggregate FDI into North America are that the leading inward investing nations are also the leading hosts to North American FDI. To this extent the intensity of cross-FDI is greatest for an established group of countries, the UK, France, Germany, the Netherlands and Switzerland. This suggests the importance of long-lived and stable economic, cultural and even political ties.

The examination of transatlantic FDI would not be complete without the inclusion of the third North American OECD country, Mexico. Unfortunately, data on Mexican FDI abroad are not available in a form adequate to conduct a country, let alone a country by industry, analysis. The quality of Mexican inward FDI information is still fairly rudimentary, and relies on the reporting of foreign direct investment projects. The best stock estimate that is available is the culmination of reported FDI project inflows since 1971. These are the data

Table 8.8 Inward foreign direct investment stock in the USA by the UK, France, Germany, the Netherlands and Switzerland, percentage distribution, 1985–95

Industry group	UK			France			Germany			Netherlands			Switzerland		
	1985	1990	1995	1985	1990	1995	1985	1990	1995	1985	1990	1995	1985	1990	1995
Mining	0.55	..	..	..	..	..	1.65	0.51	–0.14	0.60	..	..	..	..	..
Petroleum	27.91	16.11	8.31	..	..	..	..	..	..	30.98	20.51	19.16	..	0.78	1.46
Manufacturing	26.83	42.93	43.01	85.71	69.91	55.23	40.60	55.67	51.09	36.03	38.25	31.75	65.11	60.26	43.50
Food and kindred products	6.32	8.86	7.59	5.22	5.72	5.48	0.21	0.45	–0.15	9.61	11.40	4.49	..	..	4.49
Chemicals and allied products	8.35	13.35	16.90	44.90	21.87	24.69	25.15	29.65	28.10	..	12.59	12.86	20.36	18.54	24.46
Primary and fabricated metals	1.76	1.70	2.53	9.43	..	2.91	1.42	4.21	3.16	4.85	2.24	0.81	..	..	2.27
Machinery	4.54	4.80	3.55	3.21	..	12.10	6.97	11.55	10.07	8.84	6.08	6.26	6.64	16.53	5.10
Other manufacturing	5.88	14.22	12.45	22.95	19.84	10.06	6.85	9.80	9.91	..	5.93	7.34	11.73	9.30	..
Services	41.55	32.23	36.66	5.50	10.11	41.25	55.55	41.75	38.25	29.51	37.87	46.24	30.97	37.89	54.45
Wholesale trade	9.28	5.25	4.16	6.61	6.57	3.23	29.83	22.60	15.65	5.82	7.23	8.38	6.57	4.63	3.75
Retail trade	6.45	2.46	1.75	2.08	1.07	0.92	5.44	4.68	3.00	3.08	2.69	1.32	0.72	1.24	0.60
Banking	5.79	1.53	4.51	7.02	6.56	6.53	1.48	2.75	4.66	4.22	3.69	6.61	0.87	0.34	2.92
Finance, except banking	0.82	2.69	7.01	–12.25	–16.92	10.05	..	–4.42	..	5.31	1.60	3.55	6.48	6.85	25.03
Insurance	8.28	9.07	9.95	1.42	1.31	7.79	11.38	10.27	11.52	5.11	6.18	11.93	12.10	20.50	15.98
Real estate	10.94	3.64	3.21	0.61	0.96	0.18	7.42	4.64	2.64	5.97	7.62	7.31	4.23	1.14	0.25
Other services	..	7.58	6.06	..	10.56	12.55	..	1.23	0.78	..	8.85	7.13	..	3.19	5.91
Other industries	3.15	8.72	12.01	5.95	..	..	3.11	2.07	..	2.88	3.36	2.85	3.25	1.06	0.60
Total	100.00	100.00	100.00	97.17	80.02	96.48	100.91	100.00	89.20	100.00	100.00	100.00	99.33	100.00	100.00
Value in US$ m (current prices)	43 555	98 676	132 273	6670	18 650	38 240	14 816	28 232	47 907	37 056	64 671	67 654	10 568	17 674	33 070

Notes:

Figures may not sum precisely to 100 due to rounding.

.. denotes data are not available or not separately available.

Source: United States Department of Commerce (various years).

169

routinely used and published by the Dirección General de Inversion Extranjera of the Secretaria de Comercio y Fomento Industrial (SECOFI) in order to assess inward investment.

Foreign direct investment into Mexico is naturally dominated by the USA (with a cumulated share of around 60 per cent), with Canada accounting for around 2.5 per cent. Table 8.9 shows that the leading countries of Europe contribute over 20 per cent of Mexico's inward FDI. The leading share is that of the UK (7 per cent), but close behind are Germany (5 per cent), Switzerland (4 per cent), and France (3 per cent). The source country detail provided is not exhaustive of the countries of the EU or Europe. The shares of other source countries are extremely small. Some data on annual flows by source country (not reported here) show that the omitted countries often have near zero flows to Mexico. The importance of cultural and linguistic ties between Mexico and Spain is supported by the share of Spanish FDI into Mexico, which approached 2 per cent in 1995. This can be compared with the Spanish share of FDI into Mexico's North American neighbours, standing at less than 0.5 per cent in the USA and just 0.02 per cent in Canada in 1995.

Table 8.9 Inward foreign direct investment stock of Mexico for available European countries, value and percentage distribution, 1995*

	Value in US$ m (current prices)	Percentage
Europe	**13005**	**24.89**
EU	**10741**	**20.55**
France	1662	3.18
Germany	2687	5.14
Italy	81	0.16
Netherlands	1597	3.06
Spain	994	1.90
United Kingdom	3720	7.12
Other Europe	**2264**	**4.33**
Sweden	385	0.74
Switzerland	1879	3.60
Rest of world	**36989**	**70.78**
Total	**52257**	**100.00**

Notes:
* The stock estimate of FDI is the culmination of annual inflows since 1971.
Figures may not sum precisely to 100 due to rounding.

Source: SECOFI (1996).

European Foreign Direct Investment into Canada by Industry

From an overview of the FDI shares in Canada by industry, there is some evidence that European investors capitalize on their marketing and organizational, and perhaps financial, advantages, to compete in Canada. The share of other EU FDI into Canada in the food, beverage and tobacco industry has been expanding rapidly between 1985 and 1995 (from 0.77 per cent to 12 per cent), and the UK's share in this traditional industry has also increased, from some 14 to 21 per cent. This growth stands out in comparison to the more sedate increase in inward FDI in the industry from the world as a whole. The leading share position of European inward investment in finance and insurance into Canada confirms the global importance of this industry, reflected in the intensity of transatlantic cross-FDI.

The UK's FDI is heavily weighted towards finance and insurance, but other important industries are very much in common with other countries of the EU: chemicals, construction, and energy (though in relative decline in terms of share).

European Foreign Direct Investment into the USA by Industry

Since 1985 the importance of the petroleum industry's share in European FDI into the USA in 1985 has plummeted from 21 per cent to 7 per cent, very much in line with trends observed before (Table 8.7). The other extractive industry for which there are some data, mining, is deleted as a separate item by 1990, from which it can be inferred that this industry becomes so minor as to cease warranting its own category. The counterpart of these changes is again the growth of the service sector. In the case of US inward FDI, finance and insurance are separately identified, totalling an 18 per cent share. Otherwise the leading industries remain in the manufacturing sector. The chemicals industry in particular accounts for high shares, suggesting European industrial competitive strength and the attractiveness of the US market in these industries.

The importance of market-seeking strategies in the US market are evident also in the industry structure of European countries' FDI (see Table 8.8). The importance of European FDI in the wholesale trade is a case in point. It is a prominent industry for each of the selected European source countries. All the selected European hosts show a high share of their FDI in the USA as being in the chemicals industry, which includes pharmaceuticals. Prominent here is Switzerland, with its domestic industrial strength in this industry, and France. France had a 45 per cent share of its activity in this industry in 1985, slipping to 25 per cent by 1995, but still ranking in first place. The general nature of this distribution suggests that the US, or North American market, is increasingly attractive as a production base.

Apart from the general secular trends, European FDI in the USA does exhibit some source-country-specific patterns. UK foreign investment in real estate, which peaked in the mid-1980s at the time of the low exchange value of the dollar to sterling, has subsequently fallen. The two European countries with the strongest bases in finance, the UK and Switzerland, have made the greatest inroads into the USA. The UK's share rose from less than 1 per cent in 1985 to 7 per cent in 1995, and the Swiss share from 6 per cent to 25 per cent. The negative FDI position of France in this industry in 1985 and 1990 clearly is a reflection of French affiliates in the finance industry expanding their lending to their parent firms in France. Although counterintuitive as an indicator of foreign activity, negative FDI positions actually signify the use of highly integrated financial practices.

CONCLUSIONS ON THE REVIEW OF THE DATA

The geographical pattern of Canadian and US FDI into Europe is dominated by the EU, and in particular by the UK. The increase in the EU's share of North American FDI is consistent with the hypothesized impact of the SEM on North American firms' business strategies to build up their investment in the EU. Cultural affinities seem to dominate over political affinities in explaining the especially high US FDI in the UK and the significant Canadian FDI in Ireland.

The Canadian industrial pattern in the UK and the rest of the EU centres around the replacement (or overlaying in the case of Europe) of the traditional industrial profiles based on low-technology manufacturing industry. In the EU this has been dominated by finance and insurance, and in the UK by telecommunications FDI and by high-technology supplier activities in the form of electrical and electronic industries. The leading cause of these changes has been the liberalization of the telecommunications market in the UK, and the liberalization of financial markets within the EU. These policy initiatives have largely changed the complexion of Canadian FDI, and have brought forth a dynamism in Canadian FDI that was lacking in the old pattern.

From an overview of the industry pattern of North American FDI in Europe it appears that liberalization in finance, and the globalization of markets, has driven the upsurge in US FDI in Europe in this industry. The traditional manufacturing industries, such as automobiles, machinery and electrical. are now very minor elements in US FDI in the EU, and have been supplanted principally by the service sector, especially finance. and by the prominence of the chemicals industry group. Most of the adjustments in industrial structure in US FDI in Europe have been the outcome of secular trends rather than the impact of market integration *per se*, as US MNEs have adjusted to a pan-European strategy over a long period.

European FDI into North America is characterized by growth, particularly as a result of market liberalization in finance and telecommunications (especially in the UK). This has altered the industry balance, but preserved the overall identity of the established partner countries – the UK, France. Germany, the Netherlands and Switzerland – reflecting national industrial specialization. The growth of services in general has reinforced the tendency for established cross-investors to invest most heavily in markets abroad most similar in terms of economic structure to their own, i.e., to bolster the cross-intensity of transatlantic FDI. The cultural affinity thesis with Canada appears to be borne out best in European strengths in the traditional sectors in North America, for example, in the food. drink and tobacco industry group.

While the growth of the service sector has accompanied and has been part of the intensification of transatlantic FDI, nevertheless, US inward FDI from Europe in key manufacturing industries remains relatively strong. Market-seeking FDI characterizes all European involvement in the USA. i.e., production for the US or North American market. North American integration appears to have reinforced these tendencies, for example, in the chemicals group. The strong and growing attractiveness of the US market for FDI in this group certainly signifies market-seeking FDI, probably allied to the need to locate pharmaceuticals production in North America. It is likely that North American market size and integration have combined to shift market servicing strategies increasingly towards direct local production. (See also the analysis by Dunning (1993) examining the period 1950 to 1990).

CONCLUSION

It is frequently said that there is nothing so practical as a good theory. In this case theory tells us where to look for the salient features of transatlantic FDI and does not fail in highlighting the key regularities.

First, there is a clear influence from cultural similarities. Even within the integrating units (EU and NAFTA), the UK (and Ireland) are picked out by Canadian and US investors and Spanish FDI goes disproportionately to Mexico. Language is a good proxy for cultural affinity but does not tell the whole story.

Second, the impact of integration is felt on the direction of AFDI flows. The preference of European AFDI for the US over Canada and that for the UK over the rest of the EU for US and Canadian AFDI is increased by integration. Multinationals no longer need manufacturing outputs in markets fragmented by tariffs. They can centralize their market-wide activities to gain economies of scale and supplement these units by warehousing and distribution investments throughout the unifying market.

Third, cross-investment by country and industry is intense as we would expect between countries of similar income levels. This reflects both 'exchange of threat' strategies and also the underlying determinants of FDI (notably its use, as the key strategic weapon of market access, of its relationship to advertising and R&D-intensive activity (Buckley and Casson 1976, Buckley and Dunning 1976), and therefore to differentiated product industries).

Fourth, in terms of industry breakdown, AFDI in both directions has shown a marked shift from manufacturing to services and a decline in the proportion of extractive industries in the total. The key story concerns the rise of financial services in AFDI, but there is also a strong upward trend in wholesale activity, which marks a shift to centralized production plus satellite distribution in markets becoming larger as integration proceeds.

Extensions of this research could take the form of an analysis of the breakdown of AFDI by merger and acquisition (M&A) versus greenfield investments. At present, the classification of the data does not allow a country by industry analysis of M&A activity.

APPENDIX

Definition of Foreign Direct Investment

A foreign direct investment (FDI) exists when a business enterprise (or a natural person) has a lasting interest in and a degree of influence over the management of a business enterprise in another country. The normal criterion for a foreign investment to be deemed a foreign direct investment is the ownership or control of 10 per cent or more of an enterprise's voting securities. If this condition is met, the enterprise can be designated as a foreign affiliate. Any foreign investment not meeting this condition is considered to be a portfolio foreign investment. The USA adopted this definition of FDI in the International Investment and Trade in Services Act. The Canadian definition of FDI also sets ownership at 10 per cent of equity. The OECD also considers the Mexican definition of FDI to comply with the definition of FDI set out in the Fifth Edition of the *IMF Balance of Payments Manual* and the OECD *Detailed Benchmark Definition*. The value of FDI in the foreign affiliate attributed to the parent enterprise is then arrived at through the normal process of the consolidation of accounts. For an account of the pitfalls in using FDI data (in the UK case) see Buckley and Pearce 1991.

Reference

OECD (1995), *International Direct Investment Statistics Yearbook*, Paris: OECD.

Statistical Sources

Canada

Statistics Canada, Balance of Payments Division (1996), *Canada's International Investment Position, 1995*, Ottawa: Minister of Industry Canada.

Mexico

Secretaria de Comercio y Fomento Industrial (SECOFI) (1996), *Evolucion de la Inversion Extranjera en Mexico. Enero de 1995*, SECOFI.

USA

United States Department of Commerce, Bureau of Economic Analysis, International Investment Division, data provided in electronic form for various years.

NOTES

The authors are grateful for comments from John Dunning, Gavin Boyd, Alan Rugman and the HEC Montreal Conference participants.
1.   FDI by natural persons is a very minor item in statistical terms.

REFERENCES

Buckley, Peter J. (1988), 'The limits of explanation: testing the internalisation theory of the multinational enterprise', *Journal of International Business Studies*, xix (2), Summer, 181–93.

Buckley, Peter J. (ed.) (1990a), *International Investment*, Cheltenham: Edward Elgar.

Buckley, Peter J. (1990b), 'Problems and developments in the core theory of international business', *Journal of International Business Studies*, 21 (4), 155–71.

Buckley, Peter J. (1992), 'Alliances, technology and markets: a cautionary tale' in Peter J. Buckley, *Studies in International Business*, London: Macmillan.

Buckley, Peter J. and Mark Casson (1976), *The Future of the Multinational Enterprise*, London: Macmillan.

Buckley, Peter J. and John H. Dunning (1976), 'The industrial structure of US investment in the UK', *Journal of International Business Studies*, 7 (2), Fall, 5–13.

Buckley, Peter J. and Pervez N. Ghauri (eds) (1993), *The Internationalisation of the Firm*, London: Dryden Press.

Buckley, Peter J. and Robert D. Pearce (1991), *The International Aspects of UK Economic Statistics*, London: Chapman and Hall.

Buckley, Peter J. and Brian R. Roberts (1982), *European Direct Investment in the USA before World War I*, London: Macmillan.

Buckley Peter J., C.L. Pass and Kate Prescott (1992), 'The internationalisation of service firms: a comparison with the manufacturing sector', *International Business Review*, 1 (1), 39–56.

Buckley. Peter J., C.L. Pass and Kate Prescott (1994), 'Economic integration: the Single European Market and the NAFTA and their Implications for Canada-UK Bilateral Trade and Investment', *British Journal of Canadian Studies*, 9 (2), 375–400.

Buckley. Peter J, C.L. Pass and Kate Prescott (1995a), 'The Single European Market initiative – a perspective from Canadian companies', *British Journal of Canadian Studies*, 10 (1), 77–86.

Buckley, Peter J., C.L. Pass and Kate Prescott (1995b), *Canada-UK Bilateral Trade and Investment Relations*, London: Macmillan.

Buckley, Peter J., C.L. Pass and Kate Prescott (1996), *Canadian-European Union Strategic Alliances*, report for Canadian High Commission in London.

Casson, Mark (ed.) (1990), *Multinational Enterprises*, Cheltenham: Edward Elgar.

Clegg, J. (1996), 'United States foreign direct investment in the European Community: the effects of market integration in perspective', in F.N. Burton, M. Yamin and S. Young (eds), *International Business and Europe in Transition*, London: Macmillan, pp. 189–206.

Dunning, John H. (1958), *American Investment in British Manufacturing Industry*, London: George Allen and Unwin.

Dunning, John H. (1993), 'Transatlantic foreign direct investment and the European Economic Community', in *The Globalization of Business*, London: Routledge, pp. 166–89.

Flowers, E.B. (1975), 'Oligopolistic reactions in European and Canadian direct investments in the United States', *Journal of International Business Studies*, 7, 43–55.

Glaister, Keith and Peter J. Buckley (1994), 'UK international joint ventures: an analysis of patterns of activity and distribution', *British Journal of Management*, 5 (1), 33–51.

Glaister, Keith and Peter J. Buckley (1996), 'Strategic motives for UK international alliance formation', *Journal of Management Studies*, 33 (3), 233–45.

Graham, E.M. (1978), 'Transatlantic investment by multinational firms: a rivalistic phenomenon?', *Journal of Post Keynesian Economics*, 1, 82–99.

Graham, E.M. (1990), 'Exchange of threat between multinational firms as an infinitely repeated non-cooperative game', *The International Trade Journal*, 4, 259–77.

Hallen, L. and F. Wiedersheim-Paul (1979), 'Psychic distance and buyer-seller interaction', *Organisasjon, Marknod och Samhalle*, 16 (5) 308–24. Reprinted in Buckley and Ghauri (1993).

Hymer, Stephen H. (1976), *The International Operations of National Firms*, Cambridge, MA: MIT Press.

Kay, Neil M., Harvie Ramsay and Jean-François Hennart (1996), 'Industrial collaboration in the European internal market', *Journal of Common Market Studies*, 34, September, 465–75.

Knickerbocker, Frederick T. (1973), *Oligopolistic Reaction and Multinational Enterprise*, Cambridge, MA: Harvard University Press.

Rugman, Alan M. (ed.) (1994), *Foreign Investment and NAFTA*, University of South Carolina Press.

9. Atlantic strategic technology alliances

John Hagedoorn

Increased international competition and a further internationalization of corporate strategies of a wide range of companies are related to the growth of international strategic technology alliances (Duysters and Hagedoorn 1996). The broader context of these international alliances is found in the evolution of the world economy towards a system with increasing exports and imports of goods and services, internationalization of monetary and financial systems, growing flows of foreign direct investment and internationalization of technology flows. From the perspective of individual firms we can understand international strategic technology partnering as part of the spreading of their innovative capabilities over many countries. These internationalization strategies enable companies to capitalize on both market entry strategies and their internationalization of innovation and production. Internationalization enables these companies to use a large number of local sources through outsourcing part of their vertically integrated related activities to local suppliers and also to engage in market entry agreements. For technology and research-related activities internationalization allows these companies to tap into local scientific and technological sources either through internalization and equity investment or through contractual agreements.

In this chapter I shall analyse a number of trends and patterns in international strategic technology alliances, with a particular focus on Atlantic alliances, i.e. those between European and NAFTA companies. For Europe or the European Union (EU) I have taken the twelve member-states that until recently constituted the European Community plus the three new member-states (Austria, Finland and Sweden). It is important to note that my contribution focuses on international strategic technology alliances, which I define as those cross-border modes of inter-firm cooperation for which a combined innovative technological activity or an exchange of technology is at least part of an agreement. In other words, I shall only look at a particular set of alliances and disregard forms of cooperation that only deal with the sharing of manufacturing capacity or joint marketing agreements. The period studied in the empirical part of this chapter covers the most recent years in which these alliances have been formed, starting in 1980 and ending in 1994. The data is derived from the MERIT-CATI data bank (see the Appendix).

In the next section I shall discuss the competitive and technological imperatives that, according to the literature, play an important role in explaining why companies enter into alliances. This is followed by a discussion of organizational aspects of alliances and the sectoral differences found in recent research. Based on this outline of the broader picture of partnering behaviour of international companies, the next section gives the reader some empirical insight as to the trends in international strategic technology partnering since 1980, the different roles that a number of incentives play, the changes in the organization of alliances, and the roles that different industrial sectors play in this context. For each of these topics I shall not only discuss the changes over time but also compare the findings regarding the EU-NAFTA alliances with the other international strategic technology alliances formed during the same period. The implications of the above for our understanding of international strategic technology alliances, and in particular our understanding of those alliances made between companies from the NAFTA countries and the European countries, will be discussed in the conclusions.

COMPETITIVE AND TECHNOLOGICAL IMPERATIVES IN INTERNATIONAL STRATEGIC TECHNOLOGY ALLIANCES

In Ohmae's (1985) well known and popular analysis of global competition it is stated that even the largest and most diversified and 'global' companies frequently still lack the economic power to successfully enter into their foreign markets for all their products and services. Companies can use international alliances to enter into these foreign markets in a joint effort with a local partner. This joint effort compensates for the lack of economic power, competence or foreign experience of at least one of the partners. In short, this kind of competitive pressure refers to strategic alliances as to their effort to create new markets, to provide non-domestic market entry and the search for international expansion of the product range of partnering companies (see Mowery 1988 for a large number of analyses for different markets and technologies). Apart from these concrete market-entry-related pressures to form alliances, strategic alliances can also be used as a scanning device to monitor the environment in which international companies operate and to search for possible new opportunities. In combination with new product development partnerships also allow companies to monitor new product markets without fully entering into these new markets and to rely on a quasi or partial diversification of their product folio. If these new opportunities materialize further, companies can still decide whether they will pursue these new opportunities through their alliance or on their own (see Obleros and MacDonald 1988).

Although in practice it is difficult to separate the competitive pressures from the technological imperatives, as these are so interrelated and they constitute the very essence of competition in many high-tech industries, we can conceptually set them aside as different aspects of the more general explanation of partnering strategies (Hagedoorn 1993). The group of technology-related factors referred to are particularly relevant for science based companies that cooperate for the further advancement of research and the diffusion of some applied scientific or technological knowledge among participating companies. These shared activities can be related to concrete research activities, and also to other factors that are associated with some general endeavour at the technological or scientific frontier of particular fields of technology. Other relevant pressures that play a role in the formation of strategic technology alliances are the increased complexity and inter-sectoral nature of new technologies and the cross-fertilization of scientific disciplines and fields of technology. Here it is the growing interrelationship between an increasing number of different scientific and technological disciplines that builds the necessity for close collaboration between companies. Despite successful diversification strategies that a large number of companies might have chosen, even many of these very large and diversified firms lack some competence in a number of scientific and technological fields. Partnerships with competent partners can create the necessary complementary technology and scientific inputs enabling these companies to capitalize on economies of scope through joint efforts. It is also important here to note the role of alliances as a scanning device, as it can enable companies to monitor the evolution of technologies in order to assess potential technological synergies and relevant complementarities of technologies (see Mowery 1988).

A number of more specific technological factors come closer to the concrete competitive pressures mentioned above as they are related to the need to reduce and share the uncertainty which is inherent to performing R&D as well as to sharing of costs of R&D (see Mowery 1988 and Link and Bauer 1989). With increasing competition companies are also forging alliances for concrete innovative projects to reduce the total period of products' life cycles and to jointly introduce new products and services. Increased competition, in particular at the international level, forces companies to preempt markets and to introduce innovations not only relatively simultaneously in different international markets but also to be the first to these markets (Ohmae 1985). Strategic partnerships can play a role in a joint effort to contract the period between invention and market introduction for a number of projects of each individual company.

DEGREES OF PARTNERING IN INTERNATIONAL STRATEGIC TECHNOLOGY ALLIANCES

It has to be stressed that international strategic partnering takes place in a variety of organizational modes that also have an impact on the degree of partnering between firms. In order to categorize these different forms of inter-firm cooperation a number of taxonomies have been introduced (see Auster 1992, Chesnais 1988, Harrigan 1985, Casson 1987, Contractor and Lorange 1988 and Hagedoorn 1990). Basically we can distinguish between a group of equity arrangements, such as international joint ventures and research corporations, and a group of so-called contractual arrangements, such as joint development agreements, R&D pacts and R&D contracts. A wide range of contributions (Auster 1992, Buckley and Casson 1988, Contractor and Lorange 1988, Hagedoorn 1990, Hagedoorn and Narula 1996, Harrigan 1985, Osborn and Baughn 1990, Root 1988) have demonstrated that these different modes of cooperation have a distinctive impact on the character of technology sharing, the organizational context and the possible economic consequences for participating companies.

International joint ventures are probably the oldest and most well-known mode of inter-firm partnering. In the context of strategic technology partnering joint ventures are those 'firms' that have shared R&D or joint technology development as a specific company objective next to production, marketing, sales, etc. Research corporations are a sub-category of joint ventures with distinctive research programmes of which the main purpose is to supply R&D to the parent. It is obvious that the creation of a new firm with usually two parents creates a relatively high degree of organizational interdependence. In terms of Williamson's (1985 and 1991) 'markets and hierarchies' this comes close to hierarchical structures with parent companies sharing control over their joint venture. Different company strategies such as entry into new markets, repositioning and expansion in existing markets and even exit strategies in declining markets are reflected in these joint ventures.

During the past decades a number of non-equity or contractual forms of strategic technology cooperation, in particular joint R&D agreements, have become an alternative to joint ventures. We understand these contractual arrangements to cover technology and R&D sharing by two or more companies through undertakings which establish research projects or joint development agreements with shared resources. So, these agreements suggest a relatively strong commitment of companies and inter-organizational interdependence during the joint project, although the interdependence is smaller than is the case with joint ventures. This category of cooperation covers a wide variety of legal and organizational arrangements. In particular large companies seem to use many of these agreements to explore possible benefits of new technologies (Duysters and Hagedoorn 1995, Hagedoorn and Schakenraad 1994).

Research contracts are another example of non-equity alliances that regulate R&D cooperation in which one partner, usually a large company, contracts another company, frequently a small one, to perform particular research projects. For the contract-initiating party, advantages can be found in the possibility to focus on particular areas of research with substantial cost-saving compared to fully fledged in-house research facilities. Disadvantages for those companies are related to the lack of in-house expertise to assess the value of contract research and the dissociation of development expertise from manufacturing expertise (Obleros and MacDonald 1988, Teece 1987). For the other contractor benefits are found in terms of substantial R&D funding and cooperation with experienced partners.

Organizational complexity is an important aspect of these different modes of international strategic technology partnering. The choice for a particular mode is affected by the trade-off between minimizing organizational complexity and maximizing control over the alliance by each partner. The more complex inter-organizational mode of technology cooperation, such as a joint venture, raises a number of problems of corporate governance. Its quasi-hierarchical nature not only reaches intermediate level of corporate control, but also introduces dilemmas related to trust, forbearance and opportunism (Parkhe 1993. Contractual agreements appear to involve lesser intra-organizational complexity because no separate new administrative element is created. However, although contractual agreements in themselves are less complex, companies often engage in several alliances simultaneously with a variety of partners. This introduces an additional level of complexity, namely difficulties associated with both the administration of these partnerships and the need to continuously monitor the net benefits accruing from various contractual alliances (Osborn and Baughn 1990).

The international context of these alliances increases the already existing high level of complexity. In terms of control, the agreement has to be monitored from corporate headquarters over long distances or from a local or regional subsidiary. However, even in the latter case, there is often no real reduction in the 'distance of control' but it frequently merely results in the introduction of an additional level of corporate governance. Furthermore, companies of different national backgrounds are influenced by their past business experiences as well as by the difficulties of maintaining control over the alliance across borders. Companies that have collaborated on other projects in the past, and are familiar with the business practices and/or regulatory framework in which their partners operate, will perceive less uncertainty in engaging in partnerships that are less complex than with firms with which they have had little experience (Gulati 1995).

As far as the question of control in these different modes of cooperation is concerned, 'traditional' internalization theory (Buckley and Casson 1976, 1988, Dunning 1993, Rugman 1980) appears to suggest that equity agreements offer a larger degree of control over technology sharing than non-equity partnerships. However, recent contributions (Hagedoorn 1993, Osborn *et al.* 1996, Powell *et al.* 1996) suggest that in particular for technology-related alliances formal control is probably less relevant than adequate access to new knowledge, flexibility in cooperation, and mutual flows of information for which both complete and incomplete contractual agreements seem adequate.

An interesting question in this context is whether sectors differ with respect to the distribution of equity versus contractual arrangements. Studies by Harrigan (1985 and 1988), Link and Bauer (1989), Osborn and Baughn (1990) and Hagedoorn and Narula (1996) suggest that technological stability of industrial sectors is a crucial factor explaining different patterns for equity and nonequity partnerships. In sectors with low or medium degrees of R&D intensity, that we can characterize as low or medium technology intensive sectors, one will witness a larger share of joint ventures than in R&D-intensive sectors, or high-tech sectors, in which we see a general preference for contractual agreements and a higher degree of organizational flexibility in partnerships.

EVOLVING ATLANTIC PATTERNS OF STRATEGIC TECHNOLOGY ALLIANCES

If we look at the overall pattern of growth of strategic technology alliances between companies from the EU and the NAFTA countries (see Figure 9.1) we see that by and large the number of newly made alliances has grown over the years. In the early 1980s the number of alliances between the EU and NAFTA amounted up to only about 30 to 70 alliances made each year, but towards the first half of the 1990s this had risen to over 100 alliances registered each year. In 1994 the number of European-NAFTA alliances peaked with a record of over 150 new strategic technology alliances. Compared with other international strategic technology alliances we see that the growth pattern of EU-NAFTA alliances is somewhat less 'steep', but the growth pattern of the latter still essentially follows the overall growth pattern with a major exception towards the end of the period when the number of other international alliances made in 1994 has clearly dropped from nearly 250 to about 160.

In all this we should, however, not forget that strategic technology partnering as such has not necessarily become more internationalized. The number of international or global alliances has certainly increased quite strongly over the last couple of decades but so has the number of domestic alliances and the number

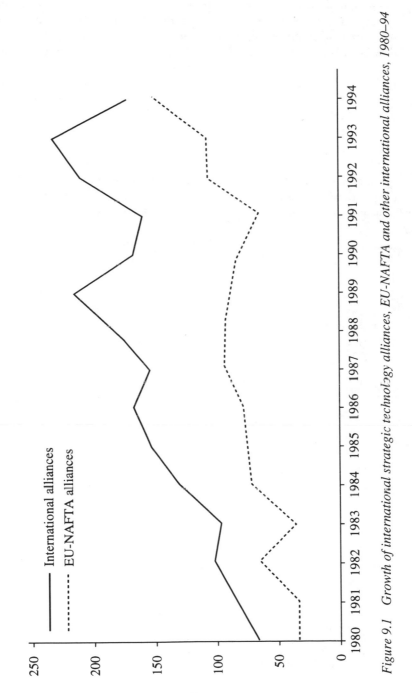

Figure 9.1   Growth of international strategic technology alliances, EU-NAFTA and other international alliances, 1980–94

of cross-border strategic technology partnerships made within international regions such as the EU or NAFTA. In relative terms these domestic and intra-regional alliances are still an important phenomenon. As with the internationalization of company R&D and other aspects of the internationalization of innovative efforts of companies there is certainly not an explosion of international activities but much more a gradual increase of international alliances in the context of an overall increase of inter-firm partnering (Duysters and Hagedoorn 1996).

In a previous section I discussed both the technological and the competitive imperatives that play a role in alliance formation. Table 9.1 presents the distribution of strategic technology alliances for which it was found that joint research and development was the only or by far the most important motive for cooperation set against alliances for which a wider range of incentives such as joint production or joint marketing was also part of the agreement. On average joint R&D appears to be the most important factor in the formation of strategic technology alliances between companies from the EU and NAFTA as over 70 per cent of these international alliances are focused on R&D. Throughout the 1980s this share was at a level of slightly over 60 per cent but during the first half of the 1990s the share of R&D-centred alliances between European and NAFTA alliances rose to over 80 per cent. Other international technology alliances seem to be somewhat less focused on joint R&D, given the about fifty-fifty distribution for both R&D alliances and alliances that have a broader manufacturing, marketing and technology-sharing orientation. However, in recent years these other international alliances also have become predominantly R&D-directed.

As we are analysing international strategic 'technology' alliances it does not come as a surprise that R&D, which plays an important role in technological development, is also a major imperative for companies to cooperate. However, the changes over time do suggest that the 1990s mark a period in which technological cooperation through joint R&D has become even more important and as such it stresses the relevance of advanced technology pressures that lay behind this phenomenon.

Table 9.2 demonstrates that this increasing role of joint R&D is also reflected in the role that different organizational forms of international technology partnering play. As mentioned above, joint ventures usually have a larger number of objectives than just the joint undertaking of R&D activities. For the other group of alliances, the contractual agreements, R&D as such appears to be more central to the agreement. Given the increasing role of technological and research-related imperatives for partnering, we might expect that the share of international joint ventures will decrease over time. Furthermore, we can also expect that, given the more dominant role of technological imperatives in Atlantic alliances, the share of contractual alliances between European and

NAFTA partners will be higher than for other international combinations. Table 9.2 demonstrates that during the 1980s European and NAFTA partners had chosen the joint venture mode for only about 30 per cent of their alliances, and this share decreased to about 22 per cent during the first half of the 1990s. Not only have contractual agreements become more important during the 1990s; Table 9.2 also shows that, as expected, joint ventures are significantly more important for the group of other international strategic technology alliances. Although for these other international alliances the share of joint ventures has also decreased, their share is still about 10 per cent higher than for the European-NAFTA alliances.

Table 9.1   *Distribution of R&D and market-focused international strategic technology alliances, EU–NAFTA and other international alliances, 1980–94 (percentages)*

		1980–84	**1985–89**	**1990–94**	**Total**
EU-NAFTA	R&D	61.3	61.5	82.6	70.7
	Market	38.7	38.0	15.5	28.3
	Unknown	0.0	0.5	1.9	1.0
	Total	100	100	100	100
International	R&D	51.2	49.5	81.0	62.9
	Market	48.6	49.8	16.9	36.0
	Unknown	0.2	0.7	2.1	1.1
	Total	100	100	100	100

Source: MERIT-CATI.

Table 9.2   *Distribution of joint ventures and contractual international strategic technology alliances, EU-NAFTA and other international alliances, 1980–94 (percentages)*

		1980–84	**1985–89**	**1990–94**	**Total**
EU-NAFTA	Joint ventures	29.4	31.8	22.4	27.2
	Contracts	70.6	68.2	77.6	72.8
	Total	100	100	100	100
International	Joint ventures	37.5	45.5	28.1	36.7
	Contracts	62.5	54.5	71.9	63.3
	Total	100	100	100	100

Source: MERIT-CATI.

Previous research (Hagedoorn and Narula 1996) has entered into a more detailed analysis of international partnering behaviour of companies from a larger number of countries and in particular looked at patterns of partnering between European, US and Japanese companies. In that particular analysis it is mentioned that during the 1980s the share of joint ventures in international strategic technology alliances between both European-Japanese and US-Japanese combinations was substantially higher than the Atlantic alliances analysed here. This suggests that formal control through equity partnerships plays a more important role in alliances with Japanese companies following the logic of a transaction-cost-based approach, whereas for Atlantic alliances other than straightforward quasi-internalization motives have begun to play a more dominant role.

Finally, we can take a closer look at the sectoral breakdown of international strategic technology alliances (see Table 9.3). If we accept sectors or fields of technology such as information technology, biotechnology, new materials and aerospace, aviation and defence as high-tech sectors that will have a substantial impact on international competition for an extended period of time, it appears an interesting question to see to what extent alliances related to these activities and sectors play a role in international partnering. Given the specific focus on Atlantic alliances the next question would be to see whether strategic technology partnerships between European and NAFTA companies are concentrated in a different set of sectors and fields of technology than the group of other international alliances.

Our data show that these high-tech sectors take the lion's share of the international strategic technology alliances. For the EU-NAFTA alliances over 82 per cent of the alliances made in the past fifteen years are found in these sectors and technologies. The share of alliances in information technology, biotechnology, new materials and aerospace, aviation and defence has risen from nearly 80 per cent during the first half of the 1980s to nearly 85 per cent during the first half of the 1990s. Much of this increase can be attributed to the growing importance of EU-NAFTA alliances in biotechnology which has reached a share of nearly 25 per cent of the alliances made during the first half of the 1990s. The other international strategic technology alliances show a somewhat similar pattern. Although the share of high-tech sectors in these international alliances is smaller than in the case of EU-NAFTA alliances they still constitute nearly three-quarters of the alliances made during these fifteen years. Also, for these international alliances we see a strong increase for high-tech sectors from slightly over 70 per cent during the first half of the 1980s to nearly 80 per cent of the alliances made during the first half of the 1990s. A somewhat striking difference with the distribution for EU-NAFTA alliances we found is that for this group of international alliances the increase of high-tech alliances seems

Table 9.3 *Sectoral distribution of international strategic technology alliances, EU-NAFTA and other international alliances, 1980–94 (percentages)*

		1980–84	1985–89	1990–94	Total
EU-NAFTA	Biotechnology	17.7	20.7	24.1	21.7
	IT	43.3	45.2	44.0	44.3
	New materials	7.4	9.1	8.3	8.4
	Aerospace/ aviation/defence	10.8	5.8	8.3	7.9
	Automotive	3.5	5.4	1.7	3.3
	Chemicals	7.8	6.5	9.6	8.1
	Others	9.5	7.2	4.1	6.2
	Total	100	100	100	100
International	Biotechnology	15.9	17.1	18.3	17.4
	IT	41.3	38.1	40.4	39.7
	New materials	9.7	10.5	7.7	9.1
	Aerospace/ aviation/defence	4.1	5.9	12.7	8.5
	Automotive	5.2	8.7	2.4	5.3
	Chemicals	12.0	11.5	12.1	11.9
	Others	11.8	8.1	6.3	8.1
	Total	100	100	100	100

Source. MERIT-CATI.

to a large extent to result from an increasing share of international alliances related to the aerospace, aviation and defence industry.

CONCLUSIONS

Complementarity between partners, in terms of either international markets or technological capabilities, turns out to be a major driving force behind the growth of international strategic technology alliances. And it is also this complementarity and the differences between companies that creates a large part of the complexity that is surrounding international partnerships. Furthermore, this complexity is increased by both the intrinsic complicated nature of modern technologies, for which we find so many alliances, and the multitude of both equity and contractual agreements that many companies have entered into.

The above discussion has shown that there is an increasing number of international strategic technology alliances in which the combination of companies from the EU and the NAFTA countries has taken a major share. Compared to other international alliances it turns out that these EU-NAFTA partnerships are particularly oriented towards high-tech activities and joint R&D. During the early 1990s high-tech sectors constituted over 80 per cent of the strategic technology alliances between the two economic regions discussed in this chapter. For instance, a highly research intensive field such as biotechnology turns out to generate nearly 25 per cent of the alliances between EU and NAFTA companies. Although other international strategic technology alliances are also quite high-tech oriented we still notice that the emphasis on advanced technologies and sophisticated inter-firm research cooperation within EU-NAFTA alliances is significantly stronger.

We also find that contractual agreements have become much more important than joint ventures and as such Atlantic partnerships demonstrate that increasingly international companies search for new forms of partnering that go beyond the traditional equity form. This could indicate that the long-term experience of partnering between European and NAFTA partners has generated a level of confidence and tolerance in cooperation that equals that of domestic alliances.

APPENDIX

The MERIT-CATI Data Bank on Strategic Technology Alliances

The empirical data in this chapter is derived from the MERIT-Cooperative Agreements and Technology Indicators (CATI) data bank. This relational database, with information on over 13 000 domestic and international technology cooperation agreements involving some 5000 different parent companies, was established in the late 1980s. After a pilot project in 1986–87, systematic collection of interfirm technology alliances started in 1988. Many sources from earlier years were consulted, which enables us to take a retrospective view. For all sectors of industry or fields of technology in our data bank, we have information on cooperative agreements from at least as early as 1980 up to 1994. In order to collect information on inter-firm alliances and their parents, we consulted various sources, such as informal reports, newspaper and journal articles, books dealing with the subject, and, in particular, specialized technical journals which also report on business events. Company annual reports, the Financial Times Industrial Companies Yearbooks, and Dun & Bradstreet's *Who Owns Whom* provide information about dissolved equity ventures and investments, as well as ventures that were not registered when surveying alliances.

This method of information gathering which we might call 'literature-based alliance counting' has its drawbacks and limitations such as inadequacy of certain sources, low profile of certain companies or industries, bias in favour of Anglo-Saxon sources, and underestimation of certain modes of cooperation such as licensing. It also introduces a certain bias in terms of the frequency versus the scale of alliances. Despite these shortcomings, which are largely unsolvable even in a situation of extensive and large-scale data collection, we think we have been able to produce a clear picture of the joint efforts of many companies. This enables us to perform empirical research which goes beyond case studies or general statements. We avoided some of the weaknesses of the database by focusing on the more reliable parts, such as strategic technology alliances, and by ignoring cost-economizing partnerships and licensing agreements.

The data bank contains information on each agreement and some information on companies participating in these agreements. The main entity is the inter-firm cooperative agreement. We define cooperative agreements as common interests between independent (industrial) partners which are not connected through (majority) ownership. The CATI database includes only those inter-firm agreements that contain arrangements for transferring technology or joint R&D. Mere production or marketing agreements are excluded. In other words, our analysis is primarily related to technology cooperation. Our focus is on those forms of cooperation and agreements for which a combined innovative activity or an exchange of technology is at least part of the agreement. Consequently, we exclude partnerships that regulate no more than the sharing of production facilities, the setting of standards, collusive behaviour in price-setting and raising entry barriers, although all of these may be side effects of inter-firm cooperation as we define it.

We count as an alliance any agreement made between two or more companies at a particular moment. Subsequent agreements between the same partners are considered as individual and separate agreements. However, if a particular agreement consists of several legal forms of cooperation that are parts of the agreement at large, such as a joint venture with a licensing agreement, we consider this as one agreement. If a partnership is extended with a new partner or a new contract is made between two cooperating firms we view this as a new alliance. Frequencies reported in this chapter therefore refer to the number of individual partnerships. Although we do have information on the value of a limited number of alliances (such as the amount of investment) we prefer not to utilize this information for two reasons. First, the coverage of this data excludes contractual agreements for which the value of the agreement is not disclosed, and second, a large percentage of technology partnerships involve interchange of knowledge rather than the exchange of funds or capital.

In this chapter, I record for each alliance: the country of origin of each partner, year of establishment of the agreement, field(s) of technology and/or industry, modes of cooperation and the degree of R&D- or market-orientation.

The country of origin of a given company refers to the country where a company or its head office is registered. Therefore, international alliances are partnerships between companies registered in different countries. This obviously has certain limitations in the case of international companies, because a number of their partnerships are between their local subsidiaries and local partners. However, many of these 'artificial' international alliances are monitored from the head office. Furthermore, there is no other choice in the context of large databases than to follow a strict procedure for categorization. Decisions regarding the possible degree of international subsidiary-level monitoring are impossible to make for a population of thousands of agreements and companies.

I make a distinction between cooperative agreements which are expected to be aimed at the strategic, long-term perspective of the companies involved and those agreements which appear to be more associated with the control of either transaction costs or operating costs of companies. In case both general motives appear possible, either because it is not feasible to differentiate between the cost or the strategic argument or because partners often have alternating motives as a consequence of the character of the agreement; I have marked such agreements as being of a mixed character. The procedure is described extensively in Hagedoorn 1993 and in Hagedoorn and Schakenraad 1994. In practice, our decision rules imply that joint ventures with R&D, research corporations, joint R&D pacts, customer-supplier agreements combined with licensing, cross-licensing, research contracts with licensing, and (mutual) second-sourcing agreements are taken as strategic alliances. Excluded are standard co-makership contracts, co-production agreements, and single licensing agreements for which the cost-economizing argument is thought to be a major motive.

REFERENCES

Auster, E.R. (1992), 'The relationship of industry evolution to patterns of technological linkages, joint ventures, and direct investment between U.S. and Japan', *Management Science*, 38, 778–92.

Buckley, Peter J. and Mark Casson (1976), *The Future of the Multinational Enterprise*, London: Macmillan.

Buckley, Peter J. and Mark Casson (1988), 'A theory of cooperation in international business', in F.J. Contractor and P. Lorange (eds), *Cooperative Strategies in International Business*, Lexington, MA: Lexington Books, pp. 31–54.

Casson, M. (1987), *The Firm and the Market*, Oxford: Blackwell.

Chesnais, F. (1988), 'Technical cooperation agreements between firms', *STI Review*, 4, 51–120.

Contractor, F.J. and P. Lorange (eds) (1988), *Cooperative Strategies in International Business*, Lexington, MA: Lexington Books.

Dunning, J.H. (1993), *Multinational Enterprises and the Global Economy*, Wokingham: Addison-Wesley.

Duysters, G. and J. Hagedoorn (1995), 'Strategic groups and inter-firm networks in international hightech industries', *Journal of Management Studies*, 32, 361–81.

Duysters, G. and J. Hagedoorn (1996), 'Internationalization of corporate technology through strategic partnering: an empirical investigation', *Research Policy*, 24, 1–12.

Gulati, R. (1995), 'Does familiarity breed trust? The implications of repeated ties for contractual choice in alliances', *Academy of Management Journal*, 38, 85–112.

Hagedoorn, J. (1990), 'Organisational modes of inter-firm cooperation and technology transfer', *Technovation*, 10, 17–30.

Hagedoorn, J. (1993), 'Understanding the rationale of strategic technology partnering: inter-organizational modes of cooperation and sectoral differences', *Strategic Management Journal*, 14, 371–85.

Hagedoorn, J. (1996), 'Trends and patterns in strategic technology partnering since the early seventies', *Review of Industrial Organization*, 11, 601–16.

Hagedoorn, J. and R. Narula (1996), 'Choosing modes of governance for strategic technology partnering: international and sectoral differences', *Journal of International Business Studies*, 27, 265–84.

Hagedoorn, J. and J. Schakenraad (1994), 'The effect of strategic technology alliances on company performance', *Strategic Management Journal*, 15, 291–311.

Harrigan, K.R. (1985), *Strategies for Joint Ventures*, Lexington, MA: Lexington Books.

Harrigan, K.R. (1988), 'Joint ventures and competitive strategy', *Strategic Management Journal*, 9, 141–58.

Link, Albert N. and Laura L. Bauer (1989), *Cooperative Research in U.S. Manufacturing: Assessing Policy Initiatives and Corporate Strategies*, Lexington, MA: Lexington Books.

Mowery, D.C. (ed.) (1988), *International Collaborative Ventures in U.S. Manufacturing*, Cambridge, MA: Ballinger.

Obleros, F.J. and R.J. MacDonald (1988), 'Strategic alliances: managing complementarity to capitalize on emerging technologies', *Technovation*, 7, 155–76.

Ohmae, K. (1985), *Triad Power*, New York: Free Press.

Osborn, R.N. and C.C. Baughn (1990), 'Forms of interorganizational governance for multinational alliances', *Academy of Management Journal*, 33, 503–19.

Osborn, R.N., J.G. Denekamp, C.C. Baughn, J. Hagedoorn and G. Duysters (1996), 'Embedded patterns of international alliance formation: the emergence of hybridization', working paper, WSU-MERIT.

Parkhe, A. (1993), '"Messy" research, methodological predisposition and theory development in international joint ventures', *Academy of Management Review*, 18, 227–68.

Powell, W.W., K.W. Koput and L. Smith-Doerr (1996), 'Interorganizational collaboration and the locus of innovation: networks of learning in biotechnology', *Administrative Science Quarterly*, 41, 116–45.

Root, F.R. (1988), 'Some taxonomies of international cooperative arrangements', in Contractor, F.J. and P. Lorange (eds), *Cooperative Strategies in International Business*, Lexington, MA: Lexington Books, pp. 69–80.

Rugman, Alan M. (1980), 'Internalization as a general theory of foreign direct investment: a reappraisal of the literature', *Weltwirtschaftliches Archiv*, 116, 365–79.

Teece, D.J. (1987), 'Profiting from technological innovation: implications for integration, collaboration, and public policy', in D.J. Teece (ed.), *The Competitive Challenge*, Cambridge, MA: Ballinger, pp. 185–220.

Williamson, O.E. (1985), *The Economic Institutions of Capitalism*, New York: The Free Press.

Williamson, O.E. (1991), 'Comparative economic organization: the analysis of discrete structural alternatives', *Administrative Science Quarterly*, 36, 269–96.

10. Systemic approaches to managing interdependencies

Gavin Boyd

In the Triad pattern of industrialized democracies structural interdependencies are being raised to high levels, diversified, and unevenly integrated into an international trading and production system by the operations of transnational enterprises, and, to a lesser extent, by the arm's-length exporting of national firms. The corporate operations are mainly individual endeavours by firms but include numerous alliances, especially in high-technology sectors, and, in certain country-specific configurations, are coordinated through industry groups. The evolution of all the production and trading is influenced, facilitated, and restricted by governments, competing and cooperating with each other, and responding to mainly domestic representations of interests, but generally losing elements of economic sovereignty to international corporations. The investment, manufacturing, and trading decisions of these firms are made while relating to numerous governments on policy issues, and cause changes in markets and economic structures, posing problems as well as opportunities for national firms whose capacities are less able to support transnational operations.

The pervasive trend is imbalanced and uncoordinated deepening integration, mainly through the development of cross border production systems. There are complex asymmetries in the spread of gains among the interpenetrating national economies, due to differences in structural competitiveness, contrasts in market openness and contestability, and the virtual shifts of economic power to international corporations, whose home country ties are tending to weaken. More integrated national political economies such as Japan and Germany have, however, more control than less integrated ones over the spread of relative economic gains, and are advantaged by higher levels of structural competitiveness and by the retention of considerable elements of economic sovereignty.

The asymmetries in the spread of gains from trade and transnational production have cumulative effects on levels of structural competitiveness, growth, and employment. Associated with these effects are cross-border market efficiencies and failures that defy engagement by national policies. Corporate competition increases the market efficiencies, but over time reduces market contestability, as international oligopoly power is gained. Government efficiencies and failures have diverse internal and external effects, with significant differences because of macromanagement contrasts between the more integrated and less integrated national political economies.

Underlying the market and structural changes are developmental issues, recognizable when appeals are made to common interests by governments interacting over questions of economic openness and of balance in international linkages. The developmental issues concern the evolution of national political economies as interdependent systems, competing and cooperating in diverse policy areas while relating to transnational enterprises – with generally limited leverage. The developmental issues set imperatives for comprehensive collective management, and, therefore, for the resolution of problems of governance that can hinder such management. The collective management imperatives are especially significant for the less integrated national political economies that are disadvantaged in the spread of gains from world commerce. Governments of all the structurally interdependent states have, however, to accept obligations of extended accountability relating to the developmental issues, that is to all foreign communities affected by their policies.

Collective management tends to be a secondary concern for policy makers because the corporate competition for world market shares drives governmental endeavours to increase structural competitiveness and to use trade policy leverage to secure favourable changes in foreign market access for their firms. Governments in the more integrated political economies have incentives to increase the gains which their economies derive from superior structural competitiveness. Administrations in the less integrated political economies have urgent reasons to work for enhanced structural competitiveness, and to resort to trade policy leverage, but tend to be disadvantaged by problems of governance. These become more serious because of conflicting domestic pressures to improve growth and increase employment.

The structural policy competition and the interactions over market access contribute to the increasing imbalances in gains from foreign commerce while the internationalized market efficiencies and failures continue. The unevenly interdependent growth is thus increasingly sub-optimal: entrepreneurship is not concerted on a wide scale, in part because governments are not sufficiently cooperative in their mutual relations. Collective management to facilitate and support broadly concerted corporate strategies and to provide a sufficiently functional environment for coordinated macromanagement endeavours is becoming a fundamental imperative.

SYSTEMIC LOGIC

Intensifying competition drives internal system-building endeavours by firms. The scale of internal system-building activity by transnational corporations is very large, and national firms, while being drawn into linkages with the expanding processes of international production, are obliged to strive for greater efficiencies in their own organizations. The extensive corporate system-building competition involves widening applications of internalization logic, through integration and diversification strategies which incorporate or displace weaker firms, altering national economic structures and making their functions more and more interdependent with those of economic systems in other countries.[1]

International competitive pressures also cause corporate managements to collaborate in strategic alliances, within and across borders. These are advantageous for information sharing, technology sharing, production sharing, market sharing, and collaborative political action. The incentives for collaborative high-technology development are especially potent, because of the breadth and pace of advances in frontier innovation. Most of the alliances are managed instrumentally, at arm's length, with discretionary shifts in cooperation reflecting changes in the ownership and profitability of the corporate allies.[2] The alliances have been multiplying over the past two decades, but their potentials for more dynamic concerting of entrepreneurial energies remain generally limited because of their arm's-length contracting.[3]

Collaboration in industry groups, such as the Japanese keiretsu, based on permanent relational ties, is an advanced application of systemic logic. The concerting of entrepreneurship in these groups is motivated by enduring solidarity, is undertaken with much security, has long-term objectives, and generates greater synergies than those in corporate strategic alliances. Collective international market strength acquired by these groups has major competitive advantages which reinforce the loyalties of member firms, and facilitate persuasive representations of interests to governments.[4] The advantages of industry groups have general appeal, but these business associations tend to develop mainly in societies oriented toward community values and the maintenance of relatively high levels of trust. In individualistic societies, with lower levels of trust, the relational ties necessary for industry groups are difficult to build, and firms have less permanent identities because of active markets for corporate control.[5]

The intensification of global competitive pressures, influencing applications of systemic logic in firms, strategic alliances, and industry groups, has occurred in a context of trade and investment liberalization, advances in information and communications technology, an internationalization of financial markets, and an uneven trend toward regional economic cooperation. *Governments*, seeking to promote systemic development in their political economies so as to increase gains from foreign trade and transnational production, generally lack the degrees of commitment and competence driving applications of systemic logic at the corporate level. Problems of governance in the less efficiently managed states tend, moreover, to be difficult to overcome, and in various ways add to the incentives of their firms to expand international operations and implement global strategies very independently.[6]

The international trade and investment liberalization has occurred during rounds of negotiations led by US governments under domestic pressures to cope with balance-of-payments deficits and to respond to corporate interests seeking improved access to foreign markets, especially in Europe.[7] The balance-of-payments deficits have resulted mainly from the import-drawing effects of heavy fiscal deficits since the early 1980s and from related losses of structural competitiveness. High-volume Atlantic trade and cross-investment have made European Union states eager to increase access to the US market, and Euro-American collaboration, virtually dominating multilateral trade and investment interactions, has been mainly responsible for the increasing openness in the world economy. The trend has derived some impetus from shifts in policy orientations, mainly in Europe, toward increased reliance on market forces as sources of growth: these forces have been given greater scope through deregulatory and privatization policies.[8]

Rivalries for enhanced structural competitiveness have tended to increase problems of advanced political development in several industrialized democracies, especially those in which macromanagement performance has been hindered by failures of allocative discipline, due to vote-maximizing political competition. The resorts to deficit spending have covered large welfare costs associated with migrations of industrial capacity and with sectoral disruptions caused by imports. The allocative failings have been serious in the states with individualistic cultures, low levels of trust, and conflicted political processes in which competition to maximize votes has limited the commitments of decision makers to the common good.[9]

Policy orientations toward maintaining and strengthening domestic system-building for interdependent growth have to develop in consensual and broadly representative decision processes, for which institutions with fairly comprehensive interest-aggregating capabilities are required, with diffuse public-spirited leadership and dedicated technocratic expertise. Integrated inter-corporate systems are necessary, for consensus and the aggregation of entrepreneurial interests.[10] All these systemic imperatives have been evident in Japan and Germany, but in the USA and other states with individualistic cultures political competition is less restrained by cooperation in the public interest, inter-corporate systems are fragmented, and decision processes are forms of conflicted bargaining, restricted to short-term concerns, with little potential for policy learning. Coping with the challenges of complex imbalanced structural interdependence is difficult for these states, and failures in this regard tend to increase their problems of advanced political development. Their firms move into international operations with incentives to avoid their burdensome costs of government, implement highly self-reliant strategies, and limit responsiveness to their structural policies, which tend to lack coherence.[11]

The contrasting domestic system-building endeavours, while evolving with the expansion of transnational enterprises as production systems, are occurring in a context of financial market internationalization which affects the entire pattern of macromanagement competition. The financial markets draw investment into high-volume speculation, give preferential service to large highly competitive transnational enterprises, and generate volatility which can destabilize national economies.[12] Superior systemic development in the more integrated industrialized democracies makes them less vulnerable to the investment diversion and volatility, and ensures substantial and stable funding for their industries. The less integrated states experience considerable vulnerability, and, in the US case, this is all the more serious because its protracted fiscal deficits have become unsustainable, posing risks of a financial crisis.[13]

Foreign economic policy orientations in the more individualistic states are typically liberal, according with domestic emphasis on entrepreneurial liberty. Liberal rhetoric commonly expresses confidence in the efficiency effects of international market forces, while attributing trade problems to the market-restricting activities of foreign governments. Retaliatory protectionist and market-opening leverage is justified by affirmations that other governments must be persuaded to accept liberal economic principles. The leverage available depends on size, and in this regard the USA is advantaged, but it is disadvantaged by the trade and investment effects of its unsustainable fiscal deficits, in part because these necessitate dependence on foreign financing.[14]

In the more integrated states with higher structural competitiveness the accumulations of gains from foreign commerce and transnational production sustain neomercantilist orientations. These evidence the autonomy and strength of integrated inter-corporate systems, active in the transformation of foreign markets and economic structures. In the Japanese case they also evidence compulsions to build surpluses in manufacturing trade in order to finance imports of food and raw materials. No other industrialized democracy is as resource-poor as Japan, and its lack of resources obligates much emphasis on maintaining a highly efficient system of outwardly oriented macromanagement. Resource imperatives are much weaker in Germany's policy, and Germany is advantaged by access to the large European Union market, in which Japan encounters formal and informal barriers.[15]

The internationalization of financial markets has resulted primarily from initiatives by the major industrialized democracies with liberal foreign economic policies. A substantially integrated international financial system has evolved, with inadequate regulatory cooperation. Large-scale investors in this system have incentives to precipitate and exploit volatility, especially through speculative attacks on the weak currencies of states with large fiscal and trade deficits.[16] The system can be a source of market discipline on the policies of such states, but the record over the past decade and a half indicates generally slow policy learning.

The United States could have been expected to have active interests in forming an international regulatory system to control speculation in world financial markets, but its liberal system of governance has failed to generate sufficient consensus. Competition between major governments to attract the operations of large financial institutions has been an important factor in US financial policy making. Another factor has been the anticipated magnitude of prospective international regulatory functions, due to the great volume of complex financial transactions that are made rapidly through elaborate communication systems.[17]

STRUCTURAL POLICIES

In endeavours to promote structural competitiveness the scope for systemic logic is determined by the dynamics of policy making and by degrees of autonomous coordinated industrial activity in national inter-corporate systems. Policy making in the less integrated industrialized democracies occurs mainly through conflicted short-term political transacting sensitive to vote-maximizing concerns, in contexts of arm's-length interactions with fragmented inter-corporate systems. Largely uncoordinated entrepreneurial strategies are implemented with little responsiveness to structural policy initiatives. In the more integrated industrialized democracies structural policies are shaped consensually in synergistic interaction with autonomous integrated higher performance inter-corporate activity. Such policies engage more effectively with issues of structural interdependence.

The liberal policy orientations in the USA and Britain, expressing commitments to limited government, are generally not open to structural policy advocacy, except where the prosperity of important national sectors is affected. Corporate confidence in the technocratic capacities of government bureaucracies is generally low, especially in the USA, where the higher levels of those bureaucracies are filled by extensive patronage, and where the structural policy record has received mainly negative assessments.[18] The representation of business interests is fragmented in the USA and Britain, as strong peak economic organizations have not emerged.[19] Conflicting assertions of corporate interests complicate bureaucratic and legislative engagement with any structural policy initiatives by the US administration, and Congressional activism tends to build contradictions into legislation authorizing institutional innovations for structural objectives.[20] Congressional groups, moreover, seek direct control over allocations of funds for specific industrial and technology projects, with interests in influencing choices about the location of those projects.[21]

Conflicting assertions of corporate interests also complicate structural policy issues in Britain; the administration can shape policy more authoritatively, because of parliamentary cooperation, but has to cope with difficulties in the aggregation of corporate preferences. The permanent bureaucracy, moreover, while operating with greater continuity than that in the USA, has been given little scope to acquire technocratic expertise: the liberal policy tradition has been matched by an institutional tradition of impartial use of generalist skills in the service of changing administrations.[22]

Structural policy options, especially in the US liberal tradition, have been seen mainly as choices between intervention and non-intervention in industrial sectors. US consultative partnering between the administrative and corporate levels is generally not considered feasible, as it would violate the principle of government aloofness from industry and commerce. Moreover, intercorporate conflicts could be expected because of clashes of interests affected by differing opportunities for political action in the consultative processes. Further, corporate confidence in proposed consultative partnering would be relatively low because of unfavourable views of the competence and dedication of officials as well as because of anticipations of frequent if not disjointed shifts in displays of administrative favour to competing sectoral interests. The consultative responsiveness between technocrats and managements which has developed in Japan, it is commonly understood, would require stable bureaucratic and corporate structures that would ensure continuing positive influences on elite psychology at each level, so that trustful and productive interaction would be possible. The restriction of policy choices to intervention or non-intervention options thus has a persuasive rationale, and interventions, through subsidies and regulatory measures, are visualized as arm's-length administrative functions performed with accountability to Congress.[23]

US structural policy endeavours have evidenced the dysfunctional effects of strong pluralism, and corporate distrust and rivalries. The pluralism has been all the more serious because of the weaknesses of national aggregating institutions and the conflicts generated by the system of divided government. The scope for technocratic judgement has been limited by the vote-maximizing concerns of administration and Congressional groups.[24] The manifest systemic imperative has been to evolve a comprehensive design for increased complementary efficiencies in sectors that have been losing international competitiveness – automobiles, electronic equipment, electrical machinery, and computers – while sustaining efficiencies in the globally competitive sectors – aerospace, chemicals, non-electrical machinery, and drugs.[25] Structural policy making has not responded to this demanding imperative because of the prominence of patronage and distributive concerns. Considerable emphasis has been given to the sponsorship of R&D over the past decade, because of public debate over losses of shares in global high-technology markets, but intense politicization of the funding decisions has caused sharp rises, falls, and shifts in allocations. The pace of change has been fast, while the intended development and commercialization of new technologies has inevitably been slow.[26]

In the European Union structural policies have been implemented mainly on the basis of traditionally close government-business relations, except in Britain, where the policy orientation has been liberal. Germany has ranked highest in structural competitiveness, because of efficiencies generated in its rather well integrated political economy, and this competitiveness is being strengthened through superior gains from commerce in the Union market. The Union needs a common structural policy, for more effective use of its own market's growth potential, and more active involvement in world commerce, but its collective decision processes are not sufficiently advanced to introduce such a policy.[27]

Structural evolution in Germany results from the synergies of relational ties in a solidarity-based inter-corporate pattern, linked through very active consultations with consensual federal and state policy processes. Industrial policy purposes are served to a considerable extent by responsiveness in those consultations and by the advisory functions of banks which have large holdings in manufacturing firms and which participate in corporate management. There is an extensive concerting of strategies through the inter-corporate ties and the exchanges with the policy levels. This is somewhat obscured by formal assertions of policy stressing freedom for market forces, but there are substantial allocations for subsidies to selected industries, and these are generally not divisive. The established policy style involves much consensual deliberation focused on the public interest, under independent review by a Council of Economic Experts.[28]

France's structural evolution has featured less systemic logic, because of policy processes seriously conflicted by ideological cleavages, personality differences, a fragmented inter-corporate system, and interest-aggregating structures that have been organizationally weaker than those in Germany. Administrations have related rather autocratically to the corporate level, with divisive effects that have contributed to its fragmentation. The private sector has included a large number of small and medium-sized firms whose resources have been insufficient to support investment in new technology. Cooperation between these firms has been at relatively low levels, reflecting strong individualism in the national culture. Private sector growth was affected by a large expansion of the state sector under a Socialist administration in the early 1980s, and then by slow privatization of numerous inefficient public enterprises through the rest of that decade. This was a major element in a policy shift toward reliance on market forces, but consultative partnering with the corporate level did not evolve on a scale that could have substantially increased structural competitiveness.[29] Political uncertainties appeared to influence corporate attitudes, because while conservative political forces were in the ascendant by the early 1990s social unrest was being caused by attempts to reduce the state's heavy welfare costs.[30]

The development of structural initiatives at the European Union level depends very much on Franco-German leadership, which dominates the Union's collective decision processes. German policy, however, is influenced by tacit preferences for preservation of its national system of administrative corporate partnering, and French policy has to engage with imperatives for building a competitive system of such partnering. Both states, moreover, have to reckon with the complexities and uncertainties of intra-Union bargaining on questions of industrial policy cooperation. Union sponsorship of collaborative technology projects has evidenced difficulties in achieving functional consensus, despite intensive consultations between the European Commission and major industrial associations, including the European Round Table of Industrialists.[31]

In Japan structural policy is a highly functional process of consultative partnering which generates synergies between the technocratic and corporate levels. This is very much a closed system, unlike the German political economy, which is experiencing a degree of Europeanization as its federal and state policies are influenced by interactions with other Union governments and firms. The principal external challenges for Japanese structural policy are posed by American trade policy activism, in a distant relationship that has become adversarial, and that motivates Japanese efforts to restrain foreign penetration of the national political economy.[32]

Systemic logic in Japanese structural policy is distinguished by the blending of macro forward-looking technocratic projections with widely coordinated long-term corporate strategies, managed with security because of relational funding. Interactive policy learning and corporate learning, with much continuity on each side, and with insulation against pressures from legislators and shareholders, tends to produce high levels of X-efficiency in what is virtually an extensive application of internalization logic.[33] Corporate as well as technocratic commitments to the entire process are sustained by a long record of successes in outwardly oriented growth, with the maintenance of leads in applied frontier technology. There has been deep penetration of high-technology sectors in the USA, and similar penetration in the European Union is beginning; the national inter-corporate system is being extended with the formation of integrated regional production networks in North America and East Asia; and global operations are being facilitated by the preservation of common managerial culture that sustains home country loyalties.[34]

MACROMANAGEMENT

Structural policies operate in the context of policy mixes which evolve under the pressures for structural competitiveness. Consensually rational decision making in the more integrated national political economies produces coherent and functional combinations of administrative activity in major policy areas, in consultative partnering with relationally linked corporate groups. The more conflicted decision making in the less integrated industrialized democracies, interacting with the strategies of firms in their typically fragmented inter-corporate systems, tends to result in less effective macromanagement. Vicious circles can thus develop as difficulties in aggregating more urgent sectoral and community demands perpetuate conflicts in the policy process.

The systemic dimensions of macromanagement are related very critically to allocative functions. Institutional capacities for building consensus in the public interest can be strained by intense competition over allocative questions. This tends to have increasingly adverse consequences as structural interdependencies continue to rise. To the extent that the political competition drives deficit spending the trade effects, the higher debt loads, the inflationary pressures, the vulnerability of the currency to speculative attack, and the caution imposed on corporate strategies all make recoveries of structural competitiveness more difficult. Where more advanced political development ensures allocative discipline, however, the reinforcing effects on institutions and consensus maintain continuity in overall performance.

Institutional restraint and guidance of political competition over allocative issues becomes more feasible if such issues are subordinated to the larger tasks of orchestrating dynamic diversified growth in the more integrated states, and as autonomous coordinated entrepreneurship becomes more active in their intercorporate systems. On the corporate side systemic imperatives relate to the breadth of productive inter-firm cooperation, the balance between foreign production and domestic production for export, and the retention of home country ties by firms moving into international operations. If there is high-volume rent-seeking this has adverse effects on productive activity, through the draining of investment into speculation, the generation of pressures for short-term profits, and the lowering of levels of trust.[35] Extensive share trading by households can contribute to rising levels of rent-seeking, and, thus, to stock market instability. The inter-corporate balance between competition and cooperation tends to reflect the overall ratio between rent-seeking and productive activity. This balance also normally reflects the balance between foreign production and domestic production for export by a nation's firms, and their overall losses or retentions of home country attachments and loyalties.

The interacting effects of consensually rational or conflicted vote-maximizing policy making, with fiscal discipline or expansion, and efficiencies or non-efficiencies in public-private sector management, together with different ratios between rent-seeking and productive activity, and between competitive and cooperative strategies, all contribute to efficiencies and failures in the markets which are being internationalized. Changes in economic structures, and shifts in the spread of gains from involvement in the world economy, also result.

In Japan the most significant institutional factors guiding interest representation and ensuring allocative discipline are the strong roles of the Ministry of Finance and the Ministry of International Trade and Industry. These ministries have commanded deference from competing political groups. The ministerial involvement, together with much self-regulation in the inter-corporate system, has contributed to a general emphasis on productive rather than rent-seeking activity, a functional blend of cooperative and competitive corporate strategies, and an expansion of the nation's integrated inter-corporate system in the development of transnational production by its firms. With all this, however, there has been considerable separation from the rest of the international political economy; domestic factors sustaining the pattern of macromanagement have operated with a high degree of continuity while foreign political and economic intrusion have been largely prevented. Much administrative-corporate control over the evolution of structural interdependencies has been possible, but the continued penetration of foreign markets has necessitated some reciprocation through gradual increases in economic openness.[36]

In Germany the systemic dimensions of macromanagement are more broadly consensual, with less concentrated administrative authority, and are more open, especially because of involvement in European Union decision making. In these respects they are more compatible with imperatives for international system-building than the Japanese macromanagement pattern. German macromanagement is based on a strong tradition of cooperation between the major political parties, between the state and federal levels of government, and between those levels and an integrated inter-corporate system. At the federal level a deliberative policy style is served by advisory functions supported by broad institutionalized aggregations of interests, and these sustain allocative discipline. Extensive consultative links with the corporate level, especially through peak economic organizations, facilitate interactive policy making that generates synergies with relationally coordinated entrepreneurial activities. There is broad productive inter-firm collaboration, conducive to economic stability, domestic production for export is much larger than foreign production by German corporations, and those producing abroad retain home country ties, although not as strongly as their Japanese counterparts.[37]

The internal strengths of the German macromanagement process facilitate engagement with issues of collective management in the European Union, for constructive interactions in which Germany is advantaged by superior structural competitiveness but is committed to integrative cooperation for interdependent growth within the Union. This requires responsiveness to the interests of other member states, and continuing dialogue with them for the building of a regional policy consensus according with the German emphasis on fiscal responsibility and monetary restraint. The involvement with European Union partners involves much reciprocal policy learning and the acceptance of informal accountability, with potentials for building trust. There is emphasis on the establishment of an effective regional monetary union in which Germany would be the central member, and, thus a force for fiscal responsibility.[38]

Systemic compatibility between German macromanagement and European Union collective management is maintained by a leadership style responsive to the concerns of France and other Union members. This induces continued acceptance of virtual German domination of the Union economy, with superior gains because of the weaker structural competitiveness of most of the other Union states. Issues regarding the spread of benefits from the integration of the Union market are, however, raising questions about the need for a strong common industrial policy, and a drive for this by the less advantaged states, although unlikely, would challenge tacit German preferences for preservation of the present pattern of regional market forces. In this context the consolidation of the powerful German role in the Union economy tends to ensure that virtual German control of the projected monetary union will be generally accepted, but divisive issues are in prospect because of German emphasis on the need for institutionalized pressures on member governments for fiscal discipline.[39]

Macromanagement in France is less broadly consensual, under more concentrated executive authority, and relatively less open, because of greater centralization, weaker autonomous inter-corporate inputs, and less participation by lower organs of government in European Union decision making. There is less cooperation between the major political parties, policy making is more conflicted, and allocative discipline is difficult to achieve. The representation of corporate interests is fragmented, and inter-firm cooperation is on a modest scale, but rent-seeking in relation to productive entrepreneurship is restrained by central authority, and foreign production is on a relatively small scale compared with domestic production for export.

The systemic dimensions of French macromanagement are on balance compatible with the evolution of collective management in the European Union, but compared with Germany the demonstration effect is a weaker contribution to the formation of regional policy consensus. Allocative discipline has been especially difficult, because of the high welfare costs in recent years,[40] and it has not been feasible to assume a role as influential as Germany's in the promotion of European monetary union. Alignment with German emphasis on fiscal restraint for the operation of the monetary union has had divisive internal effects. At a more fundamental level domestic ideological cleavages have prevented the projection of credible commitment to a macromanagement ideal that would complement or compete against the German objective of a social market economy.

Macromanagement in Britain is also less consensual than in Germany, but somewhat more representative than in France because of greater executive accountability to the legislature and responsiveness to the corporate level, although the inter-corporate system is fragmented. Political competition between the two major political parties hinders allocative restraint. Welfare costs are high, as in France, but more because of industrial decline. A major factor in this decline has been the influence of the financial sector on monetary policy, which has been responsible for upward pressure on the currency, to the detriment of manufacturing. The fragmentation of the inter-corporate system has been evident in lower levels of cooperation between firms than in Germany, higher levels of rent-seeking and higher levels of investment in foreign manufacturing, undertaken by firms that tend to lose their home country ties more than their German counterparts.[41]

The systemic dimensions of British macromanagement are compatible with integration in the European Union mainly because a liberal policy orientation facilitates cross-investment which is linking the economy rather closely to the more industrialized Union members, although the main flow of outward investment is to the USA. The rising structural links with the rest of the Union, however, are not matched by active partnership with France and Germany in the leadership of regional integration. The macromanagement record does not have demonstration effect conducive to intra-zonal policy consensus, and is associated with status as a reluctant participant in the Union system of collective management. Because of ideological cleavages between the major political parties the concept of solidarity-based Rhine capitalism associated with the German social market economy has not been complemented or challenged.[42]

Macromanagement in Germany, France, and Britain, interacting with corporate activities, has contributed to regionalized and globalized market efficiencies and failures. Administrative and corporate control over these efficiencies and failures has been greater in Germany than in France, and greater than in France than in Britain, but with effects that have been significant mainly at the regional level. Within Europe moreover market and structural changes have been shaped to a significant degree by the large and highly competitive American corporate presence, which has been well positioned to exploit opportunities for regional restructuring and expansion.[43]

The systemic dimensions of collective management in the European Union evidence institutional development lagging behind the tasks of introducing fiscal discipline and promoting consultative partnering between the Union level and inter-corporate systems. The lagging institutional development reflects collective decisional problems, and entails costs, as regional structural competitiveness continues to fall behind that of the USA. Corporate and popular support for the system of collective decision making is affected by the lagging institutional development, and by related problems of representation and accountability, which are significant in the context of imbalances in gains from the internal market, but also in the context of shifts of regulatory authority to the Union level.[44] A regional inter-corporate system which is emerging with cross-investment in the internal market is fragmented, with the cohesive German inter-corporate system retaining much of its separate identity, and links between the fragmented French, British, and other European inter-corporate systems evolving in a relatively unpatterned manner. In Union-level decision making the European Commission is open mainly to inputs from very large Union international firms with research capabilities to support advisory functions. The most influential group of such firms is the Round Table of European Industrialists, which interacts with the Commission on the basis of the shared interests of members in completing the integration of the internal market.[45]

The problems of building a sufficiently advanced system of collective management in the European Union affect its capacities to manage structural and policy interdependencies with the USA. These, because of their significance for European growth, employment, and stability, are the most important tasks in its foreign economic relations. They are especially demanding because of the difficulties of decision making in the Union but also because of US leverage to extract concessions on trade and investment issues, in line with special interests that have been accommodated in the US policy process.

Macromanagement in the USA is restricted in scope by its tradition of limited government and is made difficult by strong representations of largely unaggregated interests in a divided authority structure. Political competition necessitates extensive compromises that tend to prevent allocative discipline. Fiscal deficits have caused a high debt load, increasing the costs of government and diverting investment from productive use in a society with low savings levels. Monetary restraint to control inflationary pressures tends to prevent currency depreciation that would weaken the import-drawing effects of the fiscal deficits and facilitate adequate export expansion. Because the fiscal deficits are unsustainable and because strains have developed in the financial sector, which is quite vulnerable to volatility in global financial markets, there is a danger of instability.

The divided authority structure relates distantly to a fragmented intercorporate pattern. Relations in this pattern are overwhelmingly competitive rather than cooperative, rent-seeking is at high volumes in relation to productive activity, firms lack stable identities, managements are under strong pressures to achieve short-term profits, and domestic production for export is considerably lower than transnational production. There is extensive arm's-length networking between firms collaborating on the basis of technology, production, and marketing interdependencies in the large national economy, but this is evolving in a society with low levels of trust, and under the severe constraints of anti-trust legislation.[46]

DEVELOPMENT ISSUES

The systemic dimensions of macromanagement in the major industrialized democracies reflect problems of advanced political development, posed as the challenges of structural interdependence strain the capacities of governance systems, in some states more than in others. The evolution of these governance systems, moreover, lags behind the development of international firms as autonomous systems allocating values transnationally. This is happening in a context in which market efficiencies and failures extend across borders while government efficiencies and failures remain more distinctly national.

Advanced development in a national political economy requires institutionalized transformation of representative policy inputs into administrative functions serving the common good through sound macroeconomic policies; the affirmation of values conducive to trust, cooperation, and community formation; and the implementation of measures regulating and facilitating corporate investment, production and trading. For all these imperatives competition for office must be restrained within the limits of a broad elite policy consensus directed toward the common good and maintained through consistently active leadership, so that holistically rational decision making will be sustained. In conditions of high structural interdependence the imperatives for comprehensively functional administrative performance become very strong.

Levels and issues of advanced political development in the Triad pattern are related to market efficiencies and failures. Exploration of these efficiencies and failures has to give special attention to the public goods category. The coordination of investment, production, and marketing decisions through inter-corporate cooperation, induced by consultative interactions with structural authorities, has to be recognized as a public good that can provide growth and stability that would not be otherwise attainable. Failures to concert entrepreneurship can lead to industrial fragmentation, excess capacity, disruptive externalities, and a proliferation of uncertainties that obligate very cautious investment decisions.[47]

The growth potential of concerted entrepreneurship is especially significant for employment. Unemployment is a problem of market failure, and has increasing international dimensions as transnational enterprises restructure while driving weaker firms into decline. Unemployment demands governmental responses, but to engage with fundamentals these have to focus on the promotion of entrepreneurial cooperation for higher overall growth. This type of administrative endeavour has, of course, to be accompanied by efforts to cope with the use of oligopoly power for market exploitation. Spontaneous inter-corporate monitoring and respect for the interests of competing firms can restrain the growth and use of oligopoly power, as the Japanese experience has demonstrated, but authoritative regulation is necessary. This requires dedicated administrative skills, operative with commitments to the common good, and in this regard, as well as in the technocratic promotion of entrepreneurial cooperation, the moral imperatives associated with advanced political development are especially significant: community formation, with the social organization of trust, is essential for equity and efficiency in an advanced national political economy that must manage high structural interdependencies.[48]

Developmental levels and issues in the Triad configuration evolve through processes of continuity and change. A major feature of the configuration is the persistence of strong interest representation straining institutional capacities in the USA, and causing failures in allocative discipline, in a context in which pressures for improved performance come mainly from international market discipline. In the European Union failures in allocative discipline are subjected not only to market discipline but also to political pressure through German influence in the emerging regional system of monetary cooperation. In Japan internal state strength is sufficient for allocative discipline, and this contributes, through corporate activities, to the international market forces exerting pressure on the USA.

In the USA and the European Union states displacement of traditional moral values by instrumental ones has been a pervasive trend, expressed in more aggressive and less principled assertions of individual interests, and, to a degree, of class interests.[49] This has happened in the settings in which economic policies have given greater emphasis to freedom for market forces and the reduction of welfare costs. The emphasis on market forces has been influenced by perceived imperatives to cope with losses of structural competitiveness, experienced especially in trade with Japan. Value shifts in Japan have also been evident in more individualistic pursuits of instrumental values, attributed in part to the penetration of Western culture, but at elite levels traditional factional behaviour has been altered by developmental advocacy, reacting especially against corruption in the former ruling Liberal Democratic Party.[50]

The dynamics of the US political economy, in a social context manifesting the assertions of instrumental values, have been dominated by aggressive representations of interests, weakening and manipulating institutions of governance. In this process corporate financing, especially for public relations activity, has assumed greater significance in contests for office, while corporate political action has increased because of the prominence of foreign market access issues for US international firms. Distributional problems of vital importance for the lower social strata have been downgraded in political debate, while social inequalities have increased. At the same time general confidence in the system of governance appears to have declined. Altogether, the longstanding assumptions of liberal democratic philosophy about social and economic behaviour have been challenged.[51]

Compulsions to impose costs of macromanagement failures on other states tend to be generated in the US political economy because of national pride, the availability of strong leverage, and the influence of a climate of adversarial legalism that has evolved with proliferating disputes in competitive struggles for political and economic advantage. Aggressive unilateralism, as a form of economic diplomacy, has expressed hopes of building domestic coalitions and of manipulating popular distrust of other states and international organizations. The expected domestic political utility of aggressive unilateralism can be quite significant for a US administration because the organizational weakness of the major political parties obligate much reliance on demonstrations of presidential engagement with major policy problems. In this activity leadership idiosyncratic factors tend to be prominent because elite socialization processes tend to be quite unpatterned, due to the lack of institutional development in the political parties, and because the projection of the president's personal qualities to the nation as a whole is typically intended to be more meaningful than his specific policy preferences.[52]

The dynamics of the German political economy are more functional, consensual, and stable. Higher institutional development facilitates the transformation of more orderly processes of interest representation into effective governance. The displacement of traditional moral values appears to have been less pervasive than in the USA, and has not significantly weakened commitments to the public interest in the consensual policy making and in inter-corporate cooperation. High production costs are causing German firms to move manufacturing operations to lower wage areas within and outside the Union, but the integration of the large Union market enables them to continue serving it mainly through exports from the home economy, with the synergies of relational contracting in their inter-corporate system. The broad consensus for further development of the social market economy is, however, being strained by high welfare costs, especially in the eastern states. As economies of those states recover from socialist mismanagement their unemployment will decline, but outward direct investment by well established firms in the rest of the national economy may increase the overall level of unemployment.[53]

The French political economy functions with some major unresolved developmental problems of institution building and consensus formation. The intensely individualistic culture hinders institutional development for the harmonizing of policy preferences. A constitutionally strong executive has been intended to provide effective administration, with limited accountability to a relatively weak legislature, but contests for this high office have not forced the growth of organizational strength in major political parties. The outcomes have been determined by popular responses to the personalities and ideological stances of leading contenders. The public projection of their qualities has depended very much on their personal efforts, because of the organizational deficiencies of the leading parties.[54] The conservative parties have benefited from, and have contributed to, the regional policy shift toward reliance on market forces, but have been more affected than the Socialist Party by high-level personality conflicts. Changes to instrumental values in French society appear to have reduced interest in social justice issues that had been significant in the appeal of the Socialist Party, but high unemployment is generating social unrest.[55] Promoting higher growth while reducing welfare costs is difficult not only because of the weak support mobilizing functions and the ideological differences of the major political parties but also because of the lack of responsive consultative interactions between the administration and the fragmented inter-corporate system.

Advanced development in Britain's political economy is at a different level because of a somewhat more functional representational-institutional balance. The executive has to operate with greater accountability to the legislature, in which party representation is based on relative organizational strengths that reflect less intense individualism than that in France. This individualism, however, is evident in the quite fragmented inter-corporate system, in which managements have traditionally implemented their strategies with much independence, while relating very distantly to central authority. Adversarial relations between the two main political parties, based on class and ideological cleavages, have hindered the evolution of a broad policy consensus, despite urgent problems of industrial decline which have been demanding attention because of competitive pressures in the Union market.[56] The pressures of political competition tend to drive fiscal expansion more forcefully in Britain than in France, despite the strength of a shift in elite policy preferences toward reducing the costs of government and providing more scope for corporate freedom.

The Japanese political economy has attained an advanced level of development with institutional strength greater than in the other major industrialized democracies, that is in relation to the tasks of accommodating and guiding representations of interests. The key economic ministries which exercise most of this institutional strength have exceptional authority and relational legitimation. This sustains a very efficient form of alliance capitalism with an ethos of superior achievement orientation.[57] In this system however the strong emphasis on consensual decision making, together with the prevalence of high-level factionalism, is responsible for a lack of political leadership. On this account Japan tends to be disadvantaged compared with Germany, where the elite culture sets imperatives for leadership as well as consensus.[58]

INTERNATIONAL ECONOMIC COOPERATION

The functional significance of representational-institutional balances at the national political economy level is reflected in relations between states. Where governments cooperate for economic benefit without institutionalizing their collaboration, the initial momentum is usually lost after the short term.[59] The transnational enterprises shaping structural interdependencies are thus in effect given more scope for initiative to implement their strategies, and for political action to influence the policies of the interacting governments. Meanwhile the diminishing results of the governmental attempts at cooperation tend to cause policy makers to give more attention to the use of leverage on trade and investment issues, and to measures promising improvements in structural competitiveness.

The most productive venture in economic cooperation has been the formation of the European Union. This has evolved as a system of institutionalized collective management, in which representations of national interests are transformed into patterned collaboration through decision making in a structure that is becoming more and more federal. A vital institutional innovation has been the establishment of the European Commission as a common bureaucratic agency for independent aggregation of regional interests, the initiation of proposals for widening economic collaboration by member governments, and the exercise of regulatory powers to promote more comprehensive regional economic integration. The role of the Commission has become very substantial, despite attempts by member governments to restrict its functions.[60] The role of the European Parliament has been a secondary feature of the system, and the future of this organization is very uncertain because of the multiplicity of its political groups and their lack of effective support in member countries. The representation of national policy concerns through the involvement of member governments in decision making by the ministerial-level Council of the Union, interacting with the Commission, is basically functional, despite some manipulation of the collaborative process.[61] Increasing the very limited powers of the European Parliament, to overcome what has been seen as a democratic deficiency, could open the way for pluralistic stagnation, because of the difficulties of forming sufficiently large and stable coalitions of representative groups.

The Commission's role has evolved with advisory inputs from large corporate groups. Systemic logic in this consultative partnering has been reflected in the drive to complete the integration of the internal market, as much support for the Commission's sponsorship of this drive came from major European firms and business associations.[62] In this process the German inter-corporate system has been advantaged because of its size and internal cohesion, while fragmentation in the French, British and several other inter-corporate systems has entailed weaker potential for consultative exchanges with the Commission. The Commission's capacity to use technocratic expertise in the regional interest is, however, affected by the peculiarities of international staffing, as functional concerns have to adjust to the desires of all member governments to have important posts filled by their nominees. Overlapping divisions of functions are thus evident in the Commission structure.[63]

Economic cooperation within the Union, through collective decision making by member governments interacting with the Commission, focuses on governance of the internal market, the establishment of a monetary union, and the management of external economic relations. The most influential inputs into the decision making come from the Franco-German partnership in leadership of the Union, and are supported mainly by other industrialized northern member states. Differences over policy between the northern members are not significantly open to exploitation by the less industrialized southern members, as there are few political ties between their elites.

Governance of the internal market, in line with German and French preferences, is dominated by concerns with facilitating competitive intra-zonal entrepreneurship, under a liberal common competition policy.[64] Advancement to monetary union is to assist all forms of business activity in the internal market but is also to impose allocative discipline on member governments, and oblige them to strive for efficient macromanagement, so as to avoid trade deficits.[65] The management of the Union's external economic relations is consensually protectionist, to a degree, on the basis of understandings that Union firms require some shelter in order to enhance their international competitiveness, and that solidarity in that regard is necessary for effective bargaining on trade issues with the USA. Atlantic trade questions are overshadowed by imbalances in gains from transnational production, and on foreign direct investment issues there is less consensus. Investment bidding by member governments is competitive, and firms based in member states, especially those with less integrated inter-corporate systems, seek collaboration with American and Japanese enterprises as well as with corporations in other member economies. The expansion of direct investment and of partnering arrangements has complicated assessments of national and Union interests in the evolution of transnational production and foreign commerce.[66]

The advanced level of the institutionalized cooperation in the European Union is sustaining progress toward monetary union, with broad regional corporate support, but is not sufficiently developed to engage effectively with structural issues. While these are assuming more challenging dimensions because of foreign direct investment, the structural utility of Union foreign trade policy is gradually decreasing. Meanwhile the political effects of structural complexities resulting from foreign direct investment are tending to make initiatives for the promotion of a regional structural policy consensus less and less feasible. This state of affairs reflects the tendency for collaborative policy learning to lag behind the structural changes caused by corporate activity in a collective management system.[67]

Outside Europe there has been little institutionalized regional economic cooperation. The North America Free Trade Area has been formed without commitments to manage its rising interdependencies, and has assumed a hierarchical configuration, with strong US leverage being exercised in separate dealings with Canada and Mexico.[68] In the Atlantic context, in which the European Union relates principally to the USA, no endeavours are in prospect for institutionalizing economic cooperation. Emphasis on the independent management of foreign economic relations is a major feature of the American political tradition. European Union elite attitudes are influenced by awareness that levels of structural interdependence with the USA vary within the Union, and that a collective effort to structure a system of Atlantic collaboration could well be very difficult because of ambivalence in Britain's policy, due to strong cultural affinities with the USA and lack of rapport with France and Germany.[69]

In the global trading system the European Union and the USA have been the principal sponsors of the World Trade Organization (WTO), an institutional advance intended to promote increased openness in the global trading system. The collective regulatory function however is weak: trade liberalization is still a process of negotiating tariff and non-tariff reductions, primarily between the European Union and the USA, and as tariffs are reduced governments tend to rely more on non-tariff measures to shelter national firms, while restricting imports of price-competitive products.

The WTO is not open to complaints about corporate practices restricting market access unless these are explicitly supported by a government. Under the WTO governments are not obliged to implement competition policies, and can allow the formation of export monopolies.[70] In the dispute settlement processes the primary emphasis on promoting negotiated solutions makes the use of relative bargaining strengths very significant, especially because governments can resort to informal methods of advancing trade policy objectives. A common sequence is that anti-dumping measures directed against price-competitive imports can induce a targeted government to accept voluntary export restraints, in exchange for termination of the anti-dumping measures. Such restraints technically violate WTO principles, but of course may be agreed to informally, as outcomes of unequal bargaining.[71]

As a system for trade policy cooperation to increase openness in the world economy the WTO has representational-institutional problems. Institutional development below that in the European Union reflects the preferences of the USA, the European Union, and Japan for virtually unrestricted freedom to bargain over issues of market access: little scope is allowed for advocacy based on broad aggregations of interests in global trade liberalization. US, European, and Japanese trade practices do not reflect full acceptance of market contestability as a public good. Assessments of the WTO's prospects have emphasized that further negotiated progress toward openness in the world economy will depend on the willingness of national administrations to observe restraint in quests for advantage through trade policy leverage.[72]

Questions of openness to foreign direct investment have not been negotiable in the WTO context but have been discussed between the major industrialized states within the Organization for Economic Cooperation and Development (OECD), to achieve consensus on rights of establishment and national treatment. The principal discussions have been between the USA and European Union representatives, and have indicated preferences for maintaining unrestricted freedom to negotiate issues regarding the treatment of foreign direct investment, without working toward the formation of a common structure to monitor the implementation of foreign direct investment policies. In interactions within this policy area Japan has been rather isolated, and the USA has been advantaged because it has been able to deal separately with Japan while relating to the Europeans. There has been a similar advantage for the USA in the management of trade policy issues, but it has been less substantial. The European Union has a common foreign trade policy but has not yet evolved an integrated foreign direct investment policy, and on trade issues there is more potential for collaboration between the European Union and Japan than there is on foreign direct investment issues.[73]

European and US preferences for preserving negotiating freedom on foreign direct investment issues have evidenced concerns about questions emerging as European integration deepens. More effective exploitation of the opportunities of the Single Market by European firms is necessary for improved Union growth, but is hindered to some extent by the large and generally more competitive foreign corporate presence, comprising mainly US firms. Union efforts to promote the Europeanization of intra-zonal service industries encounter problems because of the presence of US service enterprises enjoying more than reciprocal access in the Single Market as a whole.[74] European shares of manufacturing sales in that market are considerably less than the shares of American firms in manufacturing sales within their home market.[75]

International Financial Markets

International financial markets, more integrated than those for goods and services, pose problems of collective governance with different systemic dimensions. National administrations have been more willing to accept the globalization of financial markets than the liberalization of markets for goods. The management of financial policies is an elitist process, much less exposed to domestic pressures than the direction of foreign trade and foreign direct investment policies. Financial institutions, exploiting liberal national policies, and aided by advanced communications technology, have formed an international financial system with rent-seeking operations far in excess of transactions funding industry and commerce.[76] This high-volume rent-seeking, decoupled from the real economy, can precipitate financial crises: it must be regarded as a very serious form of international market failure, because of the diversion of investment away from productive use. As those operations generate and exploit volatility, the administrations enjoying greater economic sovereignty have incentives to maintain substantial degrees of integration in their inter-corporate systems, partly by limiting foreign commercial penetration. Such system maintenance endeavours, however, are difficult for governments in less integrated national political economies.[77]

Financial markets were liberalized over the past three decades principally because of the interests of American financial institutions in gaining access to funding in countries with higher savings levels, and in serving the needs of US manufacturing firms operating in foreign markets. Rivalries between governments to promote the development of international financial centres gave impetus to the adoption of liberalizing policies. Opportunities for speculative operations, however, became far more significant than those for transactions directly related to productive activity as floating exchange rates shifted with changes in national balances of payments. Meanwhile financial management assumed greater significance for managements of trading and manufacturing firms, and, in what was becoming an unevenly integrated global financial market, firms demonstrating high short-term profits tended to secure preferential financing. General increases in short-termism were thus encouraged, but enterprises in the more integrated national political economies, especially Japan, were advantaged by relational bonds with their financial institutions which ensured lower-cost funding for long-term strategies.[78]

Conflicting pressures on the US dollar are central factors in the instability affecting international financial markets. The US fiscal and balance-of-payments deficits, together with a low US savings rate, tend to cause a continuing decline, but monetary restraint obligated by the fiscal deficits, and perversely increased whenever growth significantly reduces unemployment, tends to cause currency appreciation.[79] International monetary cooperation could be a source of discipline for fiscal reform in the USA, and could help moderate dollar volatility, but political will for such collaboration is lacking. Attempts at cooperation at the Group of Seven level have been mainly ineffective, and the International Monetary Fund has not evolved as an organization for the collective management of monetary policies.[80] A fundamental problem for the Japanese and German administrations, as the main potential partners in any arrangements for international monetary cooperation, is the absence of firm commitment to sound macroeconomic policies in the USA. It must be emphasized, however, that, as states with trade surpluses, Japan and Germany have sought to restrain appreciations of their currencies, to ensure competitive exporting, and accordingly have endeavoured to limit international use of those currencies.[81] These objectives have been pursued while coping with the basic problem of dollar volatility, without scope for initiative to promote the development of a strong system of international monetary cooperation. Only the USA has had significant scope for such initiative, but its use has been hindered by conflicts in its policy processes, and its fiscal policy deficiencies have been sources of compulsions to impose adjustment costs on Japan and Germany.

The globalization of financial markets has set requirements for a strong central regulatory institution. Some recognition of this systemic need has been implicit in many of the warnings about the dangers of instability in these markets.[82] The dangers will be less serious if a European Monetary Union is established with an effective German role in its leadership: this institutional advance would reduce the number of weak currencies subject to speculative attack, and could prepare the way for the introduction of a comprehensive mechanism for the control of financial institutions throughout the Union. Use of the US dollar within the Union would be reduced, moreover, and the governing body of the Monetary Union would be well placed to seek US and Japanese cooperation for the establishment of financial regulatory structures with a global reach. It must be noted, however, that, as a systemic advance, the European Monetary Union could be affected by ambivalence in German policy, relating to differences between the national administration and the independent Bundesbank on issues of inflation control, and the development of a monetary system that will serve the Union as a whole. Differing concepts of German-centred and Union-centred systemic logic could have diverging consequences, complicating Union decision processes on monetary issues.[83]

While there are uncertainties about the formation of the European Monetary Union the USA's fiscal and monetary policies remain unchallenged by authoritative external institutions. International market discipline, it must be stressed, is the principal source of pressure for improved performance, and the volatility in global financial markets indicates that the pressure could be intensified rapidly, with contagious effects. In the USA this danger is especially significant because of strains in the financial sector due to inadequately supervised risk-taking over the past two decades.[84] In the event of a crisis substantial monetary loosening would be expected, but as a means of restoring confidence and growth it could well be less effective than it was after the 1987 stock market crash in the USA: because of the evolution of international financial markets over the past decade there could be a swift outflow of funds from the USA to more stable economies.

PROMOTING COMPLEMENTARITY

Global financial markets and widely linked markets for goods, imposing pressures on the policies of governments and the strategies of firms, in conditions of very limited international economic cooperation, motivate endeavours to raise levels of structural competitiveness. These endeavours reflect differing applications of systemic logic, but such logic has potential applications for the promotion of structural complementarities. These could provide more balanced and more stable gains from transnational production and trade, reducing the scope for the predatory operations in financial markets, and hopefully inducing more functional policy making in the less integrated national political economies.

The Atlantic pattern of transregional relations is the main area of opportunity for government and corporate efforts to build structural complementarities, and to establish multi-group linkages for concerted entrepreneurship that will maintain and expand those complementarities. Cultural and ethnic affinities in this pattern facilitate the development of understanding and trust, and the trade comprises mainly intra-industry commerce. There is considerable complementarity, but production in Europe for Union consumers by US firms is at much higher volumes than production in the USA for its market by European enterprises, and is strategically more significant, notably in higher-technology sectors. The exposure of the US market to manufactures imported or produced in the USA by foreign firms of all nationalities is roughly 15 per cent, while such exposure is between 25 per cent and 30 per cent for the United Kingdom, France, and Germany. Foreign affiliates of mostly US firms accounted for 13.2 per cent of manufacturing output in Germany in 1990, 28.4 per cent in France, and 25 per cent in the United Kingdom.[85]

A transatlantic dialogue on trade and investment was launched in 1995 by the European Commission and the US Department of Commerce, to make recommendations for cooperation at the policy level that would facilitate the expansion of economic ties between the Union and the USA. The dialogue was activated mainly by the USA, and on trade issues US concerns focused on the Union's common commercial policy. On investment issues the USA had scope to relate to the rivalries of administrations within the Union bidding to attract US manufacturing investment. The development of a union foreign direct investment policy is hindered by the efforts of member governments to implement their own policies while observing Union rules on the free movement of capital throughout the Single Market.[86] The effectiveness of these national policies depends very much on the strength of informal bonds between governments and national inter-corporate systems, and these bonds will tend to assume greater significance if a common foreign direct investment policy with an extensive reach is in prospect, and if US diplomacy seeks to secure Union adoption of an Atlantic foreign direct investment code.

Within the Union complementarity between its members is rising to high levels, although unevenly, as the Single Market becomes more integrated. The complementarity is hierarchical, to a degree, because of German dominance, based on size and structural competitiveness, and imbalances in the spread of gains from intra-zonal commerce are the main sources of cleavages over industrial policy issues in the Union. The emphasis on free market forces as engines of growth, which is prominent in affirmations of Union policy, in line with German, French, and also British preferences, is in effect advantageous first of all for Germany, and the strengthening of the German role in the Union market contributes to the degree of integration in the German economy. This is an important factor in the regional pattern of complementarity, in which several member economies are linked more with Germany than with each other.[87]

The intra-zonal complementarity has imbalances reflecting higher levels of industrialization in the northern members of the European Union, especially Germany. These imbalances cause the complementarity to be less dynamic than would be desirable, that is less conducive to concerted entrepreneurship, with its potential for synergies. The disparities in enterprise capacities, technological levels, market strengths and forms of inter-corporate and government support tend to persist, because of continuing gains by German and other firms operating out of the more industrialized Union members.

The imbalanced pattern of intra-Union complementarity is linked with the Atlantic pattern, in which the USA is linked more with the northern Union members, but more with Germany and Britain than with France through trade, and more with France and Britain through direct investment, that is in a configuration which reflects the higher integration and competitiveness of the German inter-corporate pattern. In the linked evolution of the intra-Union and the Atlantic pattern Germany is challenged principally by the relatively higher levels of US direct investment in France and Britain, while serving the US market mainly through exports, and thus encountering challenges from US national firms and from Japanese enterprises producing in and exporting to the USA at high volumes. Japan's exports to the USA are at almost the same level as those from the entire European Union.[88]

For the Union as a whole there is a clear imperative to work toward more balanced and more dynamic complementarity with the USA, but what is in prospect is increasing asymmetry, due especially to the activities of US firms, operating with much autonomy out of the liberal policy environment of their home government. In view of the advantages enjoyed by US firms producing in the Union – due to size, resources, technological levels, and the investment bidding within the Union – the development of more symmetrical Atlantic complementarity, with synergies conducive to continuing growth and balance, will be difficult. Intensive consultative partnering between the European Commission and corporate groups throughout the Union, however, would make possible constructive interaction with US firms that are currently able to implement regional strategies rather independently. Systemic logic, in the Atlantic context, definitely requires a strong European Commission role, to promote extensive concerting of entrepreneurial strategies within the Union and between Union and American firms.

As the competitively interacting strategies of transnational enterprises have more and more extensive cross-border structural and market effects, attempts at macroeconomic cooperation across the Atlantic have to cope with greater uncertainties.[89] These tend to lower the relatively weak commitments of governments to develop such cooperation, as hopes that it can be conducive to balanced interdependent growth are discouraged. A consequence not often recognized is that imperatives for wide-ranging microeconomic cooperation become stronger: it becomes more necessary to work for collaborative management of the interdependencies between governments and firms. To the extent that this microeconomic cooperation can develop in responsive consultative partnering with enterprises, the associated information flows would reduce the uncertainties that discourage macroeconomic cooperation – that is while transregional structural complementarities increase.

NOTES

This chapter is a revised version of a paper given at the Conference on Globalization and Regionalization, University of Paris I, Panthéon Sorbonne, 29–30 May 1996
1. See Charles-Albert Michalet, 'Transnational corporations and the changing international economic system', *Transnational Corporations*, 3 (1), February 1994, 9–22
2. See John H. Dunning, 'Reappraising the eclectic paradigm in an age of alliance capitalism', *Journal of International Business Studies*, 26 (3), 1995, 461–92
3. See Lynn K. Mytelka (ed.), *Strategic Partnerships and the World Economy* (Rutherford: Fairleigh Dickinson University Press, 1991).
4. See Gavin Boyd, 'Japan's structural competitiveness', in Gavin Boyd (ed.), *Structural Competitiveness in the Pacific* (Cheltenham: Edward Elgar, 1996), Chapter 6.
5. See Mark Casson, *Enterprise and Competitiveness* (Oxford: Oxford University Press, 1990).
6. See Gavin Boyd, 'Political change, macromanagement and economic cooperation', in Gavin Boyd (ed.), *Competitive and Cooperative Macromanagement* (Aldershot: Edward Elgar, 1995), Chapter 8.
7. See Bernard Hoekman and Michel Kostecki, *The Political Economy of the World Trading System* (Oxford: Oxford University Press, 1995).
8. See Vivien A. Schmidt, 'European integration and the transformation of national patterns of policymaking: the differences among member states', paper for the European consortium for political research, Oslo, 29 March–3 April 1996.
9. See Boyd, 'Political change, macromanagement, and economic cooperation'.
10. See Boyd, 'Japan's structural competitiveness'.
11. See Roger G. Noll, 'Structural policies in the United States', in Samuel Kernell (ed.), *Parallel Politics* (Washington, DC: Brookings Institution, 1991), pp. 230–80.
12. See *Policy Sciences*, 27 (4), 1994, symposium on capital mobility.
13. See Frederic S. Mishkin, 'Preventing financial crises: an international perspective' *Manchester School Papers in Money, Macroeconomics and Finance, Supplement*, LXII, 1993.

14. On the use of leverage see Thomas O. Bayard and Kimberly Ann Elliott, *Reciprocity and Retaliation in US Trade Policy* (Washington, DC: Institute for International Economics, 1994).
15. See Ryutaro Komiya, *The Japanese Economy: Trade, Industry and Government* (Tokyo: University of Tokyo Press, 1990), pp. 126–30.
16. See Mishkin, 'Preventing financial crises'.
17. *Ibid.*
18. See Noll, 'Structural policies'.
19. See William D. Coleman, 'State traditions and comprehensive business associations: a comparative structural analysis', *Political Studies*, XXXVIII (2), June 1990, 231–52.
20. See Noll, 'Structural policies'.
21. *Ibid.*
22. See Gavin Boyd, 'Policy environments for corporate planning', in Gavin Boyd (ed.), *Competitive and Cooperative Macromanagement* (Aldershot: Edward Elgar, 1995), pp. 20–46.
23. See Noll, 'Structural policies'.
24. *Ibid.*
25. See Maria Papadakis, 'Did (or does) the United States have a competitiveness crisis?', *Journal of Policy Analysis and Management*, 13 (1), Winter 1994, 1–20.
26. See Noll, 'Structural policies'.
27. See Alan Kirman and Mika Widgren, 'European economic policy decision making: progress or paralysis?', *Economic Policy*, 21, October 1995, 421–60; Kirsty Hughes 'The 1996 intergovernmental conference and EU enlargement', *International Affairs*, 72 (1), January 1996, 1–8; and Simon J. Bulmer, 'The governance of the European Union: a new institutionalist approach', *Journal of Public Policy*, 13 (4), October–December 1993, 351–80
28. See Gavin Boyd, 'Policy environments for corporate planning'.
29. *Ibid.*
30. See Paul R. Masson (ed.) *France: Financial and Real Sector Issues* (Washington, DC: International Monetary Fund, 1995).
31. See Kirsty Hughes, 'The role of technology, competition and skill in European competitiveness', in Kirsty Hughes (ed.), *European Competitiveness* (Cambridge: Cambridge University Press, 1993), pp. 133–60.
32. See Boyd, 'Japan's structural competitiveness'.
33. See Michael L. Gerlach, *Alliance Capitalism: The Social Organization of Japanese Business* (Berkeley: University of California Press, 1992).
34. See Allen J. Morrison and Kendall Roth, 'The regional solution: an alternative to globalization', *Transnational Corporations*, 1 (2), August 1992, 37–56.
35. On rent-seeking in the USA see Gary A. Dymski, Gerald Epstein and Robert Pollin (eds), *Transforming the US Financial System* (Armonk: M.E. Sharpe, 1993) and Kevin M. Murphy, Andrei Shleifer and Robert W. Vishny, 'The allocation of talent: implications for growth', *Quarterly Journal of Economics*, May 1991, 503–30
36. See Paul Krugman (ed.), *Trade with Japan* (Chicago: University of Chicago Press, 1991).
37. See Coleman, 'State traditions'; Michael Hodges and Stephen Woolcock, 'Atlantic capitalism versus Rhine capitalism in the European Community', *West European Politics*, 16 (3), July 1993, 329–44; and Eric Owen Smith, *The German Economy* (London: Routledge, 1994).
38. See Simon Bulmer and William E. Paterson, 'Germany in the European Union: gentle giant or emergent leader?', *International Affairs*, 72 (1), January 1995, 9–32.
39. See C. Randall Henning, *Currencies and Politics in the United States, Germany, and Japan* (Washington DC: Institute for International Economics, 1994), Chapter 5.
40. See Masson, *France: Financial and Real Sector Issues.*
41. See Coleman, 'State traditions'; Hodges and Woolcock, 'Atlantic capitalism versus Rhine capitalism'; and Matthew Bishop and John Kay (eds), *European Mergers and Merger Policy* (Oxford: Oxford University Press, 1993).
42. See Hodges and Woolcock, 'Atlantic capitalism versus Rhine capitalism'.
43. The US direct investment position in Europe on a historical cost basis at the end of 1995 was $363 527 million. See Jeffrey H. Lowe and Sylvia E. Bargas, 'Direct investment positions on

a historical cost basis', *Survey of Current Business*, 76 (7), July 1996, 45–60. See also *The Performance of Foreign Affiliates in OECD Countries* (Paris: OECD 1994).

44. See Vivien A. Schmidt, 'European integration and the transformation of national patterns of policy-making', paper for the European Consortium for Political Research, Oslo, 29 March–3 April 1996.

45. See Jack Hayward and Edward C. Page (eds), *Governing the New Europe* (Cambridge: Polity Press, 1995), Chapter 8.

46. See Casson, *Enterprise and Competitiveness*, and Lawrence J. White, 'Competition policy in the United States', *Oxford Review of Economic Policy*, 9 (2), Summer 1993, 133–50.

47. On the benefits of cooperation see Michele Kremen Bolton, Roger Malmrose, and William G. Ouchi, 'The organization of innovation in the United States and Japan: neoclassical and relational contracting', *Journal of Management Studies*, 31 (5), September 1994, 653–80.

48. On the behaviour of citizens in a liberal state see Jenny Stewart, 'Rational choice theory, public policy, and the liberal state', *Policy Sciences*, 26 (4), 1993, 317–30. See also Casson, *Enterprise and Competitiveness*.

49. On the influence of instrumental values on legislative behaviour in the USA see Terry M. Moe, 'Political institutions: the neglected side of the story', *Journal of Law, Economics, and Organization*, 6, Special Issue, 1990 – Symposium on US Political Institutions, 213–54.

50. See Boyd, 'Japan's Structural Competitiveness'.

51. See Stewart, 'Rational choice theory, public policy, and the liberal state', and Boyd, *Structural Competitiveness in the Pacific*, Chapter 5.

52. See Gavin Boyd, *Corporate Planning and Policy Planning in the Pacific* (London: Pinter, 1993), Chapter 8.

53. See *United Germany: The First Five Years* (Washington, DC: International Monetary Fund, 1995), and David Mayes and Peter Hart, *The Single Market Programme as a Stimulus to Change: Comparisons between Britain and Germany* (Cambridge: Cambridge University Press, 1994).

54. See Andrew Appleton, 'Parties under pressure: challenges to "established" French parties', *West European Politics*, 18 (1), January 1995, 52–77.

55. See Masson, *France: Financial and Real Sector Issues*.

56. See Mayes and Hart, *The Single Market Programme*, and Royce Turner (ed.), *The British Economy in Transition* (London: Routledge, 1995).

57. See Shumpei Kumon and Henry Rosovsky (eds), *The Political Economy of Japan*, vol. 3 (Stanford: Stanford University Press, 1992).

58. See Boyd, *Corporate Planning and Policy Planning in the Pacific*, Chapter 7.

59. See Tommaso Padoa-Schioppa and Fabrizio Saccomanni, 'Managing a market-led global financial system', in Peter B. Kenen (ed.) *Managing the World Economy* (Washington, DC: Institute for International Economics, 1994), pp. 235–68.

60. See Schmidt, 'European integration'.

61. See Hayward and Page, *Governing the New Europe*.

62. *Ibid.*, Chapter 8.

63. See Guy Peters, 'Bureaucratic politics and the institutions of the European Community', in Alberta M. Sbragia (ed.), *Euro-Politics* (Washington, DC: Brookings Institution, 1992), pp. 75–122.

64. See Lee McGowan and Stephen Wilks, 'The first supranational policy in the European Union: competition policy', *European Journal of Political Research*, 28 (2), September 1995, 141–69.

65. See references to European Monetary Union in C. Randall Henning, *Currencies and Politics in the United States, Germany, and Japan*.

66. See Stephen Young and Neil Hood, 'Inward investment policy in the European Community in the 1990s', *Transnational Corporations*, 2 (2), August 1993, 35–62, and references to German corporate cohesion in Mayes and Hart, *The Single Market Programme*.

67. See Coleman, 'State traditions', and references to industrial policy in Frédérique Sachwald (ed.), *European Integration and Competitiveness* (Aldershot: Edward Elgar, 1994).

68. See Murray Smith, 'The North American Free Trade Agreement: global impacts', in Kym Anderson and Richard Blackhurst (eds), *Regional Integration and the Global Trading System*

(New York: St. Martin's Press, 1993), pp. 83–103, and Carlo Perroni and John Whalley, *The New Regionalism: Trade Liberalization or Insurance?* (Cambridge, MA: National Bureau of Economic Research Working Paper 4626, 1994).

69. See Gavin Boyd, 'Political entrepreneurship for collective management', in Gavin Boyd and Alan M. Rugman (eds), *Euro-Pacific Investment and Trade* (Cheltenham: Edward Elgar, 1997).
70. See Hoekman and Kostecki, *The Political Economy of the World Trading System*, pp. 252–7.
71. See John H. Jackson, 'The World Trade Organization: watershed innovation or cautious small step forward?', *The World Economy*, Special Issue on Global Trade Policy, 1995, 11–32.
72. *Ibid.*
73. There is little European direct investment in Japan. See *The Performance of Foreign Affiliates in OECD Countries*, (Paris: OECD, 1994), and *Proceedings of the Second Seminar on European Union/Japan Competition Policy* (Brussels: European Commission 1994).
74. On problems of reciprocity in financial services see Thomas O. Bayard and Kimberly Ann Elliott, *Reciprocity and Retaliation in US Trade Policy*, Chapter 11.
75. See *The Performance of Foreign Affiliates in OECD Countries*.
76. See *Policy Sciences*, 27 (4), 1994, symposium on capital mobility.
77. *Ibid.*; see also Hodges and Woolcock, 'Atlantic capitalism versus Rhine capitalism'.
78. See Boyd, 'Japan's structural competitiveness'.
79. See Henning, *Currencies and Politics in the United States, Germany, and Japan*, and Mishkin, 'Preventing financial crises'.
80. See Padoa-Schioppa and Saccomanni, 'Managing a market-led global financial system'.
81. See Henning, *Currencies and Politics*, Chapters 4 and 5.
82. See Padoa-Schioppa and Saccomanni, 'Managing a market-led global financial system'.
83. See Simon Bulmer and William E. Paterson, 'Germany in the European Union: gentle giant or emergent leader?', *International Affairs*, 72 (1), January 1996, 9–32.
84. See Mishkin, 'Preventing financial crises'.
85. See *The Performance of Foreign Affiliates in OECD Countries*.
86. See Stephen Young and Neil Hood, 'Inward investment policy in the European Community in the 1990s', *Transnational Corporations*, 2 (2), August 1993, 35–62.
87. See *Direction of Trade Statistics Yearbook*, 1995 (Washington, DC: International Monetary Fund, 1995).
88. *Ibid.*
89. On the uncertainties affecting macroeconomic cooperation see Ralph C. Bryant, 'International cooperation in the making of national macroeconomic policies: where do we stand?', in Peter B. Kenen (ed.), *Understanding Interdependence: The Macroeconomics of the Open Economy* (Princeton: Princeton University Press, 1995), pp. 391–447.

11. Planning Atlantic direct investment conferences

Gavin Boyd

Atlantic potentials for microeconomic cooperation are especially significant in so far as they indicate possibilities for collegial transregional technocratic interaction with firms, to encourage partnering for higher growth and more balanced complementarities between the European Union and North America. This partnering could develop in multi-group direct investment conferences sponsored by the European Commission and the American, Canadian, and Mexican administrations. The conferencing could be planned to facilitate corporate exploration of opportunities for collaborative direct investment decisions, identified with the aid of technocratic assessments of sectoral trends and developmental issues. With highly constructive knowledge-intensive technocratic participation the conferences could become very productive, while contributing to the formation of a transregional community of structural experts and corporate leaders.

The rationale for the conferences, which could be formulated initially by the European Commission, could stress the importance of engaging with fundamentals in Atlantic structural interdependencies, referring especially to the problem of declining growth rates in Europe and North America.[1] It could be indicated that the conferences would open the way for widely concerted entrepreneurship, and could be a source of pressure for improved macroeconomic policies on each side of the Atlantic. In that regard it could be stressed that macroeconomic policy failures have contributed to strains in the global trading and production systems, obliging cautious investment decisions by firms, while making business conditions more adverse for small and medium-sized enterprises with growth potentials.[2]

The conferences could be planned primarily for high-technology sectors. In these the benefits of corporate cooperation are especially significant because of the high costs of new technology, the diffuse effects of applied frontier research, and the scale of the market and structural changes resulting from combinations of competitive and collaborative strategies. The high-technology focus would accord with European concerns about increasing asymmetries in the gains from Atlantic commerce; it would also accord with North American interests in working toward higher shared growth in Atlantic relations.

CONSENSUS FORMATION

An Atlantic elite consensus is needed on imperatives to promote more balanced structural interdependencies between Europe and North America through integrative microeconomic cooperation, engaging with corporate strategies that are shaping fundamentals. The cooperation would be sought through intensive consultations between structural authorities and corporate managements, planned to promote harmony, in the common interest, between managerial strategies, and between those strategies and coordinated structural policy objectives, through interactive learning, with the building of trust and the acceptance of informal accountabilities.

The intended cooperation would be presented as the principal policy alternative to the common instrumental preference for microeconomic policy competition that is marginally collaborative. Pragmatic conventional wisdom can reject this integrative choice as visionary, stressing the risks of non-cooperation at the governmental and corporate levels, and can anticipate only continued assertions of economic nationalism within limits set by the retaliatory capacities of trading partners. Against this it must be asserted that governments must deal collectively with problems of internationalized market failure, and therefore must seek corporate cooperation, on the basis of shared responsibilities extending across national borders, using consultative rather than interventionist measures. The requirements for cooperations in the general interest between the administrative and corporate levels are becoming greater as problems of international market failure have wider effects, and as policy instruments weaken with the growth of corporate structural power. Moral problems are associated with leadership roles in industrialized democracies, because of the displacement of ethical principles necessary for order, justice, and growth, yet high-principled macromanagement is becoming more necessary. In the liberal political tradition there are implicit requirements for public spirited political and economic behaviour.[3]

A doctrine of integrative microeconomic cooperation could be set out in studies sponsored by the European Commission, referring to the challenging projections that have to be confronted regarding acquisitions of oligopolistic strengths as competition for world market shares intensifies. Less competitive firms are driven into declines at a faster pace as markets become more closely linked.[4] For states with many disadvantaged firms the imbalances in structural interdependence thus become very threatening.

The European Commission could work for acceptance of a basic partnering principle, stressing the potential efficiencies of responsive interaction between technocratic assessments of sectoral trends and capabilities and managerial exploration of innovative opportunities identified through discussions of those assessments, and through inter-corporate exchanges about strategic planning options. In terms of transaction cost economics the Commission's studies could emphasize that highly motivated technocratic expertise can provide, for wide ranges of firms, a type of consulting service which those firms could not readily obtain, without considerable costs and risks, from private consulting organizations that typically discriminate among their clients. It could be stressed, moreover, that while firms with large resources could bring highly capable technocrats into their staffs, these persons would in time lose their sectoral expertise, and that the potential efficiencies of technocratic interactions with and learning from numerous firms would not be attained. The partnering doctrine would not downgrade the functions of consulting firms, but would project a context in which their advising would be offered within frames of reference provided by the technocratic sectoral assessments presented in the common interest.

In Commission-sponsored studies it would be necessary to emphasize the need for technocratic-corporate consultations within the European Union as well as in the Atlantic setting. The developing pattern of exchanges would have to be expanded, and made more productive, for a broad structural policy consensus with which corporate preferences would be increasingly aligned.[5] It would have to be made clear that the intra-Union cooperation would be necessary for productive interactions in the Atlantic context, and would help to encourage increased government-corporate cooperation in North America.

The rationale for the conferencing, which could develop as Commission-sponsored studies were complemented by North American research and policy papers, could direct attention to the innovative potential of the consultative interactions, stressing the expected synergies of the interactive learning, and the need for collaborative management of the interdependencies between governments and firms.[6] These are functional relationships between policy mixes and corporate strategies, involving public goods and firm-specific benefits. With improved management of these functional relationships a cooperative spirit generated in the conferencing could give some thrust to the harmonization of European and North American trade, foreign direct investment, and competition policies, while giving more coherence to their linkages with structural policies.

The focus of the conferencing on high-technology sectors could be explained as a consequence of their prominence in global production and trade, their transmission of innovations into other sectors, and their dependence on, as well as their contributions to, major clusters of innovative activity. Technocratic expertise would be strengthened through involvement in the conferences, that is through closer and wider acquaintance with the dynamics of corporate strategies. With the corporate learning and the general building of trust, meanwhile, destructive inter-corporate rivalries would be reduced, and balances between competitive and cooperative strategies would become more functional.

The logic of the partnering, despite the diversity of the Atlantic participants, could be made persuasive in Commission-sponsored studies by identifying the basic dynamics of Japanese alliance capitalism, in which administrative guidance operates in efficient reciprocal causality with spontaneously coordinated corporate strategies. This collaboration has demonstrated the synergies of intensive task-oriented information sharing between the technocratic and corporate levels.[7] Replication in the more individualistic settings of Western societies has been considered difficult, but imperatives to learn from it have become stronger as Western governments have sought to raise levels of structural competitiveness in their economies without resorting to interventionist measures that encourage rent-seeking and have alienating effects.

Public management reforms in Western states have been responsive in part to the demonstration effects of the Japanese experience, especially because of its cost-effectiveness in the provision of administrative services. Strong task orientations have limited the interests of Japanese technocrats in bureaucratic expansion, and have restrained tendencies toward the overproduction of bureaucratic goods and services. The Western reforms have sought not only to improve administrative cost-effectiveness but also to facilitate corporate adaptation to rising vulnerabilities associated with the strains of deepening integration.[8] The policy orientations motivating the reforms have affirmed reliance on market forces for growth but have also stressed requirements to offer attractive business environments to international firms.[9]

The Commission-sponsored studies could assume wider scope by examining the logic of Western efforts to raise structural competitiveness through technology policies requiring corporate cooperation. Successes and failures in these efforts have revealed aspects of interdependence that have obligated consideration of ways of promoting structural complementarities.[10] Efforts in that direction, it has been clear, could induce macromanagement improvements in states burdened with problems of governance because of weak integration in their political economies, while also inducing constructive policy orientations in the more integrated states whose macromanagement measures have been based on economic nationalism. The promotion of complementarities, it could be stressed, would have strong growth effects, developing through the consultations integrating the entrepreneurial strategies of groups of firms.[11] For this process informal coordination and steering of the European technocratic presentations at the conferences could become a major task for Commission representatives.[12]

POLICY COMMUNITIES AND INTERCORPORATE SYSTEMS

A doctrine of collaborative direct investment conferencing would have to be spread through dialogue with European Union policy communities and corporate groups, and then with similar communities and groups in North America. Rapport on principles would have to be established despite the diversity of cultures, structures, and policy preferences.

In Europe German policy communities and corporate groups rank high in terms of institutional development and consensually rational decision processes. Their degrees of integration give them substantial capacities for advocacy and bargaining, domestically and in the Union context. Their participation in Atlantic direct investment conferences could be very active, but other European policy communities and corporate groups could be reluctant to cooperate because of concerns about Germany's dominant position in the Union. Within the German policy communities and corporate associations, moreover, there could be some ambivalence regarding a Commission-sponsored drive for consensus, because of subjective preferences for preserving cohesion within the German political economy rather than exposing that cohesion to strain under the pressures of involvement in a contentious Union structural endeavour.

Policy communities and corporate groups in most of the other Union members are institutionally less developed, are less integrated, and have weaker capacities for advocacy and bargaining. They relate to their German counterparts across considerable social distances, with conflicting interests because of the uneven spread of gains from commerce within the Union. The importance of active sponsorship of the conferencing by the European Commission would thus have to be stressed in its efforts to form a broadly supportive consensus.

To promote a European structural consensus the European Commission itself would have to learn from the Japanese system of alliance capitalism, especially to strengthen its own technocratic capacities.[13] There have been some deficiencies in its technology policy, and these appear to have been partly responsible for opportunistic choices by European firms, in conflict with the Union's need for a common structural policy.[14] There are problems of competence and bias in the international staffing of the organization, and it is vulnerable to pressures from member governments and major interest groups; it is however interacting rather effectively with member governments monitoring, influencing, and restricting their subsidies to their own industries, and the intensive learning which results could well be giving it a capacity to provide leadership for the building of a Union structural consensus.[15]

The studies which the Commission could sponsor, and its related consultative activities, would have to be directed in a special way to French and German policy communities and corporate groups, to establish strong understandings that would be associated with Franco-German leadership of the Union. The Commission's endeavours would have to encourage macromanagement convergence between France and Germany, through policy-oriented analysis of the logic of systemic approaches to competitiveness and to the management of interdependencies.[16] The system-building intent of Western management reforms could then be given more comprehensive expression, with a broadening of the dialogue with France and Germany to include policy communities and corporate groups in all member states.[17]

The promotion of Franco-German convergence would demand much effort. German policy communities and corporate groups, while more united than those in France, are strongly market-oriented, reflecting confidence in the nation's leading position in the Union economy.[18] France's political economy has a tradition of authoritative government economic involvement, relating with much less consensus to a fragmented inter-corporate system.[19] There is less openness in the French system to the functional significance of Japanese-style technocratic-corporate partnering, but, in comparison with Germany, there is a stronger grasp of the urgency of a common structural policy for the Union.

American policy communities and corporate groups could respond favourably to the rationale for Atlantic direct investment conferencing in so far as it emphasized information-sharing to facilitate entrepreneurial cooperation and promised opportunities for more active exchanges on Atlantic trade and investment issues. The conferencing could be seen as an appropriate development of the Transatlantic Business Dialogue between the European Union and American business leaders which began in 1995. This dialogue has enabled US and European corporate leaders to press for the removal of regulatory barriers to EU-US trade and investment in several sectors, including automobiles, chemicals, electronics, information and communications equipment, and pharmaceuticals.

The scope to enlist European as well as American corporate support for Transatlantic Business Dialogue objectives would be a major consideration for US policy makers and managements in discussions of proposals for Atlantic direct investment conferences.[20] Concerns to secure increased European openness could be expected to be very active because of anticipations that without increases in Atlantic economic cooperation pressures within Europe for more protection of the single market could become stronger, especially if continued European losses of competitiveness in world markets were evident. For US officials an operational consideration would be the importance of seizing the initiative in pre-conference exchanges, especially because of the possibility that the European Commission's freedom to act could be hindered by dependence on the support of member governments. The strongly individualistic orientations of US managements could be expressed in preferences for greater reliance on their own Atlantic networking, rather than through involvement in the proposed direct investment conferences These preferences could, however, be changed by conferencing initiatives taken by the US administration, especially if these dramatized European decision problems and were seen to encourage opportunistic shifts in the strategies of European firms.

CORPORATE STRATEGIES

The rationale for Atlantic direct investment conferencing would have complex implications for European and North American firms, depending especially on degrees of solidarity that might form in Europe and trends in US government-business relations. Most of the implications would be significant with respect to alliances and acquisitions. The anticipated balances of bargaining strengths and terms of collaborative options would overshadow interactions at the conferences, especially for the European participants, because of their generally weaker competitiveness and the inferior leverage of their governments on trade and investment issues. The bargaining disparities experienced by the Europeans could, however, be made less significant by intensive European Commission efforts to form a Union structural consensus. Over time, in the absence of such an endeavour, European firms would tend to be drawn into more unequal forms of collaboration with their North American counterparts. In this process the conferences would become less significant as occasions for the development of Atlantic structural complementarities.

The reduction of uncertainties through information sharing at the conferences, in line with their rationale,[21] especially as understood by the European Commission, while affected by the influence of bargaining disparities, could be of greater value for European firms if the technocratic involvement of the European Commission were very active, and if stronger bonds between those firms were being formed through the Commission's intensive consultative activities. For the present, in quests for Atlantic partnering undertaken on an individual basis, German firms are aided by their relational ties, but most other European enterprises are disadvantaged by the lack of such affiliations, that is in terms of access to information and of resources for bargaining. Linked with these disadvantages are generally lower technological levels, which are being perpetuated by smaller investments in research and development.

Most Union firms in the high-technology categories that would be attracted to the Atlantic conferencing are seeking to rationalize their operations within the single market while attempting penetration of the US economy.[22] Strategic technology partnering arrangements with US firms have been rising steadily over the past decade, and are roughly twice as numerous as those with other European enterprises, which appear to have been stagnating.[23] The growth of the Atlantic partnering suggests that European corporate interest in its opportunities would increase if Atlantic direct investment conferences were sponsored. The choices of US partners, while often made from weak bargaining positions, are influenced by growing Japanese competition in the Union market. Technology alliances with Japanese firms are at low levels – roughly one-fifth of the number of European-US alliances.[24] The interest of European firms in US partners appears to be motivated by assessments of the USA's growth potentials, and by needs for access to the technology of its firms. The size of the US corporate presence in Europe[25] is also a major factor, particularly because of its significance for the positions of European firms in their internal market. European enterprises, however, have strong incentives to preserve ties with their home governments and with the European Commission. These ties have implications regarding subsidies, procurements, marketing, trade protection, and technology-sharing.[26]

Differences in regional and global market positions influence the preferences of European high-technology enterprises. In world high-technology trade German firms have strong leads over those in France and Britain, but rank behind the Japanese share, which is rising, and the US share, which is falling. Germany's role in global high-technology trade has been declining slowly, but in medium-technology trade has been increasing gradually. The USA is the principal market for German high-and medium-technology exports, but German direct investment in the USA to build on trade successes has been considerably below Britain's. The flow increased dramatically in 1995, bringing the German direct investment position to $53 705 million, on a historical cost basis, that is roughly half the British position, but with a more significant manufacturing component. A large part of the British position has been in the financial sector. Atlantic direct investment conferencing could be expected to intensify information flows based on informal ties between German firms with interests in the USA, causing location advantages in the United States to become more significant in German managerial planning.[27]

France has a smaller direct investment position in the USA, with a smaller manufacturing component, and a more modest share of the US market, gained mainly through exports.[28] Outward French direct investment is less aided by inter-corporate ties, and is supported by weaker high- and medium-technology sectors, but has been increasing substantially, partly, it appears, to reduce exposure to bureaucratic direction and heavy taxation at home. Expanding interaction with American firms will evidently tend to increase the fragmentation of the national inter-corporate system.[29] This however could be less probable if the French administration provides strong leadership for a Commission-sponsored drive to build a Union structural consensus. The efforts of French administrations to raise levels of structural competitiveness in the home economy have, however, been hindered by heavy welfare costs, deep social cleavages, and strains in government-business relations.[30]

British firms, benefiting from high-volume information flows associated with their large presence in the USA, could engage in very active networking at Atlantic direct investment conferences. They could be disadvantaged by weaker capacities for technology partnering, however, and by the relatively weak roles of their affiliates in the US economy.[31] The interest of British managements in the conference could, moreover, be influenced by some reluctance to contribute to major increases in Germany, France, and other European flows of direct investment to the USA.

American corporate interest in the conferences would probably relate mainly to opportunities in Britain and Germany, as the principal locations for production to serve the Union market. Roughly a third of the US direct investment position in Europe is in Britain, and the position in Germany is about one-third of the British total, but includes a large manufacturing presence – $23 671 million, that is about $5000 million less than in the same sector in Britain, in 1995. Britain is the main location for US investment in the financial sector.[32]

The US corporate presence in Europe is much larger than is indicated by historical cost figures, as it includes investments that were very extensive in the years following the Second World War. The scale of operations generates high-volume commercial intelligence which would be very advantageous for US firms participating in Atlantic direct investment conferences. Potentials for collaboration are limited by low levels of trust in American inter-corporate relations[33] but could become stronger through involvement in the conferences. Interest would tend to focus on high-technology collaboration with German enterprises, because of the strength of German centres of innovation, but acquisitions of such firms might well be given higher priority, despite informal German restraints on takeovers. In the Atlantic pattern of high-technology corporate strategies over the past decade strong US preferences for acquisitions have been evident, partly, it appears, because of intense competition for shares of the single market.[34]

For US high-technology companies opportunities to collaborate with French and British firms are affected more by uncertainties about the evolution of industrial strengths and national policies.[35] Choices about locations in France, Britain, and other European countries are, however, influenced by the competitive investment bidding of host governments, which has been tending to increase because of slack growth and the disruptive effects of corporate restructuring in the single market.[36] The southern, less developed areas of the Union are attractive for assembly-type manufacturing by US firms because of investment inducements and low production costs.

SECTORS

Potentials for Atlantic direct investment cooperation can be indicated in varying degrees by contrasting sectoral profiles in Europe and North America. These profiles are constituted by differing capacities, rates of technological progress, levels of government support, and forms of corporate governance. In terms of size, technological advancement, international market shares, and supportive governmental bargaining strengths, European high-technology firms have inferior rankings, and depend more on official subsidies, procurements, and trade protection.[37] These forms of aid tend to induce excessive dependence, but the relationships could become more functional with a strengthening of technocratic advisory roles in line with those that could be intended to develop in the Atlantic direct investment conferencing.

Aerospace

Aerospace is the sector in which the USA is most competitive, with about 45 per cent of the world market. Investment in new technology, building on decades of indirect subsidization through defence contracts, is adequate to sustain the large world market share, and the national administration's interest is active. There is no significant Japanese challenge. US corporate and government attitudes to the European aerospace sector express resentment at its heavy subsidization by Union governments. That sector can expect to be aided by orders from European national airlines, especially if the Union initiates a policy of Europeanizing intra-zonal air transport. This would lead to difficult negotiations with the USA over the rights of foreign carriers presently serving routes between Union cities.[38]

Large asymmetries in corporate bargaining strength thus overshadow possibilities for Atlantic direct investment cooperation in this sector. Associated with these asymmetries are strong policy-level interests, which, for the European Union, could well motivate efforts to build a more self-reliant sector, with reduced dependence on US suppliers of specialized equipment.

Chemicals

Chemicals is a sector more open to Atlantic cooperation. There is rough parity between American and European (mainly German) levels of competitiveness, as indicated by world market shares. There is substantial cross-investment, policy-level and corporate attitudes are positive, and there is scope to expand capacity, especially to meet American demand. On each side, especially in Europe, there has been some loss of international market shares because of competition from East Asian suppliers.[39] There appears to be considerable scope for Atlantic rationalization, which could be assisted by discussions at the direct investment conferences. Locational collaboration, increased research and development partnering could increase the present levels of sectoral complementarity.

Semiconductors

Semiconductors a sector evolving rapidly with frontier research, offers possibilities for Atlantic collaboration which are especially significant because of strong Japanese challenges. This sector has fundamental importance for European and American structural competitiveness and complementarity because of its basic role in wide ranges of electronic systems. European capacities are much weaker than those of the USA, and these in turn lag behind those of Japanese firms, which have a large lead in world market shares. Government support for frontier research in Europe has been more active than in the USA, but with only modest results. European firms have sought partnering mainly with American enterprises, but the strategies of those firms have tended to focus on building links with Japanese companies. Efforts by European firms to collaborate with American corporations have been undertaken from weak positions.[40] US structural policy for the sector has been somewhat dysfunctional because of conflicting corporate pressures, lack of rapport with national firms, and the politicization of assistance for research and development.

In Atlantic direct investment conferences the potential benefits for European participants would depend very much on the degree to which they were collaborating with each other, in line with a common Union policy for this sector. Without considerable solidarity European firms would tend to be drawn into individual accommodations with the strategies of American enterprises seeking mainly to preempt opportunities for more effective competition against Japanese rivals. European restraints on Japanese penetration of the single market benefit US corporate strategies, but as these restraints are weakening there are incentives for US companies to move rapidly in their quests for stronger positions in the single market.

Consumer Electronics

Consumer electronics, closely linked with developments in the semiconductor industry, is a sector with relatively more balanced Atlantic interdependencies, but similarly challenged by Japanese competition. European policies have provided more effective protection than has been feasible in the semiconductor sector, and accordingly there could be a better balance of bargaining strengths and official interests in interactions at the direct investment conferences. American corporate incentives to undertake more equal partnering could be substantial. Large uncertainties about advances in high-definition television have, however, greatly complicated corporate decision making in this part of the sector, especially on the American side. European firms appear to have benefited from a Union-level technology enhancement programme, which has evidently improved their capacities for productive collaboration with US firms, but American research advances have altered relative capabilities in ways that have increased the significance, for US firms, of technological links with Japanese companies.[41]

Opportunities for Atlantic direct investment cooperation in consumer electronics could be explored at the conferencing on the basis of shared interests in transregional rationalization while responding to Japanese challenges. The prospects for positive results would depend very much on the prior degree of regional rationalization in Europe, influenced by consultative interactions with the European Commission. In the US market large-scale Japanese penetration is a problem for European as well as American producers, but intensely competitive relations between and within the two assortments of firms are advantageous for the relationally linked Japanese companies. These companies are, moreover, maintaining their technological leads through higher investments in research and development, financed by high-volume consumer electronic sales.

Information and Communication Industries

Information and communication industries, more research-intensive than most of the consumer electronics sector, have potentials for Atlantic direct investment cooperation which demand European policy level attention because of their structural significance and their higher degrees of government involvement through regulation, subsidies, procurement, and protection. The Japanese challenge, related to achievements in semiconductors, is more potent for the Europeans, and motivates continued administrative involvement. This assumes much significance in European interactions with the USA on questions of trade and investment liberalization.[42] Large issues in services trade liberalization between the European Union and the USA overshadow these interactions, and provide opportunities for bargaining which could restrain US corporate interest in collaboration with Japanese firms.

Information and communications technology alliances between European and American firms have become much more numerous than those between US and Japanese companies. Further increases could be facilitated by exchanges at Atlantic direct investment conferences, especially if collaborative efforts were leading to greater efficiencies in Europe. Intra-Union alliances in this sector were given impetus during the drive for complete market integration, but have been lagging behind the alliances between Union and US enterprises.[43] Telecommunications equipment development and services in Europe is a high-priority policy area in which regulatory and procurement concerns are very active, because of government and private sector interests, and Union interests in ensuring substantial Europeanization of the sector as it develops wider links with the global communications pattern. European and US decision makers recognize incentives for partnering because of the great volume of Atlantic communication flows, and the potential benefits of collaborating informally in rivalries with the Japanese. On the US side there are efforts to secure increased access to the Union's markets for telecommunications services as these are liberalized in line with European Commission directives.[44]

Automobiles

Automobiles is a sector in which European capabilities for Atlantic partnering have been weakened by substantial losses of internal market shares to US producers. European automobile manufacturers have tended to concentrate on recovering shares of their regional market, while US companies have focused on global competition against Japanese corporations. European capacities to engage US producers in dialogue on direct investment cooperation would depend very much on degrees of collaboration between the Union's automobile firms, and the extent to which Union governments would coordinate their policies under Commission leadership. The small number of large US producers would be able to exploit rivalries between the larger number of smaller European manufacturers whose positions in their own regional market are insecure.[45]

Technology factors are less prominent in corporate strategies relating to the automobile sector than in the electronics and communication industries, but US corporate interest is directed more toward Japanese innovations than to those in Europe. US market shares in Europe are indirectly protected, for the present, by Union restraints on imports from Japan, but Japanese automobile production in the Union, notably in Britain, is considerable, and is increasing.[46] US interest in Atlantic direct investment cooperation could be sharpened if a Union structural endeavour to rationalize the European industry were in prospect.

Steel

Steel, an industry of special significance for the automobile sector, is burdened with adjustment problems because of excess capacity, especially in Europe. These problems are difficult to resolve because of the sizes of workforces at risk and quite active national policy concerns with the strategic importance of steel plants, which are given much protection on each side of the Atlantic and which serve mainly their home markets. In the Union the sector is fragmented and this perpetuates inefficiencies which hinder recoveries of world market shares that have been lost in recent decades.[47] The US steel industry has also experienced losses in global competition, and since the 1960s the preservation of shares in the home market has been sought mainly through political action to secure protection. Investment in new technology has lagged and there has been little inter-corporate cooperation for adjustment and rationalization.[48]

At Atlantic direct investment conferences European and US steel producers would have to cope with issues of transregional rationalization, and with adverse trends in world markets, caused mainly by Asian suppliers with technologically advanced plants. There would, however, be opportunities for collaborative direct investment in the development of new speciality metals, and of advanced machine tools – a sector that has been in decline in the USA.

CONFERENCE DYNAMICS

Exchanges at Atlantic direct investment conferences could be expected to become cross-sectoral as well as sectoral. The cross-sectoral interactions could be quite productive, as they would supplement routine information flows within sectoral networks. There could be widening surveillance of entrepreneurial opportunities, and this could be increasingly advantageous as frontier technology advances multiply functional interdependencies between firms within and across sectors. European and American technocratic contributions in the conferencing however would probably tend to facilitate mainly sectoral exchanges.

Prospects for productive exchanges would probably depend on balances in existing complementarities within sectors. In this regard chemicals would probably rank high, but in sectors in which US firms are substantially more competitive and have to cope with strong Japanese challenges the exchanges would probably be more demanding on the US side and somewhat defensive on the European side. The asymmetries could be reduced, it must be reiterated, if the European Commission were leading an intense effort to form a Union structural consensus, supported by inter-corporate solidarity.

The conferences could provide opportunities for the formation of coalitions of firms and governments that would contend for domination of the proceedings, without interest in building more balanced Atlantic complementarities. The development of collegial technocratic advisory roles at the conferences could thus have vital importance for restraint on the activities of exclusive coalitions and the promotion of openness in the information-sharing, as well as, more fundamentally, the promotion of a spirit of integrative cooperation. For this purpose the ideals invoked by the doctrine expressing the rationale for the conferencing could be especially significant.

To promote trust and goodwill the collegial technocratic contributions to the conferences could give much attention to the encouragement of concerted locational decisions, projecting agglomeration benefits attainable with low risks and with assurances of coordinated infrastructure development. Industries in Europe are geographically quite dispersed, because of decades of market separation, while production in the more integrated US internal market is concentrated in major areas of industrial activity.[49] Agglomeration into a reduced number of industrial areas in Europe is a trend to be expected as Union and other firms restructure on a regional basis. This trend will have special significance for the central and capital city regions, many of which are experiencing industrial decline.[50] In the USA the established pattern is being altered on a modest scale by corporate rationalization to serve the North American Free Trade Area.

Locational cooperation through the conferencing could be given much encouragement by European establishment of a large pattern of high-technology research centres. A comprehensive plan for such centres would be of great value for restructuring European firms, would have a positive influence on the evolving configuration of industrial clustering, and would offer improved location advantages for American enterprises. Technocratic involvement in the exploration of locational opportunities during the conference exchanges could be expected to induce corporate acceptance of more active technocratic roles in discussions of direct investment cooperation for research and development, and for coordinated production projects. All these considerations, in a European perspective, could reinforce the case for a strong sponsoring initiative by the European Commission to launch the conferences.

The enhancement of European location advantages through an extensive development of high-technology research centres would increase American corporate interest in the Union's direct investment opportunities because of imperatives for access to new technology and because the innovative capacities of European firms would be improved. European sourcing of US and Japanese high-technology products, to retain positions in the single market, is tending to further weaken the international competitiveness of European enterprises. As their technological lags increase they will attract less US interest as partners, and will tend to be viewed more as prospective acquisitions.

To be sufficiently productive the conference arrangements would have to be more open and inclusive than the TransAtlantic Business Dialogue, which has been elitist because of the exclusion of business associations and the restriction of participation to chief executive officers of large American and European firms, on the basis of understandings between the European Commission and sponsoring US government agencies.[51] While the direct investment conferences would be intended to facilitate interactions between corporate representatives, and between them and the technocrats, leaders of industry associations would have important roles to play through the expression of sectoral and community interests and potentials, complementing the involvement of the European and North American technocrats.

The planning of conference arrangements would have to be guided by clear and emphatic affirmation of imperatives for integrative rather than instrumental cooperation, especially through overcoming problems of informational market failure. The conference exchanges would be oriented toward exploring potential complementarities between corporate strategies, within and across sectors, in the light of market linkages between industries. A further objective of more direct operational significance would be to share understandings about the planning preferences and decisions of managements in groups of firms identified on the basis of potential complementarities.

The requisite technocratic functions at the conferences would require dedicated service. Doubts about the prospects for this could be expressed by interested groups, mainly because of literature with a US focus which tends to depict officials as self-interested operators endeavouring to maximize their benefits from responsiveness to lobbyists, legislators, and organizational preferences in their administration. European technocrats, it could be expected, would be motivated by traditions of public service which are sustained to a considerable degree in the European Commission, despite its international staffing problems. Greater continuity in the processes of European technocratic participation, moreover, could be anticipated, while changes in US official involvement would be probable under each incoming administration, and would tend to prevent accumulations of expertise, but could be sources of pressure for short-term results in the development of forms of direct investment cooperation. Continuity in most if not all the technocratic participation would be desirable for the formation of an Atlantic structural policy community, based on commitments to and expertise in the service of concepts of transregional complementarity and principles of integrative entrepreneurial coordination.

LONG-RANGE PLANNING

The more balanced complementarities and higher growth hoped for through the sponsorship of Atlantic direct investment conferences would be attainable only after the medium term, as increasingly concerted entrepreneurship began to have beneficial market and structural effects. For continuity and adjustment in the coordination of corporate endeavours the sponsoring organizations, especially the European Commission, would have to plan to institutionalize the conferencing. This planning would have to take into account possibilities for adverse as well as favourable changes in the structural complementarities evolving with the conferences. International firms that substantially strengthened their global market positions could make those complementarities more imbalanced, and could become less interested in the benefits of the conferencing. Enlisting more active corporate cooperation would thus be imperative, and the conferencing could then be potentially more supportive for competition policy cooperation between governments.

The institutional requirement could be met by establishing a Secretariat for the conferences. Brussels would be the most appropriate location, because of the importance of proximity to the European Commission, as a stable source of technocratic expertise that could ensure continuity in advisory functions, and that could express the European need for more symmetrical structural links across the Atlantic. The Brussels secretariat could indirectly encourage the development of a stronger technocratic capability in the US administration and the formation of stronger business associations in the USA, while having similar effects in Canada and Mexico. It could also serve as a model for the planning of a centre that would sponsor direct investment conferences for European and Latin American corporate groups.

The Atlantic conferencing, especially if aided by an active secretariat, could encourage broad acceptance of principles, norms, and rules governing the treatment of foreign direct investment in Europe and North America. Proposals for international foreign direct investment regimes have been discussed in recent years at OECD, resulting in some advances toward consensus among experts regarding national treatment, rights of establishment, and transparency in host country regulatory measures.[52] Initiatives to build transregional corporate rapport have, however, been lacking, and there has been little recognition in the policy literature that governmental concerns with enhancing structural competitiveness are driving efforts to strengthen national firms financially, technologically, and through procurement and trade policies. A basic purpose of the Atlantic direct investment conferencing would be to redirect structural policies toward building complementarities through fundamental changes in technocratic and corporate values and objectives.

The principles on which the conferences could be institutionalized could be derived from the research papers sponsored by the European Commission. Public goods requirements, in the context of high complex imbalanced Atlantic structural interdependencies, would have to be affirmed with emphasis on the coordination of corporate activities, in line with system-building logic, through consultations dedicated to higher and widely integrated enterpreneurial endeavours. This emphasis would have to be made clear on the basis of commitments to engage comprehensively with problems of market failure and government failure extending across borders. In that context it would be especially appropriate to stress that coordinated entrepreneurship, extending beyond direct investment cooperation, would be the correct solution to growth problems. These have been tending to become intractable in North America and Europe because of the negative effects of past fiscal expansions to increase demand and more recent deflationary measures to reduce demand; it could be reiterated, moreover, that the resultant uncertainties and declines have been more serious for potentially very innovative new firms than for large transnational enterprises with oligopolistic strengths that facilitate adjustment.

The multiplication of communication links between conferencing firms would of course facilitate collusion in the use of restrictive business practices. The institutional arrangements for the conferences would have to provide for the monitoring and restriction of such practices, principally through the development of a transnational business culture that would motivate spontaneous corporate restraints. The roles assumed by European technocrats could be especially significant for this purpose. The firms at risk under the intensifying pressures of Atlantic competition are mainly European, and many of these are small and medium-sized low- and mature-technology enterprises, notably in France and the less industrialized southern European countries.

If Atlantic direct investment conferencing becomes significantly productive, and is institutionalized, the potential for expansion into more extensively concerted entrepreneurial activity would become more important, and requirements for dedicated technocratic expertise would become greater. More comprehensive cooperative management of Atlantic structural interdependencies would become possible. The demonstration effects of European advances in collective management, moreover, would become more relevant for the planning of a system of collective management for the North America Free Trade Area, and its inclusion of some Latin American countries.

Much scope can thus be seen for highly constructive European and North American political entrepreneurship. For all this inspiration could be drawn from consideration of the Aristotelian concepts of civic order and friendship, which, mainly in Europe, have been incorporated into a great theological tradition.[53] This tradition offers guidance at a fundamental level for redefining the role of the state and the role of the firm in the evolution of interdependent national communities, to build a system of truly humanistic alliance capitalism, with dynamic solidarity, overcoming problems of internationalized market failure and government failure. In the USA, over the long term, the spread of the new ethos could resolve the acute problems of social inequality that have been worsening since the early 1980s.[54]

NOTES

1. See Kumiharu Shigehara, 'Causes of declining growth in industrialized countries', in *Policies for Long Run Economic Growth* (Federal Reserve Bank of Kansas City, 1992), pp. 15–40, and *OECD Economic Outlook 58* (Paris: OECD, 1995), pp. 1–32.
2. See F. Chesnais, 'Globalization, world oligopoly, and some of their implications', in Marc Humbert (ed. ,) *The Impact of Globalization on Europe's Firms and Industries* (London: Pinter, 1993), pp. 12–21.

3. See Rabindra N. Kanungo and Manuel Mendonca, *Ethical Dimensions of Leadership* (Thousand Oaks: SAGE, 1996), and Jenny Stewart, 'Rational choice theory, public policy and the liberal state', *Policy Sciences*, 26 (4), 1993, 317–30.

4. See John Cantwell and Francesca Randaccio, 'Intra-industry direct investment in the European Community: oligopolistic rivalry and technological competition', in John Cantwell (ed.), *Multinational Investment in Modern Europe* (Aldershot: Edward Elgar, 1992), pp. 71–106.

5. See Geoffrey Edwards and David Spence (eds), *The European Commission* (Harlow: Longman 1994), Chapter 7, and Justin Greenwood and Laura Cram, 'European level business collective action: the study agenda ahead', *Journal of Common Market Studies* 34 (3), September 1996, 449–64.

6. On the logic of partnering see John M. Stopford, 'The growing interdependence between transnational corporations and governments', *Transnational Corporations*, 3 (1), February 1994, 53–76.

7. See references to coordination failures in Tsuru Kotaro, *The Japanese Market Economy System: Its Strengths and Weaknesses* (Tokyo: LTCB International Library Foundation, 1995). See also Michael L. Gerlach, *Alliance Capitalism: The Social Organization of Japanese Business* (Berkeley: University of California Press, 1992); Ryutaro Komiya *The Japanese Economy: Trade, Industry and Government* (Tokyo: University of Tokyo Press, 1990); and Martin Fransman, 'Is national technology policy obsolete in a globalised world? The Japanese response', *Cambridge Journal of Economics*, 19 (1), February 1995, 95–120.

8. See *Governance in Transition: Public Management Reforms in OECD Countries* (Paris: OECD, 1995), and references to 'soft' methods of implementing economic policies in Peter Bogason, 'Control for whom?: recent advances in research on governmental guidance and control', *European Journal of Political Research*, 20 (2), September 1991, 189–208. See also Romano Dyerson and Frank Mueller, 'Intervention by outsiders: a strategic management perspective on government industrial policy', *Journal of Public Policy,* 13 (1), Jan–Mar 1993, 69–88.

9. Direct investment bidding by European Union governments makes the development of a common foreign direct investment policy difficult. See Thomas Brewer and Stephen Young, 'European Union policies and the problems of multinational enterprises', *Journal of World Trade*, 29 (1), 1995, 33–52.

10. See Gavin Boyd (ed.), *Competitive and Cooperative Macromanagement* (Aldershot: Edward Elgar, 1995)

11. On the exploratory value of communications, especially those affirming the benefits of cooperation, see Randall L. Calvert, 'The rational choice theory of social institutions: cooperation, coordination, and communication', in Jeffrey S. Banks and Eric A. Hanushek (eds), *Modern Political Economy: Old Topics, New Directions* (New York: Cambridge University Press, 1995), pp. 216–68.

12. For a critical evaluation of the Commission's capabilities see Edwards and Spence, *The European Commission*. On problems of leadership in the Union see Neill Nugent, 'Editorial: Building Europe – a need for more leadership?', *Journal of Common Market Studies, Annual Review*, 1995, 1–14.

13. See Gerlach, *Alliance Capitalism*, and Fransman, 'Is national technology policy obsolete?'

14. See for example comments on the Commission in Xiudian Dai, Alan Cawson, and Peter Holmes, 'The rise and fall of high definition television: the impact of European technology policy', *Journal of Common Market Studies*, 34 (2), June 1996, 149–66.

15. *Ibid.*; see also Mitchell P. Smith, 'Integration in small-steps: the European Commission and member state aid to industry', *West European Politics*, 19 (3), July 1996, 563–82.

16. Such studies could build on the work of Colin I. Bradford on 'The new paradigm of systemic competitiveness'. See Colin I. Bradford (ed.), *The New Paradigm of Systemic Competitiveness: Toward More Integrated Policies in Latin America* (Paris: OECD, 1994).

17. See *Governance in Transition*, (OECD).

18. See indicators of the strength of the German position in *OECD Economic Survey, Germany 1996*, p. 38.

19. See Andrew Appleton, 'Parties under pressure: challenges to "Established" French Parties', *West European Politics*, 18 (1), January 1995, 52–77, and Vivien A. Schmidt, 'Loosening the

ties that bind: the impact of European integration on French government and its relationship to business', *Journal of Common Market Studies*, 34 (2), June 1996, 223–54.

20. See indications of US corporate and government views in Bruce Stokes (ed.), *Open for Business: Creating a TransAtlantic Marketplace* (New York: Council on Foreign Relations, 1996).

21. See general remarks on information-sharing in Calvert, 'The rational choice theory of social institutions', and references to technology and social learning in John de la Mothe and Giles Paquet (eds), *Evolutionary Economics and the New International Political Economy* (London: Pinter, 1996).

22. See Cantwell and Randaccio, 'Intra-industry direct investment in the European Community'.

23. See John Hagedoorn and Jos Schakenraad, 'Strategic technology partnering and international corporate strategies', in Kirsty S. Hughes (ed.), *European Competitiveness* (Cambridge: Cambridge University Press, 1993), pp. 60–86.

24. *Ibid.*

25. See Edward M. Graham, 'Direct investment between the United States and the European Community post 1986 and pre-1992', in John Cantwell (ed.), *Multinational Investment in Modern Europe*, (Aldershot: Edward Elgar, 1992), pp. 46–70.

26. Industrial policy problems at the Union level are, however, serious. See Andrew Cox and Glynn Watson, 'The European Community and the restructuring of Europe's national champions', in Jack Hayward (ed.), *Industrial Enterprise and European Integration* (Oxford: Oxford University Press, 1995), pp. 304–33.

27. On the significance of informal ties in Germany's social market institutions see Kirsten S. Wever and Christopher S. Allen, 'The financial system and corporate governance in Germany: institutions and the diffusion of innovations', *Journal of Public Policy*, 13 (2), April 1993, 183–202. The largest new investments in the USA in 1995 were German, mainly in chemicals. See Mahnaz Fahim-Nader and William J. Zeile, 'Foreign direct investment in the United States', *Survey of Current Business*, 76 (7), July 1996, 102–30.

28. See Fahim-Nader and Zeile, *op. cit.*

29. See references to France in Neill Nugent and Rory O'Donnell (eds), *The European Business Environment* (London: Macmillan, 1994).

30. See Paul R. Masson (ed.), *France: Financial and Real Sector Issues* (Washington, DC: International Monetary Fund, 1995).

31. Graham, 'Direct investment'.

32. See Jeffrey H. Lowe and Sylvia E. Bargas, 'Direct investment positions on a historical cost basis', *Survey of Current Business*, 76 (7), July 1996, 45–55.

33. See Mark Casson, *Enterprise and Competitiveness* (Oxford: Oxford University Press, 1990), pp. 105–24.

34. See Neil M. Kay, Harvie Ramsay and Jean-François Hennart, 'Industrial Collaboration and the European Internal Market', *Journal of Common Market Studies*, 34 (3), September 1996, 465–76.

35. See Roger Voyer and Jeffrey Roy, 'European high technology clusters' in John de la Mothe and Giles Paquet (eds), *Evolutionary Economics and the New International Political Economy* (London: Pinter, 1996), pp. 220–37, and Jan Fagerberg and Bart Verspagen, 'Heading for divergence? Regional growth in Europe reconsidered', *Journal of Common Market Studies*, 34 (3), September 1996, pp. 43–8.

36. See Brewer and Young, 'European Union policies and the problems of multinational enterprises'.

37. See Daniele Archibugi and Mario Pianta, 'Patterns of technological specialisation and the growth of innovative activities in advanced countries', in Kirsty S. Hughes (ed.), *European Competitiveness*, pp. 105–32; see also Hayward, *Industrial Enterprise and European Integration*.

38. For surveys of the European sector see Peter Johnson, 'Air Transport', in Peter Johnson (ed.), *European Industries: Structure, Conduct and Performance* (Aldershot: Edward Elgar, 1993), pp. 204–29, and Pierre Muller, 'Aerospace companies and the state in Europe' and Hussein Kassim, 'Air transport champions: still carrying the flag', in Hayward, *Industrial Enterprise and European Integration*, pp. 158–87 and 188–214.

39. See Wyn Grant and William Paterson, 'The chemical industry: a study in internationalisation', in J. Rogers Hollingsworth, Philippe C. Schmitter and Wolfgang Streeck (eds), *Governing Capitalist Economies: Performance and Control in Economic Sectors* (New York: Oxford University Press, 1994), pp. 43–71, and Frédérique Sachwald, 'The chemical industry', in Frédérique Sachwald (ed.), *European Integration and Competitiveness* (Aldershot: Edward Elgar, 1994), pp. 233–76.

40. See Mike Hobday, 'The semiconductor industry', in Sachwald, *ibid.*, pp. 145–94, and Peter F. Cowhey and Jonathan D. Aronson, *Managing the World Economy: The Consequences of Corporate Alliances* (New York: Council on Foreign Relations, 1993), Chapter 6.

41. See Martin Bloom, 'The consumer electronics industry', in Sachwald, *op. cit.*, pp. 195–232, and Dai, Cawson and Holmes, 'The rise and fall of high definition television'.

42. See Cowhey and Aronson, *Managing the World Economy*, Chapter 7; Mark Thatcher, 'Regulatory reform and internationalisation in telecommunications', in Hayward, *Industrial Enterprise and European Integration*, pp. 239–72; and Roger G. Noll and Frances M. Rosenbluth, 'Telecommunications policy: structure, process and outcomes', in Peter F. Cowhey and Mathew D. McCubbins (eds), *Structure and Policy in Japan and the United States* (New York: Columbia University Press, 1995), pp. 119–76.

43. See Hagedoorn and Schakenraad, 'Strategic technology partnering'.

44. See Oliver Stehman, *Network Competition for European Telecommunications* (New York: Oxford University Press, 1995); Noll and Rosenbluth 'Telecommunications policy'; and Willem Hulsink, 'From state monopolies to Euro-nationals and global alliances: the case of the European telecommunications sector', in Jules J.J. van Dijck and John P.M. Groenewegen (eds), *Changing Business Systems in Europe* (Brussels: VUB Press, 1994), Chapter 19.

45. See Garel Rhys, 'Motor vehicles', in Peter Johnson (ed.), *European Industries*, pp. 126–53, and Sachwald, *European Integration and Competitiveness*, Chapter 3.

46. Sachwald, *European Integration and Competitiveness*, Chapter 3.

47. See Anthony Cockerill, 'Steel', in Johnson, *European Industries*, and *The Steel Market in 1995 and Prospects for 1996* (Geneva: United Nations Commission for Europe, 1995).

48. See Stefanie Lenway, Randall Morck and Bernard Yeung, 'Rent seeking, protectionism and innovation in the American steel industry', *The Economic Journal*, 106, 435, March 1996, 410–21.

49. See Paul Krugman and Anthony J. Venables, 'Integration, specialisation and adjustment', *European Economic Review*, 40 (3–5), April 1996, 959–67, and Zoltan Acs, 'American high technology clusters', in de la Mothe and Paquet, *Evolutionary Economics*, pp. 183–219. On the evolution of more advanced and less advanced areas in Europe see Martin Rhodes, 'Globalization, the state and the restructuring of regional economies', in Philip Gummett (ed.), *Globalization and Public Policy* (Cheltenham: Edward Elgar, 1996), pp. 161–80.

50. *Prospects for the Development of the Central and Capital Cities and Regions* (Brussels: The European Commission, 1996).

51. See Maria Green Cowles, 'The collective action of transatlantic business: the TransAtlantic Business dialogue', paper for 1996 Annual Meeting of the American Political Science Association.

52. See Pierre Sauve and Daniel Schwanen (eds), *Investment Rules for the Global Economy* (Toronto: C.D. Howe Institute, 1996).

53. See Mark Neufeld, T*he Restructuring of International Relations Theory* (New York: Cambridge University Press, 1995), on the Aristotelian concept, and, on the Christian theological tradition, Kanungo and Mendonca, *Ethical Dimensions of Leadership*, and Pope John Paul II, *Encyclical Letter on The Hundredth Anniversary of Rerum Novarum* (Boston: St Paul Books and Media, 1991).

54. For a review of these problems see Hugh Heclo, 'Growing income inequalities in America? A review essay', *Political Science Quarterly*, 111 (3), Fall 1996, 523–8.

Subject index

administrative-corporate
    interdependencies 223
administrative-corporate partnering 224
advanced political development 206
aircraft 125, 186, 231
alliance capitalism 5–9
alliances 149, 150, 177–90, 194, 229
allocative issues 201, 207
Atlantic FDI conferences 222–39
Atlantic FDI, theoretical issues 157, 158
Atlantic relations
    cross investment 34, 145–7, 155–74
    current ties 16–19
    exports 34
    free trade issues 21–7
    high tech sectors 36–43
    history 2–4, 13–16
    sectoral linkage potentials 110–28
    services 35
    structural interdependencies 32 56,
        59, 60
    Transatlantic Business Dialogue 8, 22,
        29, 56, 216, 236
automobiles 125, 234

biotechnology 186

Canada
    chemicals, alliance potentials 123
    drugs and medicines, alliance
        potentials, 123, 124
    European direct investment 171
    exports, percentage of production
        117
    FDI in Europe 158–62
    import penetration 117
chemicals 231
competition policy 211
competitiveness 54, 158
computers 153
consumer electronics 124, 153, 232

corporate finance 80–106
    contrasts between systems 96, 97
    disclosure requirements 94–6
    external finance 83
    information problems 82
    institutional investors 102–5
    legal and regulatory factors 90–93
    securities markets 83–6, 98
corporate governance 80–106
    changing firms 99
    managerial incentives 82
    performance monitoring 83
    pressures for change 98, 105
corporate strategies 47
cost oriented FDI 156

electrical and nonelectrical machinery
    124
entrepreneurship 206
European Union
    collective management 202, 211
    employment 40
    European Commission 210, 223
    exports, percentage of production 117
    FDI issues 212
    FDI locational cooperation 236
    financial markets 196, 213
    firms, 99, 193, 201
    foreign economic policy orientations
        196
    gains from internal markets 205
    high tech sectors 36–43, 228
    import penetration 117
    individualism 207
    institutional development 204
    interfirm cooperation 48–51
    intraEU complementaries 217
    investment in USA 165–172
    manufacturing 35
    mergers and acquisitions 47
    microeconomic cooperation 223

monetary union 211
regulatory issues in financial markets
    197, 215
relations with USA 8, 28, 29, 205
    free trade issues 21–7
    macroeconomic cooperation 218
    manufacturing links 35
    services 35
    structural complementaries 216
    structural interdependencies 32–56
rivalry with Japan 217
semiconductors 153
software 153
structural policies 199, 200, 211
technocratic expertise 225
technology 47–51, 148–53, 226
US direct investment 145–7, 158–60,
    162–5

France
    cooperation with Germany 227
    government–business relations 199
    intercorporate system 199
    investment in USA 171, 229
    macromanagement 203
    problems of governance 203, 208
    structural competitiveness 199
    US direct investment 145–7, 230

Germany
    cooperation with France 227
    corporate finance 89, 93
    Europeanisation of policy 210, 226
    foreign economic policy orientation
        196
    governance achievements 208
    investment in USA 229
    mergers and acquisitions 87, 88
    securities markets 84–7
    structural competitiveness 199
    US direct investment 145–7

high technology sectors 222

information and communication
    industries 233
input oriented FDI 156
internalization theory 156, 193
international economic cooperation
    209–13

international technological alliances
    148–50, 180–87
internationalization of markets 201
internationalization theory 156

Japan
    automobile industry 76, 77
    foreign economic policy orientation
        196
    governance achievements 195
    industry groups 194
    information technology 186
    institutions 202, 209
    intercorporate system 200
    investment liberalization 194
    structural policy 200

locational cooperation 236

macromanagement 201
market efficiencies and failures 201
market oriented FDI 156
MERIT-CATI Data Bank 188–90
Mexico 170
monetary cooperation issues 214

national systems of innovation 141–5
new materials 186
North American Free Trade Area 16
    exports, percentage of production 117
    hierarchical configuration 212
    import penetration 117

office equipment 124

partnering in technology alliances 180–87
policy communities 226
policy issues in Atlantic relations 52–6
problems of governance 194
public management reforms 225

regionalism 21
Research and Development 178, 179, 184
    FDI in R&D 150–52
    international 150–52

semiconductors 232
steel 234
strategic alliances 111–15
    policy issues 126–8

structural competitiveness 195
structural complementarities 216
structural policies 197
Switzerland 145–7

technology 141–53, 178–90
textiles and clothing 123
theory of foreign direct investment
    155–8
trade liberalization 194

United Kingdom
  business interests 197
  Canadian FDI 159
  corporate governance 80–106
  direct investment from USA 166
  institutional development 209
  involvement in EU decision making
      210
  mergers and acquisitions 87, 88
  policymaking 204, 209
  securities markets 84–7
  structural policy issues 198
  US direct investment 145, 146, 159
United States
  aircraft 152
  automobiles 61, 67
  chemicals 63
  corporate finance 88
  corporate governance 64, 80–106
  corporate strategies 47, 63
  deficits in balance of payments 195
  electronics 62
  European direct investment 165–72
  exports, percentage of production 117

financial sector stability 215
firms 19
flagship firms 66
foreign economic policy 18, 195
high tech sectors 36–43
import penetration 117
individualism 2, 207
industrial equipment 62
investment in EU 145–7, 158–65
legislative activism 197
macromanagement 205
manufacturing sectors 60
mergers and acquisitions 87, 88
nationalism 18
petrochemicals 152
problems of governance 195, 207
relations with EU 8, 28, 29, 32–56,
    205
representation of business interests
    197
securities markets 84
structural competitiveness 148–52,
    198
structural complementaries with EU
    216
structural policy 197
technology 148–52
telecommunications 152
trade with EU 44–7

World Trade Organization
  dispute settlement 212
  institutional development 212
  EU involvement 212
  US involvement 212